A Fair And Honest Book

A Fair And Honest Book

The Memoirs of Sir Ambrose Sherwill

First published by Lulu.com 2006
Second version published by Lulu.com 2007
www.lulu.com

ISBN 978-1-84753-149-0

Cover design by Sherwill Design
Front cover image of winter sunrise over Sark by courtesy of
www.bbc.co.uk/guernsey

ACKNOWLEDGEMENTS

The handwritten notes that were the basis for *A Fair and Honest Book* lay in boxes for nearly fifty years, and were handed down through two generations before being transcribed for eventual publication in December, 2006.

Much of it was written on scraps of paper or discarded envelopes, and deciphering the close written copperplate hand writing took many hours of careful cross reference and proof reading.

This task was lovingly undertaken by two people very close to Sir Ambrose Sherwill, his second son Dick Sherwill, also a hero of the Second World War, and his granddaughter Jane Devonald.

The result is the life story of an intelligent and dedicated man, who selflessly undertook whatever task befell him. Part One describes the young life of a scholar, soldier and lawyer up until the Second World War. Part Two tells of the experiences of dealing with a situation unknown on British soil since 1066.

With no precedent on which to base his strategy, Ambrose Sherwill dealt with the German invaders of Guernsey in the only way he knew, with courage, human decency, and the rule of law.

Sir Ambrose Sherwill

Contents

A Fair And Honest Book

Part One

PREFACE

SIR AMBROSE JAMES SHERWILL

K.B.E., M.C., Kt. St. J., "Docteur" Honoris Causa of the University of Caen, (1890 – 1968).

About this book:

It was in a diary that he kept while in prison in Paris that Sherwill gave the first indication that he had it in mind to write a book. Faced with what he anticipated would be a very long term of imprisonment, in an entry dated 13th November, 1940, he wrote: *"I think when I am really settled in, I will write a book on the German Occupation of the Bailiwick of Guernsey. Not a thriller but a fair and honest book. It ought to sell well. Perhaps I may thus restore the shattered family fortunes."*

Early in 1943, together with a large party of other islanders, he was deported from Guernsey to Ilag VII Laufen in Bavaria. Here he began to work on his book. However, on 29th June, 1943, some four and a half months after his arrival, having been elected by his fellow internees, Sherwill *"became pretty fully occupied as British Camp Senior for the rest of the 'duration' and so did not continue my literary activities."*

None of Sherwill's papers is dated and, at the time of his death, many were still in the form of rough drafts, written in his meticulous but tiny handwriting, sometimes on scraps of paper and even on the backs of used envelopes. A number are legible only with the use of a magnifying glass. From their content it is possible to ascertain that some were written soon after the end of the Second World War.

In about 1965 he wrote: -

"It has been suggested to me on many occasions that, having played a fairly conspicuous part during the early days of the German Occupation of the Island of Guernsey in 1940, I should place on record my recollections of that unhappy period in the Island's history.

Until my retirement from the office of Bailiff of that Island in February, 1960, I was too fully occupied to be able to devote the time

3

necessary for the adequate carrying out of such a task. In any case, it seemed to me doubtful whether I could do so with propriety while still in the service of the Crown and the States of Guernsey. Further, in the early days, the feelings of others had to be considered.

A quarter of a century has now elapsed since the Germans first came to Guernsey, I have long since retired from public office and in the friendly, relaxed atmosphere of the Island of Alderney, where I am now living, am able to recollect in tranquillity those far-off events and, I hope to record them with at least some measure of impartiality.

Things occurred in Guernsey, in Prison in Paris and during my internment in Germany of which few, if any, on the British side except myself have any first hand knowledge. I propose, so far as is possible, to concentrate on these and not merely repeat – except where it is essential to do so in order to make my narrative intelligible – what has already been recorded in other books. Even now, I find some of the things that happened to me of such interest that I should hate them to be lost for ever and, if I should succeed in arousing anything like the same interest in some of those who may read these reminiscences, I shall feel amply rewarded."

From correspondence in March, 1967, between Sherwill and a publishing company, it is clear that by then he had decided to widen the scope of his planned book to cover some events which occurred during his childhood, the First World War and the inter-wars period, in addition to the German Occupation years.

Away from libraries and official records, he got into the habit of leaving many small and larger gaps in his writings, with the apparent intention of filling them in later. His work on the book was spread over a period of more than twenty years and it is not altogether surprising that there was considerable repetition and overlapping of the various accounts in his papers. In a number of instances it was found that Sherwill had produced several versions of the same incidents. Furthermore, it is believed that some parts of and even complete papers have been lost.

Suffering poor health in his last year, by the time of his death he had not been able to complete the book.

Soon after the Second World War, Sherwill opened his private papers to Alan and Mary Wood, for use in their book "Islands in Danger", and these papers have subsequently been made available to other authors.

Since 1997, Jane Devonald, Sherwill's granddaughter, has been working on the somewhat daunting labour of producing fair-copies of the papers. Considerable editing and pruning has been considered necessary to produce a more or less logical sequence to the main narrative. Dick Sherwill undertook to fill in some of the gaps by means of research in Guernsey. He would like to express his gratitude to all who helped in that task. He would especially wish to thank Dr. D.M. Ogier and the staff at the Island Archives Service, the Guille-Allès and Priaulx Libraries, the Guernsey Press Company Limited and Mr. W.M. Bell for their help.

R.F.S.

I

July 1904

Five weeks before, in the very middle of the Summer Term, I had been hauled away from Elizabeth College - where I had just settled in and had begun to make progress - without any sort of warning and sent to pursue my studies at the Lycée de Cherbourg. Only ten months previously I had been moved from the Guernsey High School for Boys to Elizabeth College with equal suddenness. My male parent had no particular views on education but he was susceptible to the influence of acquaintances who had. Apparently these acquaintances had, I don't know why, taken an interest in me. Well, there it was; two uprootings like that in a boy's education tend to be upsetting, they might well be catastrophic. Taking with me the prescribed two of everything and a substantially packed lunch basket (I can still remember it contained strawberries) I set off one Tuesday morning accompanied by my father and a friend whose passport for the occasion was, I gathered, a knowledge of French which he spoke with a strange guttural accent: my father was innocent of any such attainment. The "Courier" - I speak of the big Courier of 1884 vintage, not to be confounded with the little "Courier" built in 1880 - blew just as we got aboard and the old skipper, he was well over seventy then, exchanged greetings with my father who appeared to be well known to him. It was a perfect day and the journey to Cherbourg - involving a call to Alderney to disembark passengers, mails and a little cargo - quite uneventful. I remember being introduced to Monsieur "le Censeur" (Vice Principal) of the Lycée and being shown a playground and a dormitory. Then I was taken for a drive in an extremely antiquated Victoria driven by a man who turned out to have been born in Guernsey although of Italian descent, and regaled with a very good dinner at the Grand Hotel d'Angleterre et de l'Europe, then kept by Monsieur Zoppi and lying just off the Quay on the western side of the bassin de commerce. Then, gently but firmly, I was deposited at the Lycée. My education in the manners and customs of France and in the delightful language of that country had begun. I was fourteen at the time and I had not been away from home before. Let me admit it, I was horribly homesick. I was the only English boarder and there was only one other English boy (a day boy) at the Lycée. I saw him seldom and I think the inability to speak one's mother tongue and the lack of any real ability to speak any other contributed to my unhappiness. The food was good and sufficient, all the masters - except one - kind and most of the boys only faintly hostile and in some cases most friendly. The cause of the hostility was the Russo-Japanese War then raging in the Far East. France had an alliance with the Russians and we with the Japanese and naturally, national sentiments had been aroused by the conflict. Occasionally, we boarders were taken for a conducted tour of the naval dockyard. On one such visit, a French submarine lay alongside one of the jetties. It is scarcely credible - yet true - that the master in charge of us expressed great concern - in my hearing and for my benefit - at the incredible folly of exposing the closely-guarded secrets of the French Navy to a dirty little foreigner. The submarine was at least fifty yards from me and the most I learned about her after the closest inspection - in 1904 a submarine was a very great novelty - was that her hull was encrusted with barnacles and very rusty. I was receptive in those days and my French improved rapidly. Even my religious education was provided for, the French Protestant pastor of the little "Temple" at the Place Divette called each Wednesday and took me for half an hour in scripture and on Sunday mornings I attended service at his church. Initially, I was conducted thither and retrieved by a "garçon" - a bearded man in his forties - from the Lycée but I became rather sensitive about this and, on my taking the most solemn oaths to go straight there and come straight back, I was permitted to go alone. The sermon was always very long - in two parts divided by a brief interval in which, invariably, Pastor Braud produced a voluminous coloured handkerchief into which he spat with noisy gusto - and the service tended to stretch beyond midday, the hour of déjeuner at the Lycée. Accordingly, as Pastor Braud was commencing his peroration, the creaking of the door and shuffling footsteps of the "garçon" sent to fetch me would cause all heads - except mine - to turn and quite obviously caused some slight annoyance to the preacher. Then would come a series of "pssts" to which I finally responded and, the cynosure of all eyes, left the holy building. But now, as I say, I had been relieved of this embarrassment although, in order to get a complete déjeuner, I still had to leave the service early apparently of my own volition.

Well, on Sunday the 14th July 1904, I had gone to church as usual and had, as usual, left early, arriving at the conciergerie of the Lycée just as the clock was striking midday. The concierge, a dear friendly old man, emerged and, to my surprise, conducted me to the drawing room, a room with which I was not previously acquainted, and there I found someone waiting for me. It was my Mother. That such happiness should have come to me so suddenly was almost unbelievable. Instead of the usual drab routine which passed for Sunday, here was radiant joy. Away we went to lunch at the Grand Hotel de l'Angleterre et de l'Europe and to see all the sights that Cherbourg has to offer.

An excursion had been run from Guernsey leaving there at midnight on the Saturday and arriving at Cherbourg at 5 a.m., to enable the Guernsey trippers to breakfast and see the early morning "Quatorze Juillet" review in La Place Napoléon; and my Mother had availed herself of the opportunity. She had come on the little "Courier" (so many excursionists had been attracted by the opportunity to visit Cherbourg that the little "Courier" as well as the big "Courier" had been pressed into their service) and there had been a mishap on the way. The skipper had apparently partaken unwisely of the cup that cheers and an amateur had replaced him at the wheel. Entering the roadstead at Cherbourg he had taken the wrong side of a buoy and had struck fairly heavily. The little "Courier" remained poised for a moment and the people began putting on lifebelts (one passenger was reported to have had on three but I think this was an exaggeration), and then the ship slid off and continued her journey.

That Sunday was one of the happiest days of my life - I hope it was too for my Mother - but what weariness it must have entailed for her. Let me tell you why. For many years my father and mother had lived apart and my mother received only a pitifully inadequate weekly allowance under the separation agreement and, in order to exist, was compelled to supplement this. To do so she worked in a dressmaking establishment for a ridiculously - I should say criminally - small wage. She had left her employment at eight o'clock on the Saturday evening, had gone home and prepared for the journey and boarded the "Courier" before midnight; she had spent the night on deck, had spent the day doing all the things I wanted to do, and, when she left me at 8.30 p.m. she was going aboard to wait till midnight, was going to spend another night at sea in the open - this time in the big "Courier", packed not only with her own passengers but also with those from the little "Courier", found to have sustained underwater damage where she struck - and, on her arrival in Guernsey, she would just have time to walk home and make herself some breakfast before walking to her work which began at eight o'clock. Am I right or am I wrong in thinking that there was something very noble, something near heroic in the circumstances in a woman who would go through all that discomfort and bear all that weariness for the sake of brightening for a few hours the life of her schoolboy son? Right or wrong I do think it and will continue to do so.

Three years later she died after an agonising illness. I had hoped in time to repay in a practical way some of her devotion and self-sacrifice of which the example I have given was one of the least important. Her loss was to me devastating for I was, to all intents and purposes, alone in the world. It is no accident that in 1920 when I became a Deputy, I threw all I knew into getting a Married Women's Separate Property Law passed by the States or that when H.M. Procureur in 1940 (not long before the German occupation) I should feel a glow of satisfaction that a long needed and enlightened Matrimonial Causes Law was at last in operation in Guernsey. It is not customary for abstruse pieces of legislation to be dedicated to anyone. Were it otherwise, I should have no difficulty - or hesitation - as to the person entitled to be so honoured.

II

1914

I can remember as though it were yesterday that Sunday in August. I was living at Les Landes at the time and I had only been back for a week or two from a visit to France where Jack Martel and I had passed our examinations for the degree of Licencié en Droit at the University of Caen, that old-world rather smelly town of the many steeples situate in the Department of Calvados, and had then gone on to spend a short and, as we thought, well earned holiday in Paris. Before leaving for Paris we had spent an afternoon visiting Falaise, the birthplace of William the Conqueror and had there been shown the Fontaine d'Arlette, named after William's mother, and the tiny chamber - as we thought, a most unsuitable room even for a scullery - in the picturesque castle in which he is reputed to have been born. We had been shown over the castle by the "gardienne" and as we stood on its summit gazing at the rolling cornfields around us, I remember her telling us of her experiences as a little girl in the war of 1870. She was a nice, intelligent woman with an interesting fund of anecdotes. As we listened to the story of her childhood we were blissfully unconscious that within the next fortnight there was to burst over the world another period of torment.

Besides being a student at Caen University - by virtue of a "dispense d'assiduité", I was an external student having only to attend at the University for the purpose of my "inscriptions" and the payment of fees and the actual sitting for examinations though I have often thought that the "dispense d'assiduité" was somewhat of a misnomer in that it was very hard going reading French law at night after a full day's work - I was head clerk to the late Mr. H.A. Le Patourel, then an Advocate and later His Majesty's Solicitor-General and Attorney General successively in Guernsey. I earned the princely salary of £100 per annum old Guernsey Currency but, believe me, it went a great deal further than three times that sum would now. I kept, if it can be called keeping - an 8 h.p. single cylinder four-seater Darracq, the 1904 model, a good but very noisy old bus with a very fierce clutch requiring constant treatment - but not of course alone possessing that idiosyncrasy - with castor oil. I couldn't have been very flush for I remember that when the tube of the Stepney (for the benefit of those under eighty years of age, the Stepney, named after its inventor, was the spare rim and tyre which one clamped to the ordinary wheel when a puncture occurred) burst and was found to be beyond repair, I could not afford another and stuffed the cover with hay. The war broke out and took me away before I had occasion to use it but I have often wondered how my successor in ownership got on with it.

When Mr. Le Patourel became Procureur in 1929, I was privileged to serve under him as Comptroller and did, or tried to do, his job during his long and painful illness, which had a fatal termination in 1934. Everyone loved him; there was no more gentle creature. Intensely musical, retiring, without a particle of selfishness in his make-up, he had a wonderful sense of the meaning of words and his letters and speeches were models of erudition. Yet he was not a really effective speaker. He served Guernsey with all his powers; he left Guernsey the better and the sweeter for his life's work which forms part of the things accomplished forever.

Well, on this Sunday of which I was writing - when all the thoughts that I have just put on paper came sweeping along and would not be gainsaid - I walked into town to find out the exact news, if I could. At the Press Office in Smith Street the news that war had broken out was posted up. The next day a vessel, a largish German ship, laden with potatoes, was escorted into the outer roadstead, the first prize of the war.

I do not profess to have been very patriotic but, somehow, something stirred in me and I realised that I must get away from Guernsey and do something which I could justify in later years. In those days, Colonel Thomas Hutchesson, M.C., Seigneur of Fief le Comte and Dependencies, was the machine Gun Officer to the Royal Guernsey Militia and he got together a number of what he considered to be "likely" civilians with a view to forming a machine gun company and taking them to the front himself. I think he despaired of the Militia ever getting to the front in time, although he need not have, but that's a tale to be told on another occasion. Anyhow, I was one of the team selected - strangely enough I have forgotten the identity of every one of the others - and I used to attend at the Beaucamp every morning for instruction. But the project did not commend itself to the competent authorities and came to nothing.

I couldn't stand it any longer. I had seen announcements to the effect that the Royal Engineers were calling for despatch riders and, whether because I was too cowardly or too slothful to join the infantry (although I came to that in time, via airships) or whether because I could ride a motorcycle and had a reasonable command of the French language and imagined I could be more useful as a despatch rider, I know not: anyhow, I decided to have a shot at it.

Le Patourel put no obstacle of any kind in my way, although my absence was going to be a great nuisance to him, and off I went to London. I found my way to an office in Dover Street - I had never been to London before and could only get about from place to place by popping up from the Tube at or near the right spot, getting a curiously incomplete picture of the metropolis - where a gentleman, who continued to read "The Times", reluctantly disengaged his left hand and pushed a form at me, remarking superciliously as he did this to a colleague similarly occupied "It's literally snowing despatch riders today" as I, very diffidently, put forward the qualifications which I hoped might induce my acceptance. Clearly, my impatience had been wholly unjustified. In this 'extension of Whitehall' the talk of beating the Germans was not one of the least urgency. I was accepted and told to return home and there await a further summons. I did so and gave Mr. Le Patourel a month's notice. Before that was up I received my call to join at Wormwood Scrubbs (Aerodrome) of all places. I duly arrived and paraded outside the big airship shed there and, at the first parade, the King's Regulations, or so much as was good for us to know, were read to us. I remember how offended I was when I heard that the penalty for desertion was death; I had come quite a long way and gone to a lot of trouble to join; was it likely that I would desert? But of course these things do happen and no doubt the reading of the Regulations, though tactless at that juncture, was necessary. But the thing that astounded me most was the fact that I was enlisted with the rank of Petty Officer Air Mechanic in No. 8 Squadron of the Armoured Car Division of the Royal Naval Air Service. The whole outfit was under the command of Wing-Commander Boothby. The pay and allowances were most generous. I had never been so well off in my life. It seemed that my search for adventure was going to be gratified. Our hectic rushes about England on what was termed training, our service in Belgium where I acted as despatch rider to the British Attaché to the Military Governor of Dunkirk, my experiences in the latter town under the shell fire of the "Big Bertha" installed near

Diksmuide, our return to England, how we were ordered to the Dardanelles and then had our orders countermanded; how the Division was broken up and our own Squadron disbanded; how we joined the Airship Section of the R.N.A.S. at Walney Island, Lancashire, with the reduced rank of Air Mechanic, the break-up of the old non-rigid dirigible "Silver Queen" one very foggy morning after she had collided with the Airship Shed and dropped all her water ballast on us, how I was offered the job of Second Coxswain on the newer non-rigid dirigible but asked instead to be, and was, recommended for a commission in the infantry, although in themselves interesting, would take too long to relate.

On a January evening in 1916, I left the Airship Station for the last time to walk across to Barrow-in-Furness to catch the night express for London and in my pocket I had a railway voucher through to Guernsey and a letter from the War Office informing me that, with effect from a certain then future date in that same month, I was gazetted a Second Lieutenant in the East Kent Regiment and, moreover, I had been given a week's leave. I am ashamed to say that, at the time, the East Kent Regiment meant nothing to me but, when on arrival in Guernsey I showed my letter to a knowledgeable acquaintance, he said "Good God, man, you ought to be proud and consider yourself lucky, you've been gazetted to "The Buffs".

III

JUNE 1917

The subaltern of a regiment of the line who has joined for the duration is not usually a very knowledgeable person with regard to the science of war but, even to those of us in this category, it was apparent that something big was afoot.

Of course we knew, and were proud of the fact, that we formed part of General (afterwards Field Marshal Lord) Plumer's Army and had he not an incomparable Chief of Staff in General Sir Charles Harington. But the preparations of which we saw signs on every hand went beyond our wildest expectations. Railways, both broad and narrow gauge, had been constructed, vast dumps of shells and wire and stakes and bombs and S.A.A. and every other sort of thing that goes to the active making of war had been accumulated along our divisional front and presumably elsewhere in the Army's sector and guns of all calibres had been and were being brought in in greater numbers and varieties than we had deemed possible. Yes, clearly, something big was afoot.

There were rumours, too, that a vast tunnelling scheme had been engaged in designed, at the appropriate moment, to blow the summit of the Wytschaete Ridge and all thereon sky-high.

Now, at the time of which I am speaking, my own Battalion the 8th Buffs. was back in rest billets and one of my jobs was to take a working party up every other night to a spot somewhere in rear of Scottish Wood where one of many deep and very capacious dug-outs was being constructed on the reverse slope of a small hill. It was not a popular task for Tommy Atkins doesn't altogether approve of working parties, especially at night, when he's supposed to be resting. But it had to be done and, with some curses and a good deal of grumbling, it was. So far as I can remember, we suffered no casualties although one evening as we were going to our night's task, the enemy threw quite a lot of shells near us, although I am sure he could not see us and was merely searching for possible targets. Anyhow, at the point which we had reached when he opened fire there was no natural cover of any kind but away slightly to the left was a long line of apparently empty waggons. These would afford some cover from splinters and such cover as was obtainable we took advantage of. I was always a naturally curious person and, while we were sheltering, I pulled myself up the side of one of the waggons to see what, if anything, was inside. You can judge of my feelings when I tell you that that waggon, and all the others, were full of that most unpleasant missile, the "football" type of ammunition that we used to fire with such effect from trench mortars. The cover of which we had so promptly availed ourselves was as hurriedly discarded. Our dug-out and all the others were completed at last and then one day we heard the news that the show - which became known as the Battle of Messines - was to come off on June 7th, zero hour being 3.10 a.m. We were not to go over then but were to be in support until 3.10 p.m. of the same day when we were to move off and, going through our new front line, were to take up and hold a line some little distance east of a raised roadway known as the Damstrasse. The night before the battle my battalion had moved up into some of the dug-outs of which I spoke earlier and the one to which I had been directed was a magnificent affair with a wire bed for everybody and holding some four hundred of us. It was very deep, deeper than anything I had known previously.

Before turning in I had asked Baker, my servant, to call me at 3 a.m. so that I might be up in time to see the mines go up on the Ridge. He and I overslept, however, and I was awakened by a terrific rumbling. The dug-out rocked and appeared to be about to collapse. But the Durham miners who had done the timbering had worked well and truly and it stood up to the test. We kept touch with the front line and at last our zero hour arrived. As we were advancing, we met many prisoners, some bringing back our own wounded on stretchers and, without opposition, reached the line of the Damstrasse. Whether it was heat or a touch of gas, I don't know, but I remember I was violently sick and had a splitting headache. Here was I in the midst of a battle when there was nothing I should have liked better than to be tucked up in bed with a couple of aspirins. But it passed off and, a little later, we moved on to take up our position on the line allotted to us. It had been a very successful day and our troops had met with little resistance. Usually, the days or even weeks preceding a battle were occupied in cutting wire and knocking out the enemy's guns and mortars and, of course, as fast as they were knocked out they, or a large part of them, were replaced elsewhere. But, in this battle, new tactics had been tried. Careful aeroplane spotting had fixed the position of practically the whole of the enemy's defensive weapons and these had been left intact until the morning of the battle and then, just before the infantry went forward, the most formidable bombardment of the war so far experienced had knocked them out. It was a battle brilliantly commanded and brilliantly carried into execution.

As the day progressed, however, the enemy brought in his guns and reinforced his new front line. At about 7 p.m. our guns opened up and the enemy replied and soon every gun and machine gun that could be brought to bear was firing. It was terrible and yet magnificent. It seemed as though each side had a 'crise de nerfs', the Germans apparently thinking that a further thrust was imminent and we that they were about to counter-attack.

The troops who had taken part in the morning's attack and through whom we had passed had moved on again through us to hold a new front line roughly a thousand yards ahead of our position, and in the midst of the evening's bombardment, they signalled back using the newly issued signalling panels. I was signalling officer of our battalion at the time and went out with a signaller to try and get the message. It meant signalling to the front line in full view of the enemy but it couldn't be helped and soon they began lobbing 4.2's at us. At last I got a reply that the front line battalion was trying to get brigade signals and didn't want me; my signals asking them to give me a message to deliver were either misunderstood or ignored. There was only one thing to be done. I must find out what was wrong with brigade signals and try to put them in touch with the battalion calling them. I knew the location of the brigade signalling post and that it was manned in part by some of my own signallers lent them for the battle, among them Davey, a Post Office telegraphist with a phenomenal turn of speed. So, picking up a runner, I got back as quickly as I could. I had just reached the post, a former German pill-box facing, from our point of view, the wrong way, that is to say with the only means of ingress or egress facing the German front line, when a 4.2 shell burst almost under me. Half jumping and partly blown by the force of the explosion, I found myself inside the pill-box. I was obviously hit in the shoulder, and peppered all down the left side; pretty badly shaken too. But I took a stiff gulp of rum from my flask and felt better. Conditions inside are bad; the enemy is lamming the pill-box with

5.9's, all of them landing unpleasantly close and some falling on the pill-box itself. The concussion inside when this happens is terrible and the concrete won't stay the hammering very much longer. It's impossible to keep a candle burning and, in fact, impossible for the signalling post to function at all under these conditions. It must be evacuated. One by one, bringing out the gear, we must get away between the shell bursts. It wanted a surprising amount of will-power to leave this illusive shelter for the open and a possible shell full in the face.

We got out, however, without loss and moved to the flank and there, in a short length of trench, set up the post anew. We picked up the front-line battalion, received their message and despatched it. And then it was time for me to get looked at. I went back to battalion headquarters to find that my runner, who had seen the shell burst close to me and did not know that I had disappeared into the pill-box by the time the smoke dispersed, had reported that I had been blown to bits. The M.O. was not there at the moment and the C.O. (Lt. Col. F.C.R. Studd D.S.O.) and the Adjutant, always known to us as the Duchess, dressed my wounds with their own fair hands and despatched me to the base. I was en route for Blighty, one of those very lucky people, the walking wounded.

Two months later, I was at home on leave and about to walk into town when the postman met me at the gate and handed me a letter addressed to me in my C.O.'s handwriting. On the flap at the back were the pencilled words "I have just heard that your M.C. has come through". This was the first I had heard of it but the letter told me that he had recommended me for the coveted decoration. Arriving in town, I am surprised to receive congratulations on the matter and to find that, by a coincidence, the award was referred to in the *"Daily Mirror"* which had arrived that morning. The tailor, all smiles and congratulations, sews on the purple and white ribbon while I wait.

In the following September, I received a free warrant and a command to attend at Buckingham Palace. There, in the Throne Room, with a Band of the Scots Guards playing in the minstrels' gallery, I, with many hundreds of others, receive my decoration from the hands of King George V, who smiles kindly, shakes hands warmly and utters a brief word of congratulations. It is very quickly over and I go out to lunch to celebrate the occasion. But I am not wholly satisfied for there was no-one to accompany me to the Palace and no one to lunch with me. Sometimes, life can be a very lonely affair.

Postscript

Colonel Studd of The Buffs was a most unusual character, the kind one comes across in popular fiction. Brave beyond the ordinary, he always pretended to be scared stiff. He liked the finer things of life and hated war. I have always been grateful for the privilege of serving at his Battalion H.Q. and watching his reactions to triumph and disaster. They were those enjoined in Kipling's "If". When, his Battalion having had a particularly tough time and come through reasonably creditably, he was awarded the D.S.O., he refused to 'put it up' on the ground that it was the Battalion and not he - that had earned it. We, his immediate entourage, protested that he was letting the Battalion down and swore that we would all remove our own ribbons if he didn't heed us. With his usual disarming smile, he listened to his 'stupid' junior officers and allowed the necessary ribbon to be procured in Béthune and sewn on his Service jacket. When our battalion was disbanded in February, 1918, Col. Studd was sent to command a Battalion of the Northumberland Fusiliers. Not very long afterwards, we who had known and loved him were horrified to learn that he and every member of his H.Q. staff had been killed instantaneously - without a mark on any of them - by concussion from the explosion of one German shell. *Sic transit gloria mundi.* A great man and a great Regiment to whom my affections are pledged forever.

IV

March 1918

It is amazing what can be done, if you know how, in the way of turning a collection of men of all ages and classes of society and of varying outlooks and temperaments into a really efficient, well-disciplined battalion. But you must know how, as Major Corrall did.

The battalion to which he and I had belonged - the 8th Buffs - had been disbanded in February in accordance with the fiat which had gone forth that henceforth brigades were to consist of only three battalions instead of four as hitherto - the supply of cannon fodder was failing by now - and Major Corrall had been appointed by Major General Daly, the G.O.C. 24th Division, to command the 24th Divisional Depot Battalion whilst I, a mere Lieutenant with only fourteen months' seniority, was sent to a Camp to await further orders which, I anticipated, would probably direct me to join our 6th Battalion. I had absolutely nothing to do except tuck away four meals a day and this, to me, has always been an unendurable existence. I found it so - this time without the meals - at the Cherche Midi Prison in Paris over twenty years later; but in between my life seems to have been very full, not of big or important or even interesting things, but always full and so perhaps, unknowingly, I have achieved a considerable measure of happiness. But I digress. I learned that Major Corrall's command was not far from my Camp and, having obtained a day's leave, by lorry-jumping and other like means, I duly reached Curlu or rather the place where Curlu had been because, neither then nor thereafter, did I see a sign, except upon the map, of any village. I was warmly greeted by Major Corrall, to whom I offered my services ad interim and by whom they were accepted subject to the sanction of higher authority which Corrall said he would apply for. I returned to my own Camp, explained the position to my temporary C.O., who was quite indifferent as to whether I stayed or went and said as much. This was good enough for me and on the morrow, complete with equipment, I proceeded (I forget how) to join the Depot Battalion.

Corrall was doing wonders with it and with the camp at which it was stationed. It lay in a valley with a small river flanking it and there were dug-outs in the side of a hill in which the officers slept. The N.C.O.s and men had huts with wire beds, there was a first class guardroom and paths with white-washed stone borders had been laid out. Most of the material had been scrounged in the neighbourhood - I myself took part - with about a hundred others - in the removal in one piece across the river of a huge hut on which the C.O.'s covetous eyes had fallen - much to the dissatisfaction and annoyance of the Salvage Corps. Discipline was excellent, the men were contented and their precision at arms drill was almost worthy of the Guards. We worked tremendously hard at our job of putting the final touches to the soldiers who had come from England to us to be trued up before being thrown into the line and, as we had all by now a good deal of experience of the line ourselves, what we taught wasn't only theory. Corrall's fame spread abroad and all sorts of "Red Tabs" looked in - as though by accident - to see what he was up to. Every officer had to know Kipling's "If" by heart and carry a copy in his left, I repeat "left" - breast pocket. So did every man in the "stunt" platoon trained by Corrall personally.

Very early on the morning of the 21st March we became conscious of a violent drumming. It was unmistakable as one of the biggest, if not the biggest bombardment we had heard. It was a long way off and it wasn't ours or we should have known about it. It must be the long expected German attack. All that day and part of the next it continued and it appeared to get closer although whether that was due to a change of wind or not we didn't know. Rumours filtered through of terrible things. Our front line entirely shattered with all the troops therein blotted out. The withdrawal of our support and reserves, and so forth. And then on the night of the 22nd, Corrall called us together and told us that all of us who were fit for the front line were being taken up there in lorries on the following morning. We gathered that reserves were conspicuous by their absence and I think I am right in saying that our battalion was the only reserve the Division could call upon.

We duly "embussed" the next morning and were deposited at a little village whose name I now forget but which was about equidistant from Vraignes and Le Verguier. There was a brigade headquarters there and I remember we were given welcome cups of tea and a cap full of revolver ammunition, for we officers each had a revolver but not a round between us. It was very foggy as we fell in on the main road preparatory to marching off to - in the words of our orders - "extricate the G.O.C. 17th Brigade". He was one of the youngest Brigadier

Generals in the Army clearly destined for very great things. It is a measure of the fickleness of human memory, but, try as I will, I cannot recollect his name. The Germans were shelling at random, a procedure which always got on my nerves much more than the shelling of a definite objective. To my amazement and inexpressible delight, Corrall put me in command of the "stunt" platoon, which he had himself trained to a very high pitch of perfection, and away we went in the direction of the front line. I suppose it was merely because he and I were the only two Buffs' officers in the battalion but, to me, it was the greatest honour ever to have befallen me. Going as we all thought, to certain death, the platoon and I walked on air. We soon discovered that the 17th Brigade and its G.O.C. were not in need of extrication; in fact they retired through us after inflicting as much loss as they could on the enemy and there didn't seem anything left for us to do just then. The whole division was being moved back and was being replaced by fresh troops and there seemed no point in our not moving back with it. But, on the left of the road as we moved back, there was a gap of about a thousand yards entirely unheld and we learned that a battalion has got mislaid. Corrall takes a snap decision and orders us to fill the gap, so in we go. The place is well wired but the trench is but one spit deep. We get busy remedying this and are getting dug in when at about 3 p.m. we see the Germans advancing in great numbers. We are short of ammunition and have very little food or water. If they make a determined attack we can't hold them for long. But they are apparently impressed by the show we put up and dig themselves in and send out stretcher bearers under cover of red cross flags to pick up their wounded. It was the only time I ever saw this happen. We ceased fire immediately.

I'm in the reserve line in command of a lot of lads of about eighteen. They're dear boys but I don't like the prospect of things if there's real trouble, for not one of them has been in the line before. A German plane flies overhead the length of our line and very, very low. Obviously he is photographing us. I try several rifle shots at him without any result. Then, later, they open up on us with the high velocity Austrian guns which they're using these days but we sustain no casualties and our morale doesn't suffer nearly as much from this as it does from the shelling we get from our own artillery who are apparently unaware of our presence. The Germans send out patrols and we take some of them prisoner. As one of the poor devils passes me, I, wanting more than anything else to know the time of the coming

German attack, ask him this in my slowest most distinct English and, to encourage a reply, draw my revolver. It is clear that he has not understood a word, it is clear, too, that my stupid gesture has not disturbed him, so I grin, put my revolver back and wave him on. Between ourselves, he got the better of that little encounter. And then comes the news that at 3 a.m. we are to be withdrawn under cover of a show to be put up by the Machine Gun Company on our right. Three o'clock arrives and we get away without having sustained a single casualty. We form up on the road and march interminably, or so it seems. Millions of our shells are stacked on either side of the road, being abandoned to the enemy. Eventually we reach a village and our C.O. reports, apparently to some strange Brigade Headquarters. He is told to turn us about and go up the line again. He explains that we are without ammunition, without food and without water. He is told that if he says any more he will be placed under arrest. The chap who treats us thus is presumably 'compos mentis', although I doubt it. Weakly we drag ourselves to our feet and march eastwards again but we haven't gone a hundred yards before commonsense operates on someone at Bde. H.Q. and we are recalled by runner and allowed to resume our withdrawal westwards. We reach another village and are halted. Immediately and as one man, the entire Battalion lies down in its tracks and the bulk of us are soon asleep. A batman comes and whispers to me that he has a cup of tea for me. This pulls me together and I explore the village. I find in a shed a heap of raw carrots and spread the news. They are not to be recommended, as a rule, for a breakfast dish but on this occasion they prove extremely palatable.

Then on again and we find ourselves in open country, traversing ploughed fields, some six hundred yards from a village. Here we are told to form a line but not to trouble to dig ourselves in. We are covering the retirement of the Division across the Somme bridges but it's only a formality having us there at all for there isn't a German within miles.

Unknown to us - and where ignorance is bliss 'tis folly to be wise - Roisel, our railhead, has long since been taken and, within half an hour of our taking up our position, shrapnel is bursting uncomfortably close to us, so close that one sees the loose earth splashed like the surface of a pond into which a handful of gravel has been thrown. To get as close to us as that means that they are observing us from that village, probably from the church tower.

Then we see the German infantry emerge from the village and advance in open order in our direction. The shrapnelling ceases and in its stead they chuck high explosive at us and do so very accurately. And then the word is passed along and reaches me that we are to retire. Remembering the text-book on the subject of withdrawals, I pass suitable orders to the forty odd men who have attached themselves to me when bang! I am hit in the right upper arm so that the rifle I am aiming at the time falls from my grasp; bang! I am hit under the right eye and imagine that most of my cheek on that side has been shot away. I find on feeling it with the hand I can still use that it is relatively intact but pouring blood. Bang! I get a nasty one in the right thigh from which I pour blood. Taking the time from the others, my own command has withdrawn and I am alone. The Germans are now about three hundred yards away advancing steadily and I can just get to my knees and that's all. I see two riflemen of the 2nd Bn. The Rifle Brigade away on my right. I shout to them. They look at me and carry on. I shout again and they come and pick me up. They have to put me down every now and then for I'm fainting from shock and loss of blood but gradually we get back. I get them to tie my wounded arm around my neck with a bit of string for I can't bear the weight of it. The going over the ploughed land is heavy with my damaged leg but we reach a road running parallel with our original line and then I see our Medical Officer. I ask for a stretcher. "My dear fellow", he says, "there isn't one for a mile, you'll have to go on walking." And then, on a motorcycle, along comes an Officer of the 73rd Brigade whom I know slightly. He stops his motorcycle and I beg a lift. He says he's sure I can't hang on: I'm just as sure that I can and I do and off we go. A few hundred yards down the road we come across Major Corrall and stop and, on my demand and after much hesitation, he gives me a tot of rum. This bucks me up tremendously and I hang on like grim death till we run into a cutting and there find an ambulance with one vacant stretcher. I am soon on that stretcher bound for the Casualty Clearing Station and Blighty.

V

MAY 1920

I was badly wounded on the 23rd of March 1918 in front of Peronne in a rearguard action in which the body of men (it had ceased to have such a determinate form as would entitle it to any other appellation) to which I was attached was engaged. In the nick of time to prevent my being taken prisoner, I was propped up on the carrier of a motor-cycle ridden by the Intelligence Officer of the 73rd Brigade, I reached the Casualty Clearing Station, had my wounds dressed and was despatched by train and was bombed on the way reaching No. 8 General Hospital, Rouen, some days later to be operated upon and rested a bit before being taken across channel in a palatial hospital ship and finding myself at length in a hospital bed in the great dining room of the Great Central Hotel, Marylebone. That, so far as this story goes, is by the way. But if it hadn't happened, it is at least certain that this tale would be quite different.

My wounds were such as to keep me in bed until the middle of July and, having no relatives or friends in or around London at that time, I found life rather monotonous. I had been reading for the Guernsey Bar when war broke out and, in July 1914, had taken my Licence en Droit at Caen University, Calvados, France. Between me and call to the Guernsey Bar there still stood two hurdles, call to the English Bar and the examination in Guernsey Law, Evidence and Procedure, and Conveyancing which is conducted by the Bailiff, the Procureur and an Advocate appointed by the Royal Court of Guernsey. There seemed little chance of my getting back to Guernsey for the time being but here was I, disabled for at least another four months or more in so far as the war was concerned, set down by providence within a taxi ride of the Middle Temple, the Inn of Court that I had long hoped to join when the opportunity allowed. There came a day when I was fit enough to get into a taxi and on that day I went to the Treasury of the Middle Temple and paid my entrance fees and called on Dr. W. Blake Odgers LL.D., the Director of Legal Education. I purchased enough books to be going on with and started in on Criminal Law. In those days you could take the subjects in the first half one by one in any order you chose, the second half had to be taken in one dose. It wasn't easy after nearly four years of mental idleness and fairly vigorous outdoor pursuits (I suppose war can be termed a pursuit and it certainly had been during my last few days of it, though not previously) to concentrate on the authors on Criminal law prescribed for my enlightenment but it would have been more difficult still to tackle any of the other subjects. By diligence I duly obtained a First at the following exam., was ploughed once in Constitutional Law and eventually after nineteen months, had passed all my examinations for call to the English Bar and had obtained a Second Class Honours Certificate and had bracketed equally with a man called Garland for the Powell Prize for Evidence and Procedure.

Meanwhile I had, on the 11th November, 1918, been discharged from hospital and sent to join the 2nd Battn. Royal Guernsey Light Infantry stationed at Fort George, Guernsey. Back in January when my Battalion, the 8th Buffs, had been disbanded in connection with the reduction in the number of battalions per brigade then brought into effect, I had volunteered for service with R.G.L.I., for I knew their Service Battalion had been badly cut up and that they were in need of reinforcements and, after all, as a Guernseyman born and bred, my duty lay with them. This had not been forgotten and so the 12th November 1918 saw me in Guernsey. But the war was over, although peace was not to be signed for some time yet. I was not really a soldier at heart and, to tell the truth, I found it infernally dull after service in France.

I still had some bits of shell in me and one of them caused quite a bit of discomfort so I went sick and was operated on. I was in hospital just over thirty days and this meant, under a rule then in being, automatic demobilisation. I was free to pursue my legal studies.

There were lectures to attend at whichever of the Inns of Court was the venue thereof for the time being. There were dinners to be eaten in the magnificent old Hall of the Middle Temple but between times I found it cheaper and more congenial to live in Guernsey where I went through the books of precedents, read Gallienne on "Renonciation par Loi Outrée", "Jeremie on the Law of Inheritance" and performed the mental gymnastics passing for study which are customary in the case of would-be Guernsey practitioners, and passed my local examination "with credit to myself" so I was informed by that genial Bailiff, Mr. (afterwards: Sir) Edward Chepmell Ozanne. The Parliament of my Inn had, on my application, excused me, on the ground of my war service, from eating the full number of dinners, and now the time had come, as it seemed to me, for the crown to be set on my achievement. I was to be called to the English Bar. Honourable as that call is, it is not the end but the beginning, the commencement of the realisation of the minute extent, for practical purposes, of one's legal knowledge. This I soon discovered afterwards and it does not form part of this particular tale. Attired, then, in white waistcoat and tails and wearing for the first time the brand new stuff gown purchased from Ede & Ravenscroft in Chancery Lane a few days before and complete with bands and wig, I might have been seen wending my way to the Parliament Chamber at half past five that evening. Then, proceeding two by two, we made our way with great solemnity the length of the Great Hall where, before the Reader, we signed our names in the Register set out on a table made from timbers from the "Golden Hind". I was an Utter Barrister. Then came dinner in Hall at 6 p.m. Although the port is very good, dinner never lasts very long and it is over in time to enable me to catch the boat train for Southampton en route for Guernsey.

My luggage is already in the Left Luggage Office at Waterloo and as, nicely mellowed, I trudge across Waterloo Bridge carrying my blue bag containing wig, bands and gown, I feel strangely elated and that God's in His Heaven and that all's well in this best of all possible worlds.

Two days later, I appear before the Royal Court of Guernsey and ask to be admitted to the Guernsey Bar and the Procureur (Mr. Arthur William Bell) having certified to the Court that I am a Licencié en Droit and a Barrister-at-Law and that I have passed the local examination in Legal Knowledge and that I am otherwise entitled to be admitted, the question is put to the Jurats by the Bailiff. They assent and, having advanced to the Greffier's table, the latter official reads to me the solemn, dignified and yet very practical Oath of Advocate of the Royal Court. I kiss the Bible in sign of my taking the Oath, the Bailiff leads in the cry "Dieu sauve le Roi" and I am invited to retire and robe.

Conscious that the Court is waiting, one's fingers become thumbs as one tries to tie the unaccustomed tapes of one's bands but one does it somehow and takes one's seat in the humblest place at the Bar. And there falls from the lips of the Bailiff (Sir Edward Ozanne K.B.E.) one of those charming speeches of welcome of which he is such a master and which are not the least of those characteristics which endear him so to the people of Guernsey.

VI

THE CHURCH IN PERIL ON THE SEA

One summer's day in 1934, a distinguished party set out from St. Peter Port on the motor yacht Mandolin, belonging to the Reverend Peter Thomas Mignot, C.B.E., C.F., en route for Sark. It consisted of H.E. the Lieutenant Governor, Major General Lord Ruthven, C.B., C.M.G., D.S.O., His Lordship the Bishop of Winchester (Dr. Cyril Forster Garbett, D.D., afterwards Archbishop of York), the Very Reverend Agnew W.G. Giffard, M.A., Dean of Guernsey and Col. F. Brousson, D.S.O., Government Secretary in Guernsey. I went along as legal adviser.

Mr. Mignot was in command. He had an English skipper who was a most competent seaman but had little, if any, knowledge of local waters. The sole deckhand was a Guernsey lad named Harold Hobbs. His father was the coxswain of the R.N.L.I. lifeboat stationed in Guernsey and young Hobbs later became a member of her crew and was to lose his life when, on June 28th, 1940, a German plane machine-gunned her off Noirmont Point, Jersey. Harold Hobbs, as it turned out, was the only member of Mandolin's ship's company with any local knowledge worth talking about.

Directly after we left the harbour, the Lieutenant Governor told me that the Bishop wanted to talk to me on the legal aspects of the Church matters in Sark which were the reason for our journey and that he was below in the saloon awaiting me. I joined him and our talks lasted about a quarter of an hour.

The sea was very calm but there was some fog about and, when I came up on deck, I noticed that it had thickened and that no land was visible. Harold Hobbs passed me and I enquired which way we had come. He replied that we had passed the Lower Heads Buoy three minutes earlier. I glanced at my watch and, unconcernedly, noted the time. But for that it is virtually certain that we would have been wrecked less than half an hour later. Of that possibility I had no inkling until it occurred.

As, about twenty minutes later, we sighted land there was a murmur of: "Ah! there's the Bec du Nez" (the northernmost point of Sark). The land was shrouded in mist and its details were only partially discernible. I looked at my watch and was startled that we had made the Bec so soon. Unless we had been doing about twelve knots (and I knew she didn't do more than nine), it couldn't be done in the time. Alerted, I watched closely what was happening. Clearly, Mr. Mignot thought he had rounded the Bec and he starboarded his helm to take us inside the tail of the Pécheresse Rock. And then, as we got nearer, I realised that what he had taken for the Bec was the west point of Brecqhou and the rock he proposed to go inside was not the Pécheresse but La Moie Batard, between which and the land there is no passage. I think he must have realised there was something wrong for he left the glass-fronted wheelhouse to get a better view. Meanwhile, we were moving to certain destruction and the presence of the Bishop, the Dean and the Clerk in Holy Orders who had just left the wheel did nothing to reassure me. Now, in all normal circumstances, it just is 'not done' to interfere in the navigation of another man's yacht. I had, in many years boating in Sark waters, never been in so close to Brecqhou as we now were on our present course. I had no other knowledge of the underwater profile of La Moie Batard than that its western face was bold. Something had to be done and done quickly. All the others, including Mr. Mignot by now, were grouped right up forward apparently fascinated by what they saw ahead. I rushed up the two steps to the wheelhouse and yelled to the skipper to put both engines full astern. He did so at once but I had no hope of doing more than slowing her before she struck.

The skipper started to starboard the helm so as to turn her away from La Moie Batard but it was near high water and the tide was pouring up between Brecqhou and Givaude. She must have been about 75 feet long and I was afraid that, as we swung and the tide caught her bow and accentuated the effect of her helm, she would rip her bilge open on the port side aft as she came into contact with any underwater protuberances on the rock's southern face.

Rightly or wrongly, I took a split second decision and brought the helm back so that, with any luck, her stem would strike La Moie Batard fair and square. She had a slight overhang forward and it was my hope that all the damage would be above the waterline. The skipper was as cool as a cucumber and I am sure he thought I had panicked because he said to me: "Steady, sir". There wasn't time to explain to him why I was doing what I was for all my attention was on the approaching rock and the group of people forward who, if they didn't get away from where they were, were either going to be badly bruised when she struck or else thrown in the water. I didn't even shout to them; the effect of the approaching rock on me was mesmeric. The yacht stopped with her stem about 8 or 9 feet from the rock (I had almost lost sight of it over the stem and it is my firm belief that it was the tide rushing up inside Givaude, quite as much as the engines, that stopped her from striking. I told the skipper to keep her engines going full astern until we were well out of danger and then gave him the direction of the Bec du Nez, which now loomed up out of the fog. He told me afterwards that her reversing gear had never operated properly until that season and I was glad that I hadn't known that earlier. The rest of the journey to Sark was uneventful and we anchored near the Gull's Chapel in Grève de la Ville and were ferried to the Creux Harbour (the Maseline Harbour had not yet been thought about).

For some reason, I got aboard before the others. Mr. Mignot did not mention the morning's adventure but it must have shaken him very badly for, while we were having tea, he suddenly asked me if I would like to buy the yacht. I explained to him that I could not afford to run her let alone buy her. He was a very rich man and I suppose it hadn't struck him that I was most decidedly not.

The others came aboard and we started for home. By now, it was after half tide down. We returned the way we had come. Off the Bec, Jolicot was now virtually in danger for us (at L.W. Springs it dries 5 or 6 feet) for we could not have been drawing less than six feet. It looked to me as though we were going to pass over it. Harold Hobbs, who was standing up forward, thought so too, for he signalled frantically to Mr. Mignot to port his helm. This he did promptly. Rounding the Bec du Nez, we pointed for the Lower Heads Buoy and, in due course, picked it up. It seemed impossible that we could run into any further danger and then, to my amazement, instead of rounding it or passing reasonably close to it on its northern side, Mr. Mignot, when we were about 200 yards short of it, turned and headed direct for St. Peter Port Harbour. The marks on Guernsey were too indistinct to be sure whether we actually passed over the Lower Heads which are awash at Low Water but if we didn't, we passed perilously close to them. The Bishop was sitting next to me and, a few moments later, said he was very grateful for my intervention in the morning and I then told him that he had been in danger not once, as he thought, but three times that day and I begged him to promise me that in no circumstances, would he ever go to sea with Mr. Mignot again as it was much too dangerous. He said that he gladly gave that promise.

Mr. Mignot sold his yacht at the end of the season.

The following year I was promoted from part time Solicitor General (as such, I was entitled to carry on such private practice as was not incompatible with that post) to Attorney General and that meant a diminution in my income of about £500 p.a. I could no longer afford to keep my little motor cruiser "Mary Rose" and advertised her for sale. To my great surprise Mr. Mignot bought her. He pulled out the 12 h.p. engine with many years of service still in it and installed a most expensive 30 h.p. Thornycroft engine which merely made her squat aft and increased her speed by not more than half a knot. She was moored in the Harbour at the time of the German bombing and a great splinter tore out most of the port side of her cabin top. After the war, she was sold to a fisherman and, so far as I know, is still afloat and earning her living as a fishing boat.

VII

April 1935

It had been an exceptionally long trial but it terminated just before the luncheon interval. The accused had been sentenced to death. Ignorant of this, the afternoon queue had already formed and was waiting patiently for 2.30 p.m. An interesting trial in many respects; interesting because of the enigmatic character of the accused, the nature of some of the evidence, the eminence of certain of the witnesses and also because such a crime as this occurs only once in every half-century or so in Guernsey. When it opened I was Solicitor-General and acting as Attorney-General, for the holder of that office had died during the previous year and the new appointment had not been made. It was during the course of the trial that I became the new Attorney General. Advocates H.H. Randell and W.H. Arnold defended the accused. But having whetted your appetite, perhaps you'd like to hear about it.

You will have gathered already that the crime of which the accused was alleged to be guilty was that of murder and these, briefly, are the facts.

Gertrude Elizabeth de la Mare, a young married woman separated from her husband and having a small daughter, was housekeeper to Mr. A. Brouard an old bachelor living at Camp Joinet, St. Andrew's, Guernsey. The old man was careful with his money and Mrs. de la Mare evidently believed him to be an old miser possessing a considerable fortune. Actually the strict economy he exercised was necessary owing to his limited means. Anyhow she appears to have made up her mind to become his heiress and, with that intent, she cut his throat with a breadknife as he lay in bed early one morning. She also made a will for him in writing resembling his calligraphy and she also prepared a last letter from the old man explaining his motive for committing suicide and speaking highly of herself. She rushed to neighbours and telephoned for a doctor and saw that the "deceased's last letter" was read by the latter, who, incidentally, was deceived by it, and she produced the "will" at the old man's Bank later in the day. Now in the will and in the last letter were certain curious mistakes and, when Mrs. de la Mare was asked to write a concise statement of all the facts for the purposes of the enquiry, strangely enough many of the same mistakes were found in that statement. She was originally charged with uttering a document knowing it to be forged but this was only a holding charge. The second doctor called to view the body was of the opinion that murder had been committed. So, by now, was the first doctor but it was clear that, originally, he had thought it a case of suicide and who, having read the "last letter" could blame him. But there was scope for the defence here and as you know, under English law and Guernsey law as well, the prosecution have the burden of proof on their shoulders and if in the mind of the Jury - in Guernsey, the Jurats - there is any reasonable doubt as to the guilt of the accused, the latter is entitled to an acquittal. So I decided to call in Sir Bernard Spilsbury to conduct an immediate post mortem examination. We asked Scotland Yard to handle the matter for us and that was why that genial detective officer Chief Inspector Duncan and his assistant Detective Sergeant came to Guernsey. Their methods, their care, patience and diligence, were a revelation to the local force.

Well, there was no doubt in Sir Bernard Spilsbury's mind that murder had been committed and he was able, out of his vast experience and knowledge of morbid pathology, to reconstruct the crime. There were some delicate blood tests to be done, too, and so the services of the eminent toxicologist Dr. Roche Lynch were requisitioned. Gruesome as the raison d'être of that visit was, I believe the great men enjoyed their visit to Guernsey and we were charmed and honoured at having the opportunity of meeting them. Guernsey is usually off the map but it wasn't then.

The question of the handwriting in the "will" and "last letter" was of course crucial and much too important for us to depend upon the evidence of a Bank Manager. And so Mr. Gurrin, whose fame as an expert in calligraphy extends far beyond England, was brought into the picture. There was the evidence too, of a very large number of local people. The jig-saw puzzle was at length complete, every piece fitting perfectly and it showed one thing only, that no one but Gertrude de la Mare could be guilty of this foul murder and that she, in fact, had committed it.

She was committed for trial before the Royal Court in due course.

The case had attracted considerable attention and the great daily papers sent reporters and one of them commissioned Mr. E. Philips

Oppenheim, the novelist, to write an impression of the last day's proceedings. Crowds thronged the public gallery throughout the trial. Queues waited patiently outside the Court for hours to take the place of those who vacated their seats.

The Bailiff sat with eleven Jurats - the twelfth had received a letter from the accused some months previously applying for a post as housekeeper. It contained similar mistakes to those which were so material in the relevant documents and so, on the representation of the prosecution, he did not sit except as a spectator. As a potential victim, he would have been a much greater financial prize.

Day succeeded day but the interest was sustained throughout, being heightened as the eminent experts gave their evidence - incidentally Sir Bernard Spilsbury who had not been admitted to practice as a doctor in Guernsey, was described to the Court by Counsel for the defence, much to his and the Court's amusement, as, for that reason, a quack in the eyes of Guernsey law. I remember in this connection Mr. Randell asking him whether he expected to be paid and Sir Bernard, with a twinkle in his eye, replying "I hope so". Then the accused went into the box and put up a tremendous fight against overwhelming odds. On the thirteenth day there remained only the speeches of Counsel and the summing up and at last these were over. The Jurats were invited one by one - as is the custom - to cast their votes. All agreed that the accused was guilty but five added the words "but insane". And so by a verdict of six votes to five Gertrude de la Mare was sentenced by the Bailiff to death in customary form. Asked if she wished to say anything as to why sentence should not be passed on her, she replied "Yes, Mr. Sherwill knows I'm innocent". This the court appeared to consider unimportant. As is customary, the execution of the sentence was deferred until the pleasure of His Majesty became known and we all felt confident that, with so narrow a margin in the vote justifying the death sentence, the latter would not be carried out. It was not. All the papers including a transcript of the evidence were transmitted to London and in a surprisingly short space of time, for the Home Office moves very quickly when a human being is in such suspense as was Mrs. de la Mare, His Majesty had pardoned her upon condition that she undergo penal servitude for life. A strange form, this pardon, but that is the form it takes. And so Gertrude Elizabeth de la Mare did not amass a fortune but served the term of years which a life sentence connotes and actually came back to Guernsey to thank her counsel who had put up such a terrific fight in the teeth of overwhelming odds.

AJS on motorcycle near Dunkirk : Leaving for England

AJS from a group photograph of Royal Guernsey Militia officers, 1925

Mary Rose being launched at St. Peter Port *(circa 1933)*

Dick and John, with dinghies, at Omonville

John and Mary Rose aboard Ariel

Painting Warwick at Longy Bay, Alderney 1938

Warwick at Omonville

Warwick towing Ariel on last lap to Omonville against the tide

Havelet House, Guernsey

VIII

GRÈVE DE LA VILLE

There was a time, not so very many years ago, when bombs and rationing did not play the part in our lives - or make havoc with them, as the case may be, - they do now but it's a strange and rather distressing thing that we none of us seem to appreciate our blessings until we lose them. It is so with health, with occupation, with home comforts, with liberty, and even with love. Presumably it is unavoidable but what a pity. Now in those days the seas and coastal waters were free and safe, the ingredients for preparing a picnic lunch were easily obtainable, petrol could be produced in unlimited quantities and one's salary was at the pre-war level.

When you live in Guernsey, which as everybody knows is very, very small, you soon tire of the delights of touring the Island in a motor car. The countryside is - most of it - very beautiful, and some of the seascapes visible from heights or shore entrancing; but nevertheless (I think because the motor car is too effortless a means of transport, and probably if one "worked one's passage" on a bicycle the reward would be commensurate with the effort), although, particularly on Sundays, there was an almost endless procession of vehicles, on the faces of the majority of the occupants a keen observer would have observed a look of resigned boredom.

We, the salary being, as I say, still intact in those days, had taken to the sea. Our first ship was a converted naval pinnace which, we discovered subsequently, had had the considerable defects of her hull veiled by an extra thickness of outside planking, itself by then not too sound. She was fitted with an ancient Parsons 28-36 h.p. engine of the type, long since outmoded, wherein the exhaust and the inlet valve stems were housed, one inside the other, in the same guide. The propeller shaft emerged on the port side of the deadwood and, as this was very sturdy, one of the three blades of the propeller was always almost fully out of action and she thus carried a certain amount of "port helm". She was 29 feet 4 inches in length and had a beam of 10 feet 6 inches, was very heavy and unhandy and did not satisfy me for long and I sold her as a work boat to the tenant of an adjacent island.

My next venture was more ambitious, not in size but in quality. I sent a knowledgeable person to Southampton to try to pick up something near the dream ship I described to him and after an absence of some days I had word that he thought he had found what I wanted but she was still on the stocks; would I come over and look at her?

Needless to say, I went and was taken into Lallow's yard at Cowes and there, in a corner, was the completely planked hull of a duck of a launch capable of being finished in accordance with the owner's wishes. She was 26 feet 4 inches in length and 7 feet beam with nice lines and first class workmanship. We gave her a teak cabin-top with a beautifully rounded fore-end. When finished she was a picture. We fitted a more powerful engine later and had many a trip in her - she did the run to Alderney in 2 hours and 35 minutes - for Guernsey with its subsidiary islands is the happy hunting ground of the amateur yachtsman. And then I received promotion as a result of which my income decreased and I sold her. She passed into good hands and was re-engined with the best that money can buy; but when last I saw her, her beautiful cabin-top had been nearly blown away on the port side, for she had been caught by part of a bomb or the blast of one dropped in St. Peter Port harbour on the 28th June 1940.

But having once owned a boat one is never quite happy without one. One haunts the waterfront and gazes with longing, covetous eyes on one's nautical friends and gets little consolation in the trips which their generosity and understanding provide.

And so I came to acquire "Warwick". I had long been hankering after a new boat and I felt that I could probably afford one if I economised in other directions. The whole of my working life is spent indoors and I felt, despite my family responsibilities, that I required and perhaps deserved a little recreation.

A marine engineer showed me a photo of her and one or two other craft but I liked her lines best and she appeared to be well found and reasonably well engined. She had to be a one man craft, for I couldn't afford a man, and so must have no brass requiring constant cleaning. Dirty brass-work is an eyesore and the constant work of keeping it clean a weariness of the flesh and a terrible handicap to enjoyment for, with limited spare time, one finds it almost entirely eaten up in polishing. Her Ford engines commended themselves to me principally because they make a very reliable marine job and because the renewal of spare parts can be effected relatively cheaply.

Let me describe her to you; if you are interested in boats, the description won't bore you but if you're not you can always skip it.

"Warwick" is 35 feet 4 inches in length with a beam of 9 feet and half an inch. Her port of registry is London. Built by Messrs. Short Bros. of Rochester in the late twenties, she has rather pronounced flare forward and equally pronounced tumble-home aft. Excellent in a head sea, she has rather full lines aft, and, according to persons versed in these matters, she would be at her worst running before a sea. Right forward is a chain locker, then a shallow cupboard and next a very comfortable little two berth sleeping cabin with locker and cupboard space and a good skylight over. Not much floor space but I personally prefer it to the saloon for sleeping in. Then coming aft, a lavatory with wash-basin on the starboard side and a well appointed little galley opposite with a very useful two burner petrol stove, a good sized sink, plate racks, with saucepan, kettle, cutlery and crockery. Then the saloon is mahogany with two wide berths with lockers under and a sideboard on the port side. In both forward cabin and saloon are V Spring mattresses. Aft of the saloon is the engine room fitted with two Panther engines, that is to say engines of Ford "T" model converted to marine use by Messrs. Hylands Ltd., a very excellent conversion. During the first few minutes after starting up it is necessary to juggle with the gear lever putting it almost into "astern" to prevent the ship running ahead and charging whatever may be there. This is the usual "T" model fault and the moment the clutch plates get unstuck there is no further trouble. The starboard engine drives a dynamo for lighting purposes and the port one a bilge pump. Over the starboard engine is a small engine driving another dynamo also for lighting purposes, over the port engine a hand-operated bilge pump. The late owner was connected with an electrical firm and the electrical installation was of the best, all compartment and navigation lamps being so lighted.

Her cockpit is very roomy and nicely panelled in mahogany and the aft compartment houses the helm and two petrol tanks holding 18 gallons each. There are extensive lockers in the cockpit.

Fitted with a 24 feet mast in a tabernacle, she carries a big foresail and mainsail and will sail after a fashion. She has over a ton of inside ballast in small pigs. She carries an 8 feet 6 inch mahogany dinghy which can be hauled on deck by means of the boom and a tackle and then housed. Painted buff with green waterline she's a nice looking craft. She can roll but so do all of her size.

Well now that you know all about her, come with the family and me in her this Sunday bound for Grève de la Ville. The weather is glorious, the sea like the proverbial mill pond. The flood tide has made, let's take advantage of it. Leaving St. Peter Port, we steer E. $^{1}/_{2}$ N. crossing the "douit" of the Little Russel, passing south of Brehon Tower and between the Petit Creux and Alligande not bothering to keep to the steamer channel for there's plenty of water for us, then rounding Epec and leaving Vermerette on our port hand, we are in the Passe Percée with Jethou and Crevichon and Tinker on our right and the Percée Rock and Herm and Meulettes on our left. As pretty a land and sea scape as any you will find. The Fourquies lie ahead, there's water but we won't go over them but, leaving them on our starboard hand, we head for the Baie de la Jument on the west side of Big Sark, passing Le Pigeon in the Herm cliffs and the Selle Rock on our port side. There's Noire Pute away to the north-east but we shan't go near it as the tide is [sic].

Brecqhou stands out clearly in the middle distance with Sark lying ahead on the other side of the Gouliot Passage now coming into view. The tide is taking us crab fashion up the Big Russel and we shall just about make the Bec du Nez on this course. We pass twenty yards to the north of the Bec and rounding it, pass inside Jolicot, now well covered, and outside Moulinet lying off the Courbée du Nez and then haul in a bit to clear inside the tail of the Pécheresse. We needn't bother about the Boue de Pignon which always carries plenty of water for us and we are outside the Demie and the Boue de la Fontaine. We pass Noire Pierre and the Petite Moie and, heading towards the Chapelle des Mauvres, run in until we are well inside the buoy in Grève de la Ville and drop anchor. Well, what about it? Lunch on board and then a lazy afternoon ashore? Agreed: my wife produces and we consume an excellent lunch. By Jove, the little woman can cook. John's a cadet in "Worcester" and is home on holiday. He's a little superior about "Warwick" and my seamanship is not (don't I know it quite apart from his comments) up to his standards. Mary Rose is with us with a pal, Dick is much in evidence and is extraordinarily useful in a boat (I think his discipline lacks something in finish) and Joly and Rollo, not old enough to take an active part (except for standing on a box and steering) are among our passengers.

I'm not sure whether you know La Grève de la Ville. There isn't any "Ville" nearby except a holding so called but let that pass. It has a beach for the greater part covered with shingle with, near low water, largish round stones enveloped in a slippery green weed. It nestles at the foot of a high cliff, leading to the summit of which is a zigzag path reached by climbing over some rocks. That picturesque work of nature resembling a great Gothic doorway - The Gull's Chapel - lies S.E. of it and, around the corner to the southward, overlooking the narrow channel between the main land and La Grande Moie, stands Cap Robert Lighthouse whose red light you may have seen. I take a rather personal interest in this Lighthouse for, on a January morning in 1907 or 1908 I was sent to Sark in the old "Alert" (couldn't she - and didn't she on that occasion - roll) to obtain the signature of the Seigneur of Sark to a Petition to His Majesty in Council praying that Sanction might be granted to the transfer to the Brethren of Trinity House of a piece of land at Cap Robert forming part of the Tenement called "La Valette de Haut" belonging to M. Robert S. de Carteret for the purpose of the construction of a lighthouse. The lighthouse being now in existence, ça va sans dire that the petition was granted in due course. Sark law, or rather the Charter of James I, forbade the parcelling of a tenement. But we are spending a Sunday in Grève de la Ville, not in la Cour de Sercq.

Carrying our tea, we climb the zigzag and go across fields to La Ville and La Rue du Sermon (so called because a former Vicar prepared his sermons walking up and down it) and, turning right, pass La Seigneurie and find a suitable spot for tea. Sark is very lovely at this time of the year even if the first freshness has gone: the smell of the clover, the hum of the bees, the warm drowsiness over everything are charming. The children pass us on their way home from Sunday School and later the bells of St. Peter's summon the faithful to evening service. Is there anywhere in this troubled world where peace is so all-pervading. And yet man doesn't develop to his fullest capacity in such an atmosphere. Something more stimulating is needed for that. But what a place in which to recuperate or to which to retire when the great world outside proves too relentless. And so we muse over a cigarette until we are reminded that we have a long way to go and that someone is coming to supper. We get back to the beach. By now the tide is well down and we shall have to handle the dinghy carefully not to damage her on the stones. And then, quite suddenly, a breeze springs up from the north-east. The beaches of Sark are steepish and it takes little to set up a nasty swell on them and so, in a few minutes, we realise that it's going to be a ticklish business getting the party off without swamping. We get the dinghy away with John and Dick in her, Dick to let go an anchor and John to bring her in keeping head on to the sea. I go in nearly up to my waist to steady the dinghy and, with only one casualty, my wife, who goes completely under, we get away in two boatloads. We elect to go home south about. Past Point Robert, the Baie de la Maseline, where the new jetty, enabling passengers to land at all states of the tide without being ferried ashore in small boats and hated, accordingly by the fishermen, is fast taking shape; past Founiais, between Les Burons with the cat-like southern portion and the Pierre du Goulet.

The tide's running very fast here and we sweep through, past Le Creux Harbour with its two tunnels, past La Conchée and its cormorants, past Point Derrible and Point Château, then towards the cliffs and past Dixcart Bay and the Coupée and Brenière out again into the tide-way between the reef stretching in from L'Étac de Sercq, and La Pierre du Cours, past Bretagne Uset[1] and Sercul, past the old shafts of the one time silver workings and away in the direction of the Lower Heads Buoy. We can't pick it up yet but we soon will on this course. Yes, there it is and in another quarter of an hour we shall be on our moorings in St. Peter Port Harbour, bronzed with the sun, with our lungs filled with sweet and scented air, satisfied, well satisfied with our day's outing and the good company which our family affords to its members.

---oOo---

Postscript to the above which was written in prison in Paris in Dec. 1940, when whatever else has failed, my memory for the names of rocks hadn't. It has since.

In the spring of 1941 a German officer stationed in Guernsey insisted, despite my protests, on taking "Warwick" over for his own use. His batman kept her in perfect condition and I could not help feeling that she was far better used in this way than being laid up near the Model

---

[1] Bretagne Uset is now known as Moie de Viet.

Yacht Pond right through the summer. Then the officer left Guernsey and I found her lying in the Old Harbour with both engines submerged in bilge water. I protested to the German Harbourmaster, who sympathised and had her towed to St. Sampsons. There I found her when, in 1945, I returned from Germany. Her general condition was such that I sold her for what she would fetch. So difficult was it then to find a boat and so much had the £ depreciated in value that, a virtual wreck, she fetched more in £s than I had paid for her in first class condition. She found a really good owner who restored her and fitted diesel engines. She comes to Alderney from England each summer, often on more than one occasion and I am always invited on board.

IX

CORONATION NIGHT - MAY 12TH 1937

Looking back across the war years it seems incredible that there was a time when humanity did indulge in innocent amusement, when life was fair and when one looked upwards to admire the stars, to look upon the Milky Way and to speculate upon the immensity of space and not in fear and trembling lest there should rain down high explosive and incendiary missiles. Yet there was such a time and perhaps it can best be depicted by a glimpse of the Coronation Night Regatta in St. Peter Port Harbour. We had listened earlier in the day to the broadcast of the solemn, inspiring service in Westminster Abbey where His Majesty had dedicated his life to the service of the nation and now we were going - mainly, be it admitted, for the benefit of the children - to take part in the Regatta organised to round off a memorable day. The weather was perfect - typical 'royal' weather - and the Harbour of St. Peter Port looked a picture viewed from the lookout in the garage yard. I had been heavily engaged in making a network of wire and string in the shape of a jib and mainsail on which to hang the hundreds of Chinese candle lanterns with which we had provided ourselves for the night's festivities. There was a hook for each, each hook in its right place. If all went well, this preparation would save much time and enable us to illuminate "Warwick" very speedily, particularly if my team of lamp lighters worked as I intended. True the network when packed up appeared likely to be anything but tractable in the unpacking for the wire hooks caught in everything they touched but it will be daylight when we rig the thing and with patience or, at worse, with impatience, we shall be able to manage. Besides this "upstairs" illumination, if I may so term it, "Warwick" was to be flood-lit. This meant, for various reasons, that we should have to stay on our moorings but there didn't seem very much point in steaming about a very congested harbour - as St. Peter Port was certain to be, and we hoped that no one would think of flood-lighting their ship.

I should explain that "Warwick" is a cabin cruiser of thirty-five feet in length and so the work in rigging flood-lights was not very difficult nor expensive. We used bulbs from car head-lights with reflectors made from tin and arranged for these to protrude from the ship's side by means of battens. The juice was provided from our two 24 volt batteries used for the ordinary lighting of the ship. It was a heavy drain on them and we had to get our little charging engine going to keep the lights bright throughout the evening. What with looking after the engine, re-lighting Chinese lanterns that went out and extinguishing those that caught fire I was fully occupied and so didn't have a chance of seeing how we looked from a distance. I was assured, however, by those who did that we looked grand.

Now, besides May and all the children, including Joly and Rollo who had never been up so late before and were - in the early part of the evening only - in the seventh heaven of delight, Vera and Herbert Stephenson had joined us. I don't think I've introduced you to them before but they're dears. Herbert has spent a good many years in South America, is a profound student of unusual things, can argue the hind leg off a donkey, can say - and often does - the most outrageous things, delights in shocking the prim and proper, declares himself to be entirely without religion and is at the same time the kindest of mortals, feeling keenly and striving to remedy the inequalities of opportunity and the injustices which he sees around him, a thoroughly good sort, likely to put one off and even to offend one mortally if one doesn't know him but, when really known, a most loveable mortal. And Vera, his wife, rather disapproving of his 'tactlessness' but used to it by now, a charming, loyal helpmeet if ever there was one.

Now in those days, strange as it may now seem, rationing wasn't thought of. You went into a shop - of course it had to be the proper kind of shop - and ordered eggs or butter or tinned fruit or whatever it was you were after and you got it without having to have finicky bits cut out of your ration book and - believe it or not - without limiting yourself to a given number of ounces. And so, for supper that evening in "Warwick's" cockpit there were boiled eggs and tinned salmon and lashings of bread and butter and bananas and a host of other things. As I write this in Paris in December 1940 it makes my mouth water and I wonder if we shall see such days again.

Great ingenuity has been shown in the decoration of some of the boats and never has the harbour looked prettier set, as it is, between the grim pile of Castle Cornet - which once held out for King Charles when the Island was Cromwellian - and the town of St. Peter by the Haven, as it used to be called, rising tier upon tier to the westward with lights in all the windows: air raid precautions had not then been invented.

Gradually, our Chinese lanterns go out or catch fire and have to be cast overboard hurriedly. Joly and Rollo are getting very tired and peevish and Mummy is getting cold; it's time to go. So roughly tidying up - what a business the removal of the scattered candle-grease will be tomorrow - we go ashore in the big dinghy, landing at the steps by the broken wall and, so, home to bed.

A delightful lazy evening with fresh air, good food, children's voices, and excitement and laughter - and tears - and friends, and somewhere behind it all, the thought of England's greatness and the simple nobility of our King and Queen so bravely taking up their life's work, come fair weather or foul, and another thought for that King who delighted in the simple things of life and whose Jubilee we had celebrated not so very long before who, full of years and of honour, had handed on the torch he had borne so long, and for that other King - now Duke - who, never crowned, had gone without the realm. An evening to look back upon, full of those simple things, the ones - the only ones, really, that make life worth living. Little did I think that Coronation night, as I sat up forward idly gazing at the lights that lined the White Rock from St. Julian's Weighbridge to the Spur, that several years after in the Cherche Midi prison, Paris, one dark December day, the memory of that Coronation night would come flooding back with all the intimate little details that I would have sworn I had forgotten, to illuminate and render bearable for a space the ordeal through which I was passing.

X

AUGUST 1938

As I looked out of the old fortress window, the young flood had already made inshore and the very tiny wavelets were to be seen just beyond the Brinchetais Ledge and Blanchard. Elsewhere, the Race of Alderney was a flat calm save where, here and there, an unevenness of the sea-bed, some minor current or the gentle breeze, or perhaps all three, caused a ripple or a whirl in the blue green water. Although it was only six o'clock by summer time, it was already warm with the promise of one of those perfect days which are so rare. From Mannez Common a mist was rising and France, away across the Race, was quite invisible.

My family and I were spending our summer holiday in Alderney in the flat forming part of Essex Castle - that picturesque and, in parts, venerable fortification perched on the summit of the hill wherefrom juts the Hanging Rock and overlooking Longy Bay whose ancient name was Baie du Castel - a flat which my wife had furnished with some taste and much care and which we of the family had come to regard as a home from home.

There were seven of us and the maid; my wife, petite, dark, vivacious, fond - sometimes I thought inordinately fond - of bright colours and startling jewellery, altogether a colourful being whose tastes in this direction did not prevent, or even hinder, her from being a model housekeeper, a splendid cook, an extremely dutiful wife and a devoted mother. Then there was me. I hesitate to mention myself next for the family incline to the view that, however good I might once have been, I am now somewhat outmoded, a sort of Model T and not the right sort of man of which their generation is or will eventually be composed. Of course they admit I'm useful at times and for certain purposes for they have at least grasped the idea that my earnings come in useful and do tend to increase the richness of the ingredients found in the stock-pot called life. I'm not really being fair to them in saying this. Actually we are a most happy united family by no means disdainful of an occasional scrap. I've had a harder life than they have or, I hope, will. Humble beginnings, too much striving, too little recreation, have tended to make me "earthy", dictatorial and intolerant. Perhaps this recognition of it will help me shed the fetters that have so far prevented me attaining to the full stature of humanity. Then there's Mary Rose, a tall, good-looking girl of seventeen without much personality or rather, I think, with a strong personality much repressed, having no apparent ambition, extremely idle and untidy; John, an absolute darling, over six feet in height and as strong as an ox, not over-endowed with brains, not yet sure of himself but possessing the most generous instincts; a Cadet on H.M.S. Worcester and lately appointed a Probationary Midshipman in the Royal Naval Reserve; Dick, aged 13, masquerading as a student at Elizabeth College, of curious disposition who has rather outgrown his strength, inclined to be disgruntled with everything and everybody and yet at times the most delightful of companions, mad on animals and devoted to and highly skilled in dinghy-sailing; Jolyon, aged 7, with lovely eyes and hair and such a sense of humour yet withal frightfully sensitive, very observant but not so very brainy and Rollo, aged 5, a real tough constantly quarrelling with and being teased by Jolyon, and yet when by himself the most charming and interesting of companions. Well, here we all were once more spending our annual holiday in Alderney. And today has been selected - weather and circumstances permitting - for a trip to Omonville la Rogue, a little fishing port lying roughly half-way between Cap de la Hague and Cherbourg: not a long journey, in fact a run of less than three hours from Braye Harbour but those who know the Race of Alderney when it is feeling only moderately vicious will appreciate that what the Merchant Shipping (Safety at Sea) Convention and Legislation would describe as a short international voyage can be when partaken of (I have an unhappy sort of feeling that this phrase should be reversed but cannot alight on the correct expression) across that troubled stretch of water, not only highly unpleasant but extremely dangerous. Those who have been caught in the overfalls in the Race of Alderney in a thirty-five foot boat will not desire a repetition of the experience. But today the glass is high and the Race is in a mood "des plus adorables".

"Warwick", my thirty-five foot twin-screw motor cruiser, lay on her moorings in Longy Bay below me. The dinghy in which we were going aboard was hauled up on the beach just beyond the Nunnery. By craning my neck, I can just catch a glimpse of "Ariel", the cutter belonging to our friend Mr. Rutter who, with his wife and part of his family, is spending a holiday in the flat next door to us. Oh! I forgot to tell you that the Rutters are going to Omonville as well and so is

Abbott Cheever, the American artist who came to Alderney by accident and is, we think rather wasting his time and labour here. A dear fellow, we're all very fond of him.

After a hurried breakfast - for we must not miss our tide - away we trudged down the rough-surfaced road on the very edge of the cliff leading to Longy Bay and bearing sharply to the right at its foot went over the grass to the slip under the shadow of the Nunnery wall and so to the dinghy.

Mary Rose and John elected to go in "Ariel" and, as the latter's speed is less than ours (she was fitted with a converted Austin Seven) we let her get away first. By this time the full flood had made and "Ariel" left Longy under full canvas and not using her engine. When, a quarter of an hour later, "Warwick" came out from between Raz Island and Queslingue and headed south of Cap de la Hague so as to get sufficient offing to clear the end of the Brinchetais Ledge, "Ariel" was miles away to the south-eastward. The strong spring tide and the light morning breeze were conspiring to give her a quick passage. "Warwick" soon overhauled her, in fact much sooner than I had expected and the wind, which had been becoming lighter, dropped altogether and "Ariel", as we could see, had got her engine going and was getting no help from her big Bermuda mainsail. She was steering a course which would take her about two miles clear of Cap de la Hague lighthouse and "Warwick" was on a parallel course about one mile further from land. Never had I seen the Race so calm. We slowed down so as not to get too far ahead of "Ariel" and I remember that while we were running dead slow Dick clambered over the transom into the dinghy and pulled her till he got tired. But going dead slow like this was monotonous and so we revved up a bit and, it having become misty under the land, we soon lost sight of our companion vessel.

Away past the Anse de Saint Martin with that most charming but, I understand, treacherous little fishing harbour, Port Racine, and the Red Buoy out in the middle of the bay. The mist is thickening a bit. We must keep a good look out so as to avoid the dangers off the Coque. We pick up the Coque and, giving it a good berth, we bear in towards the high land with our eyes skinned trying to pick up the marks which clear to the northward of the Tataquets outside Omonville.

It gets thicker every minute and not only can we not pick up the clearing marks but we have lost sight of the land altogether. How are the others in "Ariel" getting on? Mr. Rutter, though an experienced seaman, it not too familiar with this coast. Ought we to go back and look for them? On second thoughts we decide that the proper thing to do is to locate Omonville and then, if it's still thick, to run out again on a very careful compass course and meet the others.

We run on in, straight for where we judge the high land to be, - we can't risk putting Warwick's head straight for Omonville and eventually pick it up and then, coming almost south, suddenly pick up the Beacon - reputedly red in colour - which lies just off the end of Omonville Breakwater. Now then, around with her and out to meet the others. For about eight minutes we head north-east so as to make sure of clearing the Hures de la Coque - for by now it's past high water and the inshore ebb tide has made and would, if one didn't make suitable provision against it, put one right into danger - and then we get Warwick pointing N.W. by W. On this course we should soon pick up "Ariel" if she has kept the course she was on when last we saw her. But there's nothing to be seen and the weather is of the kind when it's difficult to estimate how thick it exactly is and in all probability we can see for a much shorter distance than we imagine we are doing. Shall we miss them altogether and ourselves become uncertain of our position? For even with engines stopped, the Race tide, which, off the Cap, runs as fast as ten knots when a spring tide has fully made, bowls one along so that, in the absence of a sight of some fixed recognisable object, one is quite unable, within a mile or so, to estimate one's position.

But what is that black spot away on the port bow? If it's "Ariel" she's hauled down her mainsail and she hasn't made the headway one would have expected. It is her, we feel certain a few moments later, and head in her direction. She's coming along very slowly rather close inshore and would do better further out where the tide isn't so strong at the moment. As we come up to her we put "Warwick" about and throttle down to "Ariel's" speed. We sight the Coque with the Semaphore Station at the end of the little promontory and we notice something else: "Ariel" and "Warwick" although doing about five knots through the water are hardly moving at all over the ground and the tide is strengthening against them all the time. Mr. Rutter notices it too and John, who is with him, hails us and asks for a tow. We get a line aboard her which is secured around the mast and, taking up the slack, we give "Warwick" full throttle on both engines, "Ariel's" engine is also going all out.

We begin to pull away and gradually pass the Coque and will soon be able to head inshore. But it really is thick. A diesel engined fishing vessel coming out of Omonville looms up quite close to us outward bound and a deck-hand, guessing that we are bound for Omonville, indicates our course. We are not making much progress and haul out a bit to the eastward, to see if the tide is a little slacker there. It is, and watching the dim outline of the land we begin to make progress. The tide is setting us strongly to the westward and we see the ripple of the Baissettes and turn off to avoid them. There's water over them for us but the longest way round is often the shortest way home. Ah! there's the high land of Gréville dead ahead; with luck we'll spot the red beacon any minute now; yes, there it is. We round it leaving it on our starboard hand and run into the little harbour protected from the northward by its sturdy breakwater and the mass of rocks outside. There's a mooring chain laid across the bottom and many an anchor has fouled it but we know its approximate position and anchor clear of it. And now to get ashore and haul the dingy up the shelving beach, pay our respects to M. and Mme. Mauger of La Buvette du Port and then, trudging past the lifeboat house, the house whose entire gable is dedicated to the glory of Amer Piquant, and the rather grim grey-stoned and chimneyed dwellings surmounted by quaint terracotta cats and dogs, in the direction of the twelfth century church, sadly dilapidated, whose belfry clock would not dream of stooping to tell the lie of summer time. But we are not, at least not immediately, bound to the church but to another building - separated from it by a quaint old water lane where the villagers do the family washing - the Hotel Restaurant. It is one o'clock - the journey has given us healthy appetites, and is not Madame's poulet en casserole des plus delicieuses that one can find along the whole length of the Cotentin. This afternoon, a wander through the village, a careful look at the church, very simple inside but with an air of gracious dignity, perhaps a short chat to the Curé, blind and a "mutilé" of the Great War, perhaps tiring of the confines of the village - and it is certainly limited - a long country walk or, better still, up the coast close inshore past the Raz de Bannes to Cherbourg. But enough for the present, Madame's poulet is done to a turn and déjeuner absorbs all our thoughts.

XI

SEPTEMBER 1938

For some time the war clouds had been looming ominously and now it looked as though war was inevitable. Defence Regulations had been drafted and an adaptation prepared for the Channel Islands and now there had come a summons from London. Harrison was to go from Jersey and I from Guernsey to attend a conference. I consulted Duret Aubin of Jersey by telephone as to whether the Jersey emissary was going by boat or plane and it was decided eventually that we should go by plane. Neither Harrison nor I had flown before and we were a little dubious about taking to the air. But it would save such a lot of time and trouble.

The next morning, seven o'clock found me aboard the St. Helier having breakfast while waiting to leave for Jersey (for those were the days before Guernsey possessed an aerodrome of her own) and, accordingly, I had to join the plane at St. Peter's Aerodrome. On board was the French Consul, returning to Jersey after one of his periodical brief visits to the other island within his jurisdiction. A charming raconteur, we spent an hour together and the journey, usually tedious though quite short, was almost over before we realised it. Why here we are almost abreast of La Corbière; and there's the Ruaudière Buoy and the stretch of St. Aubin's Bay. We're due in St. Helier in another twenty minutes. I see Duret Aubin on the quay awaiting me and find that he's arranged for me to leave the ship first which I do and he hustles me into a motor car and drives me to the Royal Court House where I have a chat with the Bailiff and Harrison. Then I'm taken along the picturesque road leading to the Airport where we find Lord Portsea and his sister also awaiting the plane's departure.

Well, we clamber aboard and ascertain that there's a lifebelt under the seat, read the instructions as to how to inflate it and adjust it, look for the paper bag (in case of accidents, for you can be just as ill in an aeroplane as you can on a steamer), try the chewing gum supplied by a thoughtful transport company and plug our ears with the cotton wool provided for the purpose.

Our seats are those nearest the pilot's compartment and at the angle at which the plane is when at rest, we lie back as in the seat of the most modern of motor cars, only more so. Ah! here's the pilot coming aboard; the door of the plane is closed and the steps leading to terra firma pulled away. One by one, the four engines are started and revved up and I have the uncomfortable feeling that I should like to get out while there's time while realising that, unless I throw a fit or do something very dramatic, it's too late. Then, with a tremendous roar, we start careering across the landing ground, gaining speed all the time. But we're reaching the other end and we'll never leave the ground in time. That means we'll crash into the fence. And then I realise that we're off the ground, though I am quite unaware of the moment at which we left, and gaining height rapidly. We wheel, and, instinctively, as the plane heels over I grab my seat. She comes back on an even keel and then we are over the cliffs - in the neighbourhood of Bonne Nuit Bay, I should guess - and I see the Paternosters away to the left. We bump badly at this juncture and, as we leave the cliffs, we seem to drop bodily some few feet and then we're out over the sea in lovely sunshine but with great masses of white cloud away in the direction of Guernsey of which Island we see nothing. We get a glimpse of Sark and then a real view of Alderney looking glorious bathed in sunshine and then we're over Cap La Hague and St. Martin and then Omonville where we branch off seawards. Away to our right can be seen the long breakwater containing the big roadstead at Cherbourg. And then we run in and out of cloud for the rest of the journey. Ah! That must be the Isle of Wight and this Portsmouth for there's "Nelson" and there "Victoria and Albert". And now we begin to descend and, turning, appear to head for a small green patch on which it seems impossible that we can hope to land safely. But the patch gets bigger and bigger and we glide in very gently and hardly conscious that we have touched the ground, run up to the tarmac and come to rest. A very few minutes and we are off again bound for Hendon, this time flying for quite a while in cloud so dense that our wing tips are only barely visible. I notice that it's much more bumpy over the land than over the sea but I gather from more experienced travellers that we've had a perfect journey. Arriving at Hendon, we quickly pass the Customs and jump aboard the palatial bus which is to take us to Victoria. As we pass the various suburban parks and open spaces, trenches are being dug everywhere, some mechanically, others by hand. It's evident that no chances are being taken. We've heard, of course, of Mr. Chamberlain's departure for Munich and speculate as to the likelihood of his succeeding in preventing, or postponing the calamity which looks like overtaking Europe. The thoughts of millions are similarly occupied.

We reach the Hotel Victoria, Northumberland Avenue, and have lunch and then go on to the Home Office where we find we're not expected until the following day, and where they are too busy to attend to us. We go there the following day and spend most of it getting the Guernsey and Jersey drafts of the Defence Regulations into conformity with each other. From where we sit we can see a Recruiting Office. They seem pretty busy for there's a queue outside. And, then, the queue melts away and the rumour reaches us that the news is good. A cynic tell us that the volunteers of a few minutes ago are now vainly endeavouring to give their shillings back but we - green as we are and unversed in the ways of this great city - doubt the complete accuracy of this. We go out and, in Leicester Square, we buy a newspaper and so great is the excitement and so tremendous the crush that it wasn't easy to get a copy. And thus we read what the poster has conveyed, that Chamberlain's efforts have succeeded. Harrison and I feel light-headed with joy, the cloud that, we felt convinced, was on the brink of bursting, had been conjured away; yes, we were light-headed with joy and thankfulness. We decide to go to a cinema and so celebrate the occasion. The film is one in which Edna Best appears. We don't think it one of her best and it isn't suitable for the occasion but we enjoy it. And the next day we see Chamberlain's return. We're at the Home Office again saying au-revoir before preparing to catch the boat train on our way home and rumour has it that he has landed at Croydon and is on his way. Knots of people gather along Whitehall till, gradually, there is a continuous line and, at the junction of that thoroughfare with Downing Street, is a biggish crowd carefully shepherded by police. Mounted police arrive from the direction of Westminster Bridge, the waiting crowd thickens and then, without fuss or display, a car, well over near the pavement on its correct side, comes into view. The crowd roars a welcome. We catch a glimpse of a spare figure, of an alert face, the face of a man much younger than the seventy years of the Prime Minister. And then we see humble members of the public jumping on the running board to clasp his hand. And he responds and the police hanging on to the car on each side do not interfere. Chamberlain has been on a mission on behalf of the man and woman in the street and it is fit and meet that they should have this opportunity of showing him thus their gratitude and their thanks. And then the car turns into Downing Street and is lost to sight. We feel as though, if only for a moment or two, we have been somewhere near the centre of world events, as perhaps we have.

XII

CLOUDS ON THE HORIZON

The clouds of war had long been gathering but the storm, when it eventually came, would not touch Guernsey. At least it would not be touched to an appreciable extent. Travel to England would be restricted, certain commodities would have to be rationed, the labour problem in the glasshouses might become difficult, the prices of and profit from the export of tomatoes would rise and might even soar, the flower of the island's manhood and womanhood would volunteer for national service, many more would be conscripted; a proportion, perhaps a high proportion, of young men would die in action or be more or less severely wounded, some so badly that it would have been kinder had they died outright: an appropriate War Memorial would be erected and, then, we in Guernsey would return wholeheartedly to the pursuit of peaceful occupations and recreations in our own insular way.

Such was the prospect; what was the actuality? I will try to describe it as seen through my own eyes. The field of vision must necessarily be narrow and possibly superficial but I cannot overcome my limitations and the reader must put up with them or now decide against reading any further.

Since April, 1935, I have been His Majesty's Attorney General in Guernsey, a relatively unimportant but at the same time rather arduous post. Guernsey is not the capital of Jersey, as so many people appear to imagine, but is a separate island (Capital: St. Peter Port), being the principal island of the Bailiwick[2] of Guernsey, consisting of the islands of Guernsey, Alderney, Sark, Herm and Jethou. The official language of the Bailiwick is still French,[3] the 'parler' of the countryman in Guernsey is Guernsey French,[4] and in Sark, Sark

---

[2] A Bailiwick is the jurisdiction of a Bailiff i.e. Chief Judge and President of the Legislative Assembly.

[3] Not the French of modern France but an attempt at a modernisation of old French while retaining masses of outmoded legal expressions.

[4] The old Norman dialect interspersed with English expressions e.g. "Tommy, as-tu frumaise les toplights dans le greenhouse? Oui, father, all spiff."

French[5] whilst in Alderney virtually no one speaks anything but English. Each of the islands of Guernsey, Alderney and Sark has its own legislature and its own court, that of Sark being a feudal one. Herm and Jethou belong to the Crown[6] and are leased to tenants. The populations of the three principal islands at the outbreak of war were approximately as follows: Guernsey, 42,500; Alderney, 1,300[7]; Sark, 600.

As Attorney General in Guernsey I had a busy time, being assisted by a part-time Solicitor General, one full-time legislative draftsman and two clerks. Responsible for the drafting of all legislation whether by way of 'Projet de Loi' or 'Ordonnance' and for piloting it through the Royal Court and the States in the case of the former and through the Royal Court only in the case of the latter, having to attend most sittings of the Courts and many meetings of States' Committees, to prosecute in all criminal cases other than those minor ones dealt with in the Police court, to represent and advise upon the interest of Crown and States, to act for and advise the constables of most of the ten Parishes, to do all Crown and States' conveyancing, to advise and assist, when asked, in relation to the government of Alderney and, very occasionally, of Sark, I had little time for leisure but that little was, as far as possible, spent at sea. What delightful family cruises we had (my wife thinks otherwise) between the islands of the Bailiwick and between Alderney (our usual holiday centre) and Cherbourg, Omonville la Rogue and Dielette. And what genuine kindness and hospitality we met with wherever we touched land. My friend, Monsieur Mauger of the Café du Port, Omonville, where are you now, I wonder, and you, Monsieur Dufay of the Hotel Restaurant du Port, Dielette, purveyor of the most delicious meals, have you survived the German invasion of the Cotentin?

I had often looked at our 1914-18 collection of 'DORA', reposing dustily on a shelf in the Greffe[8] and the idea of compiling a somewhat

---

[5] Sark French resembles Jersey French far more than Guernsey French. Sark, derelict and deserted, was in 1565 repopulated with forty families drawn mainly from the Manor of St. Ouen in Jersey. Its spiritual home is still there.

[6] Herm was purchased from the Crown by the States of Guernsey in December, 1946 for £15,000.

[7] In late June, 1940 Alderney was completely evacuated and the inhabitants only returned in December, 1945.

[8] The Record Office.

similar but more up-to-date version filled me with dread. But it had to be done. The Home Office supplied us with a copy of the first draft of the Defence Regulations and I started on the task, the unpleasant task, of adapting them to Bailiwick needs. That first draft was followed by numerous others as the brains at Whitehall really got busy, so much of what I did in the early days was completely wasted. Throughout, I was able to collaborate on the matter with my good friends the Bailiff and the Law Officers of Jersey. Their advice was often of great value. The island routine work went on much as usual and I was much plagued around this time by innumerable meetings in committee and conference over the Bill by which we were introducing divorce for the first time and which was designed to be the most up-to-date in Christendom. Indeed, some wives and husbands (I place them in that order not out of bias but because of my life-long admiration of the fair sex) appeared to believe that it would, so far as they were concerned, usher in the millennium.

Then came Munich and I received an urgent message to repair to the Home Office. What occurred in London has been related in an earlier chapter.

Early in August, 1939, my wife and I and the children went for our accustomed holiday to Alderney where, at Essex Castle, we had a flat of spacious dimensions and microscopic rent. We renewed old acquaintances and made new ones; we made our usual trips to the French mainland in my motor cruiser 'Warwick'. Then, the end of the holiday, so far as I was concerned, was approaching but my wife and the children (including our John, a Cadet in 'Worcester') were staying on till the end of the school holidays. And so we decided on a final cruise to Omonville in company with 'Ranger', with Judge French in command of that stout little ship. As, replete with the delicious 'omelette' and 'poulet rôti' provided 'moyennant finance' in that charming little old-world spot, we steered to clear Les Tataquets and La Coque on our homeward journey, we sighted the 'Bremen' outward bound from Cherbourg for New York. I stuck my neck out and predicted that, when next we saw her, she would be wearing the Red Ensign. How wrong can one be? On arrival at our flat in Alderney, I found a telegram from the Bailiff of Guernsey urgently summoning me to return there.

The next day, Mary Rose drove me down the rough cliff-side track from Essex to the road leading to St. Anne's and Braye Harbour so that I might catch the morning tide. As we lurched about in the ancient Armstrong-Siddeley (once the wedding carriage and pride of Alderney and long since mine for a tenner) we met a telegraph boy. At his urgent signal, we slithered to a standstill and I tore open a wire addressed, as I thought, to me but intended for my John (by now a Midshipman, R.N.R.) directing him to report at once at Portsmouth. So back to the flat to unearth him and get his kit packed while, feeling no end of a dog, he beat it across the fields to say 'au-revoir' to his then dearest and fairest. Then his mother and Dick decided that they, too, must come to Guernsey to see him off properly so, leaving the car for them, I walked into St. Anne's where Sergeant Pilot Teddy Odoire R.A.F. (now Group Captain Odoire D.F.C. and Bar, A.F.C., until recently Air Officer Commanding, Malta) under similar orders, asked me to give him a passage. Then on to the harbour where I got my ship ready for sea and took my passengers out to her in the dinghy. I looked at my watch as I rounded the end of the breakwater; I was already two hours late on tide; it would be a slow passage with a head tide for the latter part of it. There was a steady drizzle with low visibility but a dead flat calm so I headed to pass west of the Pierre au Vraic and counter the tide setting me down on Sark. Nearing Guernsey, we cheated it a bit by slipping down the Douit Sauvary. We got a late and very scratch meal at the Hotel de Normandie and, - shock number one - when I tendered a Guernsey £1 note in payment, it was refused and I was asked for an English one. Although an Englishwoman by birth, my cautious creditor's husband was a Swiss. It was fortunate that she did not insist on being paid in Swiss francs. The next morning we saw John off by plane at 6 a.m., Dick left at 8 a.m. by plane for Alderney, my wife at 9 a.m. by the S.S. 'Courier' for the same destination. At 10 a.m. I started work.

The closing months of 1939 and the earlier ones of 1940 were uneventful in Guernsey and, so far as I was concerned, a continual round of wartime legislation, regulations of every shape and size; I seemed to ooze them at every pore. Ridgway, Grigs and I finally settled the draft of our Divorce Law and I drafted the National Service (Armed Forces) (Guernsey) Law which, through no fault or delay on the part of anyone in Guernsey, had not received the approval of His Majesty in Council by the time disaster struck us and so could not be put into operation.

Life, for me at all events, was just a dull routine and I often felt tempted to rebel against the directions given to the Bailiff of Jersey and to me when, at the outbreak of war, we had both sought permission to relinquish our posts for the duration for more important work, even if still chairborne, in the United Kingdom. We had been told that we would best be doing our duty by remaining at our respective posts.

I still had no inkling of what lay before us.

XIII

January 1940

Some people, whose activities are mainly of a physical order, will tell you that brain work cannot possibly be as tiring as hoeing parsnips and that any modern ideas to the contrary are just nonsense. Be that as it may, my own experience is to the contrary. Without professing to have mental powers above the average, I have a job which, for some years past, has used up the bulk of my energies and the coming of the war and of the extra legislation attending upon the war, my time seems to have been less my own than ever. Towards Christmas then, I was annoyed, though not surprised, to find myself getting irritable at little things and beginning to lack that zest which accompanies good health. It was no good thinking of going to Alderney, whose air is to me a never failing pick-me-up, for the flat which we had furnished with such excited interest had been requisitioned by the War Department under the Defence (Compensation) Act, 1939, together with all the other flats in Essex Castle, for the purposes of a military hospital. And then, stronger, much stronger reason for staying in Guernsey over Christmas, were not Mary Rose and John spending their leave with us, Mary Rose from her aerodrome in Wiltshire and John from his destroyer. The mere thought of seeing them again was a tonic in itself. And Dick and Jolyon would have broken up for the holidays and there was Rollo, who hasn't started school yet, to consider. Who knows in war time what a year will bring forth. But this year, at all events, the whole family was to gather around the table to celebrate the gladdest of all festivals, gladdest, I think, because it is essentially for celebration en famille. But then I'm old-fashioned. I think the family had a really happy Christmas but, like all experiences which are redolent of happiness, it seemed just to slip past one and there we were, Mummy and Dick and I, on the Jetty at St. Peter Port Harbour, with the rain just starting to pour down, watching Mary Rose and John going up the gangway and disappearing into the bowels of the "Normannia" on their return to duty.

And now the Christmas holidays are over and Dick and Joly have resumed what they are pleased to term their studies at Elizabeth College. And I am still very tired, "épuisé" is I think the word giving the nearest shade of meaning to my condition. And so it was that my wife and I decided on a week (I couldn't spare longer) in Jersey.

We left Guernsey on a Saturday evening in really filthy weather, at least it was pouring with rain although there was little wind. Two hours later we were crossing St. Aubin's Bay on the South coast of Jersey with the lights leading up to the Dog's Nest dead in line. And then the lights leading into St. Helier's Harbour became visible, just those lights and nothing else. But they suffice and in a very few minutes we have passed through the narrow entrance and have swung round and are gradually being hauled alongside by the ship's winches. It's raining harder than ever and, the immigration formalities - very brief ones - over, we are glad to find a taxi and get to the Grand Hotel as quickly as possible for its warmth will be acceptable and the journey has given us quite an appetite.

Although we had been to Jersey many times before, we had neither of us had an opportunity of exploring it for, on short visits with time lacking, one takes a car or a bus on every possible occasion and thus sees nothing, or next to nothing, of anything.

But this was all to be remedied and so it was. I don't mean to say that we entirely disdained all modern means of locomotion rather did we turn them to the best account in carrying out our plans.

Which of our several journeyings was the most enjoyable?

Was it the really terrific walk the whole length of St. Aubin's to St. Brelade's, with lunch at the delightful hotel and a visit to the fascinating old Church, on to the Airport and to St. Peter's Church, the vain attempt to cross the valleys and thus reach St. Lawrence, and the return to St. Helier down St. Peter's Valley and along the Esplanade, with our legs numb with tiredness and aching for days afterwards?

Was it the bus ride and walk to Bonne Nuit Bay on the North Coast with the excellent lunch excellently served in the delightful Chalet Hotel nestling in the sun on the cliffside?

Was it the visit to the prehistoric tomb at La Hougue Bie and then on to Gorey and Orgueil Castle which, after a light lunch served amid shining brass and pewter, we explored as thoroughly as our limited, very limited, archaeological knowledge permitted, and the bus ride back along the east and south coasts?

Was it the wonderful hospitality shown us by Charlie Duret Aubin and Cecil Harrison and their charming wives at the Palace Hotel and the rural drive which followed, with tea with Jay and her husband (and such a tea to which, after such a lunch, we were incapable of doing justice,) and then the visit to the fowls and the pigs?

Or was it the day we spent with the Bailiff and Mrs. Coutanche, when after a delicious lunch we were conducted over the Seigneurie de Noirmont and taken by the most delightful cliff paths to points of vantage overlooking St. Aubin's Bay (why, there goes the mailboat bound for Guernsey), Noirmont Tower and the perfectly lovely cliffs and sea beyond and then back to toasted scones and hot tea by a roaring fire in Mrs. Coutanche's pretty drawing room, the warm being such a contrast to the cold outside?

Or the walks we took such as the one up Waterworks Valley and to Elizabeth Castle?

You may select whichever you prefer. So far as I am concerned, each was delightful, each exactly satisfied the mood and the hour. We got very wet, did we, on occasion. Well, what of it, we didn't mind.

And now we're just running into Guernsey Harbour. It has been bitter on deck but much too fine to go below. We passed a Norwegian ship shortly after clearing the north coast of Jersey bound, one would guess, for Bordeaux.

Seaplanes are practising landing and taking-off in the outer roads but we're alongside and there's a taxi-man trying to attract my attention. By Jove, it's cold, I hope Katie has a hot cup of tea ready for us.

XIV

THE GATHERING STORM

Towards the end of May, Major-General Telfer-Smollett, our Lieutenant Governor, had at his request been given a more active command and his successor-to-be paid a visit to Guernsey to have a look around before taking over. Chatting to him after lunch one day during his visit I asked him whether he thought we could hold the Germans in Belgium and France and he replied that he thought we could. I remember feeling very dubious about this but hoping that he was right. Soon afterwards, he was sworn in as Lieutenant Governor.

Things worsened rapidly and at a conference attended by the Bailiff and me, the Lieutenant Governor had a nervous breakdown and we were without an effective head. He went home to bed and I never saw him again for he went when the troops (The Royal Irish Fusiliers) did. After the war I was to hear from him again. In the rush to get away his wife had left a lot of clothing (purchased, no doubt, at great expense and intended to bewitch the population). These vanished during the German occupation and now he was alleging gross neglect on our part, who had remained, and claimed heavy damages. He could have had no conception of what we had been through or that we were never permitted access to Government House. I fear I returned an answer not designed to turn away his wrath but rather to augment it.

At about this time Jurat John Leale and I met from time to time and talked things over. Leale, a Methodist Minister, a former Cambridge don, an expert in finance and economics and the owner, by inheritance, of one of the largest and most profitable business concerns in Guernsey, but withal modest, self-effacing and abstemious in all respects, had probably the most penetrating brain in Guernsey. Possessing all the qualities I lacked and completely different to me in character, he and I had worked in the closest harmony for years and there was no one whose views I respected more. As it turned out, we were destined to collaborate even more closely - for a time - in the future. Together we had discussed the situation likely to arise in the Channel Islands and had reached the conclusion that the German troops would reach the coast of France nearest to the islands and, in that event, would occupy them. This latter probability was discounted by the Home Office, who thought that, if we kept very quiet, the Germans might leave them alone. Much earlier, when it had appeared that our only danger was that a swift surface vessel or a submarine might seek to destroy the shipping in our harbours and, perhaps, to shell St. Peter Port and St. Sampsons, we had asked to be supplied with a couple of twelve pounder coast defence guns. Our request was acknowledged to be a reasonable one but, we were told that such a shortage of armaments of all kinds existed that it would be at least two years before the guns could be supplied to us. (It is interesting to record that, within days of the Germans arriving in Guernsey, their only transport being planes of the troop carrier variety, they had massed field guns at a number of strategic or tactical points in Guernsey. I saw them myself, standing wheel to wheel in great numbers.)

It now appeared to Leale and me that, before the Germans arrived, provision should, if possible, be made for the evacuation of Guernsey children, young women and men of military age. We saw the Bailiff on the matter but suggested that, at that moment, the British Government had so much on its plate that it would be unfair to worry the Home Office with this additional burden. The days passed and the Germans crossed the Seine. It then seemed to us that we could no longer, in justice to our own people, defer the matter and the Bailiff agreed. Accordingly, the Home Office was communicated with and our views and fears made known to them. The military situation on the continent continued to deteriorate. Finally, word came from the Home Office that the Cabinet had the matter before it and eventually the subject of the Channel Islands - insignificant in relation to the vast and perplexing problems awaiting solution but, to us, all important - was reached and a decision taken. That decision was to the effect that the Channel Islands were to be demilitarised and that shipping would be provided for a limited evacuation.

A gracious message from His Majesty the King was telephoned to the Bailiff of Jersey and - by pre-arrangement - telephoned to me for transmission to our Bailiff (he heard badly on the telephone) late one evening, the text being confirmed by letter the following day. This letter and a letter of instructions concerning demilitarisation reached the Lieutenant Governor and a conference was held at Government House. Our instructions were not to make public the position in Guernsey until it was announced in Jersey and, the mail arriving later in the latter island, it was arranged to hold sittings of the Royal Courts of Jersey and Guernsey by 3 p.m. that day. Until then, consultations had to take place under the pledge of secrecy.

The Bailiff convened a secret meeting of educational officials at which the rough outline of what was to happen was given them. The Principal of Elizabeth College (The Reverend W.H.G. Milnes M.A. M.C.) who, it appeared, had already given considerable thought to the possibility of the evacuation of the school children, was asked to elaborate his view and a second meeting (not this time secret) of Parish Constables, Parish Rectors and School authorities was called to assemble immediately after the court sitting. At that sitting, His Majesty's Gracious Message was read and a statement concerning demilitarisation and evacuation approved for publication. At about this time a message came through from the Home Office that three evacuation ships would arrive at 2.30 a.m. the following day and that they must be loaded and must be put to sea again at once. Bearing in mind what this would mean in discomfort for children of tender age, I asked for and obtained permission to hold the ships till 6 a.m.

We then had to improvise registration centres in the ten Guernsey parishes and to make transport arrangements to get some 2,000 young children and their teachers to the harbour by such time as would enable the ships to sail by 6 a.m. They would be leaving probably for the duration of the war.

The Rectors, Constables, Douzaines, school teachers and many States' officials were roped in and registration centres (a separate one for each category of evacuee in each parish) were set up whereat (a) school children (b) mothers of children under school age and their children and (c) men of military age could be registered. Everyone concerned behaved magnificently and it is a measure of the amazing efficiency with which everybody worked that, with everything still to be arranged at 4 p.m., by 5 a.m. the following morning, nearly 2,000 children, each with spare clothes, gas mask, food for the journey, had been transported to the harbour ready to embark.

I woke at 6 a.m. and telephoned to the Police Station to enquire how the operation had gone. I was told that the children were already aboard. It seemed to me that it was a near miracle that arrangements, so hurriedly improvised, had succeeded. I made myself a cup of tea and went to get a bath. As I turned on the water, doubts assailed me - I am of a pessimistic turn of mind - and I turned it off and telephoned to the harbour. The Harbour Master (Captain J.T. Franklin) answered and told me that the children were there looking rather miserable in the cold of early morning but that, far from being safely on board, no ships had yet arrived. Throwing on some clothes, I drove down to investigate for myself. There were two small ships at anchor in the roadstead and the Harbour Master told me he had sent out a pilot to bring them in but that the masters had no orders as to where they were to make for on leaving Guernsey and preferred to remain at anchor. I was on the point of telephoning to the Ministry of Shipping when he called me back and, pointing to a ship which had that moment come into sight, he said: "It's the old 'Antwerp'". It was although (unless because he was an old L. & S.W.R. man) how he knew at that distance beat me. She arrived and dropped anchor near the other ships. A ship taking aboard troops and military stores was moored on one side of the jetty. On the other side was the cargo vessel 'Ringwood'. Franklin sent the latter out to anchor in the roads and directed Pilot Charlie Ferguson to bring in and berth the 'Antwerp'. She had lost several lifeboats through enemy action a few days before. Going aboard, we found a Sea Transport Officer with orders for the evacuation ships; he speedily got to work and, within a short time, embarkation was begun. One of the three ships was found to be completely unsuitable and so the 'Ringwood' was pressed into service instead. She, the last to get away that day, left at 2.30 p.m. The poor children had long since eaten the sandwiches provided for the journey timed to start at 6 a.m. The only casualty was a case of appendicitis which was successfully dealt with on arrival in England.

The registration of would-be evacuees went on steadily and, as ships arrived, they were embarked, military and civilian evacuation going on simultaneously. Deeply worried by the incipient panic I noted at the harbour which seemed likely to increase when it became apparent that all who wished to go would never get aboard the limited number of vessels available, I asked the Government Secretary to keep back twelve rifles and bayonets, but no ammunition, from our militia stores and equipment being sent away to comply with the Cabinet's order to demilitarise. I intended to issue them to the police and was confident that the sight of cold steel would have the necessary steadying effect. He kept back the rifles but forgot about the bayonets. Then, on our urgent and repeated representations, as fast as the ships unloaded their passengers, they turned around and came back for more. The original

Home Office orders limiting the evacuation to school children, children of under school age and their mothers and men of military age, were progressively relaxed and a veritable armada of ships, some quite large, was sent to us and, when it was over, the last ships left, they could have taken at least five thousand more. The need to arm the police with rifles and bayonets had long since vanished. In all, besides the military, some 17,000 persons had left the island. The town of St. Peter Port seemed strangely deserted, no children played in the streets and mothers mourned the loss of their children and would not be comforted.

I almost forgot to relate that, before any promises of ships was given, the Home Office - moved, presumably by the Treasury - required an undertaking that Guernsey would be responsible for the transport costs. I consulted Leale - our Finance Committee President - who acquiesced and I gave the necessary undertaking over the telephone. I added that as we were bankrupt, the chances of our ever being able to honour it were slender. The Home Office comment was that that didn't matter to them.

The period of evacuation was, I think, the most difficult and painful I have ever experienced. Waves of panic and indecision swept over people; official notices were misread, words of advice completely misinterpreted and the most grotesque rumours passed for truth. There was a run on the banks, one evacuating publican gave away his entire stock of liquor. One official, at his own expense, had posters with "Keep Your Heads. Don't be Yellow" printed in black on a yellow ground put up all over the town. He then suddenly remembered that he ought to go and did so, without telling anyone in his department. The emergency organisation set up to try to deal with the situation worked untiringly; registration clerks worked until exhausted, dropped off to sleep, woke and worked on. And their efforts were matched by the Merchant Seamen who carried all those thousands without a single fatal casualty.

Grave criticisms have been levelled at us for not giving people more notice. We couldn't. We had to wait thirty-six hours for a Cabinet decision and, I would assume that, at this particular time, the latter had so many much graver matters on its plate that it simply couldn't deal expeditiously with so relatively tiny a matter as the evacuation of the Channel Islands. Do let us keep a sense of proportion. Meanwhile, we were pledged to reveal nothing, presumably because had we revealed anything to our people, it would have been splashed all over the front pages of the London dailies. Then, we were ordered to synchronise publication with that in Jersey, and had to postpone publication for some hours. If you doubt anything of this, I suggest that you read Chapters I and II of Ralph Durand's book.

The evacuation over, we who were left behind drew a sigh of relief. Many, completely exhausted, caught up with some of their lost sleep. But more trouble was to follow. In Sark, under the leadership of La Dame, calm reigned. We had offered them a ship to bring away those wishing to leave. Our offer was declined. Scarcely anyone left or sought to leave. Such is the effect of leadership. Communications with Alderney was by radio telephone and we, and those in Alderney, were under an absolute prohibition against using it in that the Germans, now approaching the French coast only some eight miles away, would be picking up what was said. I had known Alderney and its people pretty intimately for at least twenty years and I thought it likely that their reaction, living, as so many did, close to the soil, would be much like that of Sark. Nevertheless, but only after much persuasion - German aircraft had been seen in the vicinity - the Master of the 'Sheringham' was induced to go there - and I thought I made it clear to the carrier to him of the message - that anyone who wished to come away might use her. She was a largish vessel and well appointed and could, at a pinch, have brought away the whole population. She returned with less than twenty people on board. She brought no message from the Alderney authorities. I concluded that Alderney, like Sark, was staying put.

Meanwhile, things of which I had no immediate knowledge were happening there. The Machine-Gun Training Unit stationed there was withdrawn and, leaving their vehicles behind, they wrecked them before leaving. The Trinity House ship 'Vestal' arrived there to collect the keepers from the Casquets and Mannez Lighthouses. At Cherbourg, the dockyard and oil installations were dismantled and set on fire. Vast clouds of smoke drifted as far as Guernsey and, I am told, even as far as Jersey. The explosions and the smoke must have been far more terrifying in Alderney. With glasses, the German army could be seen moving down the Cotentin peninsula in the direction of Cap la Hague. In the late afternoon of June 21st. Pilot Jack Quinain Senr. of Alderney arrived in Guernsey with a letter from Judge French for the Lieutenant Governor and found me still at work. I told him the

Lieutenant Governor had been recalled and that the Bailiff, who had been directed to assume the civil functions of the former, had gone home. Did he know what the letter contained? He said that he understood it asked for some essential supplies. I decided to open the letter in that the shops were on the point of shutting. It was a perfectly rational letter and its main purpose was to ask for a supply of barm. I was puzzled and asked if they were contemplating brewing beer. Quinain didn't know. I phoned de Guerin's Mills and asked for enlightenment. They said that that was what Alderney called yeast. I asked them to send the quantity requested down to Quinain's boat, penned a letter to Judge French and Quinain left for Alderney.

The next afternoon, Pilot Quinain returned with a letter from French of an entirely different kind. It upbraided me for daring to open a letter intended for the Lieutenant Governor's eye only (this was nonsense, in view of its contents) and charged me with the utmost callousness in evacuating Guernsey completely and leaving Alderney without any help whatever. I thought about the 'Sheringham' and how she had come back from Alderney practically empty and came to the conclusion that something approaching panic must exist there and that it appeared to have engulfed those in authority. Having no ship to send (the crew of the 'Staffa', the little cargo vessel that carried part of Alderney's requirements had refused, because of the danger from German planes, now very evident, to take their vessel there the day before) I gave instructions for the Ministry of Shipping to be informed by telephone of the position there, as I saw it, and asked that two or three small ships should be despatched to Alderney immediately. They were and arrived the next morning. Unknown to me, Judge French had asked the Master of the 'Vestal' to break wireless silence and summon vessels for an evacuation. Whether he did or not, I do not know nor do I know for certain whether, if he did, it was his message or mine which brought the small ships. In any case, it matters little but an enthusiast has worked it out, knowing the earliest time at which the Vestal's message could have been sent, that the ships could not possibly have reached Alderney at the time they did if they were summoned by the Vestal.

The evacuation of Alderney was completed on the morning of Sunday the 23rd June. Nineteen stout-hearted people remained behind and Judge French sent me a list of these by Pilot Jennings, who deviated for this purpose on his way to England in his pilot boat and was then to rendez-vous with the Pilots Nick and Dick Allen off the Casquets. The rendez-vous there was missed. Of those remaining, one was a man of 92, one was the Greffier of Alderney, Charles Batiste, and two were the former Rector of Ste. Marie du Castel, Guernsey (an Alderneyman) and his wife. I understand that the behaviour and work of Mrs. Mesny both before and during the evacuation of Alderney were outstanding and deserving of the highest praise.

Knowing that within a week they would be starving and believing that we were about to be cut off from Alderney by a German invasion of that island or of our own, I at once despatched the lifeboat with instructions to the coxswain to bring them all to Guernsey 'by force if necessary'. When one gives an order, one never knows how it will be obeyed. The coxswain strapped a great Colt revolver to his waist and proceeded on his mission. The passengers were as cool as cucumbers. The old Rector and his wife had been busy attending to the needs of the hapless cattle which had been abandoned by their owners. The Greffier brought down all the Alderney registers in his possession that he and helpers could lug along to the lifeboat. As soon as the little ships (the 'Courier' and the 'Isle of Alderney') which usually served Alderney returned from their missions to England, they were sent up to Alderney to bring away the cattle and pigs and a party of farmer volunteers was sent with them. This included Capt. Don Bissett D.C.M., our noted Bisley shot, with instructions to put to sleep all the dogs and cats he could get his sights on. The party reported the most pitiful conditions. Newly calved cows had not been milked for days, young calves had been found dead in the fields, a horse had jumped a gate into the roadway and had died of a broken neck, cattle were roaming about on the breakwater and pigs rooting in the streets. One cow, still tied short by the head in her stable, had a half-full pail of milk and a milking stool by her side, where they had been left by her distracted owner when he quitted. Somehow, the party of skilled farmers eased the animals' sufferings, starving dogs and cats waiting outside their homes were killed and the cattle were brought to Guernsey without incident and, we having no readily available grazing land, were placed on the grassed airfield. (When the Germans arrived a few days later, they accused us of sabotage in doing this and they had to use troop-carriers with which to shoo the cattle to a corner of the airfield before they could land.) The party had collected all the meat in the refrigerators used by the troops although the electricity that operated them had been off for days. We put it in our own cold stores and saved the lot, but only just. Then the 'Courier' brought down the pigs. She was machine-gunned and bombed when off Guernsey and went aground. Refloated, she berthed at St. Peter Port. Our cold stores were filled to capacity and we had no spare pig-food so we dispatched her, with the pigs still on board, to Plymouth that very night.

It amazed us that a working party had not been left behind to tend the animals whose sufferings - but for our intervention - would have been terrible. The old people who stayed had done their best for them but it was beyond their strength and capabilities. I wonder if the administration, in their dash for safety, gave any thought to what they were leaving behind for those in Guernsey - who were staying put - to rectify. Leadership is always important but how much more so in times of calamity.

More trouble followed swiftly. At 4.30 a.m. on Sunday the 23rd June - the day of the Alderney evacuation - one of our doctors rang around to all his confreres in the profession explaining that, in his view, total evacuation was essential. They all met at 7.30 a.m. and their Secretary, who and whose junior partner happened to be my own family doctors, asked me to meet them all and, asking Leale to attend, I met them at 11 a.m. The original convenor, who sat close to me, put forward an impassioned plea for a statement by them all that, for the avoidance of starvation, it was essential that evacuation of Guernsey should be total. Our partial evacuation operation had been completed and I knew that total evacuation was impracticable and moreover that, whatever hardships before us, it would be the wrong thing to do. I thought it impolitic to express my view at the moment. The whole thing was argued out by the doctors who, with the one exception, were quite cool and collected. I had never before, nor have I since, felt waves of panic emanating from a person near me. They were affecting my own judgement and, but for politeness sake, I would have asked the source of them to go and sit at the other end of the room. In contrast, I well remember the resolution of the oldest doctor of them all - Dr. Arderne Wilson - who argued stoutly that, despite grave hardships, we would survive. It should be remembered that at this time we in Guernsey were certain that the Germans would arrive shortly and that it was not in the contemplation of anyone that we would be able to secure supplies of things like flour and meat from the continent. During some lull, my doctor told me that his partner was a

Jew and that he feared the worst might happen to him at the hands of the Germans. Could I not somehow get him out of the island? We resumed our conference and I suggested that this doctor should be sent by me to the Home Office to put the case advanced to me by the doctors and ask for total evacuation. I knew he would fail but said nothing of this. The meeting agreed and it was closed. Now my wife, who knew why I had gone to the meeting, came along to hear the result. She was originally to have gone with our two small boys and was to have been attached to Elizabeth College as a sort of additional matron but she had changed her mind and had told lots of people that she was staying. Now the doctor entrusted with the mission to the Home Office insisted that she (we were all great friends) and the boys must come with him. She consulted me and I wavered for I had originally intended her to go. Then Leale stepped in and very rightly reminded her that a lot of people had relied on her example in deciding to stay. I came down heavily on Leale's side and she reluctantly came to heel. I instructed Dr. W.J. Montague that, having completed his mission, he was on no account to return. As his wife and children were already in England, this inflicted no hardship on him and I had no hesitation in so insisting. Unhappily, he died in England from natural causes and I never saw him again. I realised, of course, what my wife was going through from the opposing forces working on her for she had it firmly implanted in her mind that her two boys were likely to attain manhood as stunted sickly dwarfs. They certainly looked pretty pallid when, after the end of the war, I returned to Guernsey but their experiences do not appear to have adversely affected either their health or stature. I don't think fear of the Germans ever entered my wife's head either then or when, later in my absence, our house was full, to the attics, with them.

While these things were happening, a German plane flew very low over St. Peter Port and then flew backwards and forwards over the island of Guernsey for hours. She appeared to be mapping it by photography. Then, on Friday the 28th June at about 7.30 p.m. German planes appeared from the northward and started machine-gunning. As it began, I was speaking to Markbreiter of the Home Office on the telephone and - with the words "Here they come" - I held the mouthpiece to the open window so that he could hear it for himself. The subsequent bombing of the long line of tomato lorries waiting to ship their fruit for England (a reduced mailboat and a cargo vessel service had been resumed) was a dreadful business. Twenty-seven men and four women were killed and thirty-eight men and nine women were seriously wounded. Our lifeboat, of characteristic build and with a large Red Cross painted on her deck, on passage to Jersey, was machine-gunned and a member of the crew killed.

As soon as the partial evacuation was completed and one had time to think, it became apparent to some of us that, to cope with the emergencies that were crowding and likely to crowd upon us, some modification of the leisurely methods of insular government was urgently necessary.

Others were thinking this, too, and it came to my ears that there was a movement on foot to appoint a member of our civil service as a sort of dictator to supersede the existing organs of government. I rang him up and asked what he knew of it. He replied with the utmost frankness that he had been approached and had turned it down flat. I then rang the man who had supposedly started it and asked him to come and see me. He did and I told him that, if he pursued the matter I would have him arrested and (I think I said) interned. He denied everything but he was so uneasy that I felt he had something on his conscience.

Now, it was clear to me that what we needed above everything was active, courageous, level-headed leadership. In my view, one man stood out above all others in the person of the Reverend John Leale. He excelled in finance matters and finance was going to be one of our major problems. I undoubtedly chatted to him on the subject generally but cannot remember whether I ever put it to him that he should be in the lead. I was the Attorney General with instructions from the British Government to stay at my post and, in any case, I was also a States civil servant and it would have been most inappropriate for me to be put in that position. It never occurred to me and I was only too willing to serve to the best of my ability anyone lawfully appointed.

The Lieutenant Governor was recalled and had left. I was very exhausted mentally at this time and I played about with the idea of getting the Home Office (we were still in telephonic communication) to appoint Leale as a Civil Lieutenant Governor. Then came a Home Office letter addressed to the Lieutenant Governor dated the 19th June, 1940, to the following effect:-

"Sir,

I am directed by the Secretary of State to say that, in the event of your recall, it is desired

by His Majesty's Government that the Bailiff
should discharge the duties of Lieutenant-
Governor, which would be confined to civil
duties, and that he should stay at his post and
administer the government of the Island to the
best of his abilities in the interests of the
inhabitants, whether or not he is in a position
to receive instructions from His Majesty's
Government.

The Crown Officers also should remain at their
posts.

I am, Sir

Your obedient servant,

(The letter was unsigned)..........................."

I rang up the Home Office and asked who should have signed the letter
and was told it was intended to be signed by Sir Alexander Maxwell,
the Permanent Under-Secretary of State. I had: '(Signed) A. Maxwell'
typed in at the foot and presented the letter to the Royal Court for
registration.

(It is amusing to recall that, months later, Dr. Brosch, of the German
Feldkommandantur, called on me and said that he was puzzled as to
how the Bailiff had been appointed Lieutenant Governor. I took him
to the Greffe and showed him the letter and he never so much as
questioned the fact that it bore no original signature.)

This letter put paid to the proposal I had in mind but it effected
nothing. I investigated immediately and it was clear beyond doubt that
the Military Lieutenant Governor had possessed no civil powers and
therefore that none had been conferred upon the Bailiff.

Then, one morning, Leale came to me and told me that he and Mr.
Ridgway, the Solicitor General, had approached the Bailiff and
persuaded him that I should be appointed as a virtual dictator and that
they had drafted a resolution which, if passed by the States, would
make me the president of a Controlling Committee with power to
appoint and dismiss its members and that the Bailiff was already in
course of summoning the States to a meeting that very afternoon. I
had previously known nothing of this and had not even suspected it. I
felt that I could better serve my Island as adviser to the President,
whoever he might be and I felt myself to be without the training or

experience or special qualities for the post. As a lawyer and within my range of experience, I felt reasonably competent but to embark upon this task, treading unknown and untried paths was, I felt, outside my capabilities. Worn out as I was by the tasks of the previous weeks, I had not the energy left to resist Leale's arguments and reluctantly consented, if the States so desired. At the Meeting of the States - there had been no opportunity to inform them of the nature of the business they were to discuss and, in fact, the meeting was technically unconstitutional - there was surprise and considerable misunderstanding. From memory, Deputy Stamford Raffles and Deputy Cross opposed my appointment.

I fully appreciated their views. I made it clear that, in my view, the right candidate was Leale himself and that, as Attorney General, my services would be given him, if appointed, with all the energy and loyalty at my disposal. I think I said that I was not of the stuff of which dictators were made. (I had it very much in mind but did not, I think, say that Leale had been elected to a Juratcy, which meant that he was in office as the result of an expression of will on behalf of the people of the whole island for life whilst I had been appointed not by islanders but by the Crown.)

After a short debate, in which Leale, as proposer, made the final reply, I was appointed without a vote being taken and, so far as I can remember, without any cry of 'Contre'. I had power to appoint the members of the Controlling Committee to be and, after consultation with the Bailiff, to dismiss any of them. By now, I was nearly prostrated by a blinding sick headache but went to my office to decide on my 'Cabinet', The appointments were published the following day and were as follows:-

Jurat the Reverend John Leale M.A. (Economics)

Jurat Sir Abraham J. Lainé K.C.I.E. (Food)

Dr. A.N. Symons (Medical & Nursing Services)

Jurat A.M. Drake (Horticulture)

Deputy R.H. Johns (Unemployment, Re-employment and Public Assistance)

Mr. R.O. Falla (Agriculture)

Deputy Stamford Raffles O.B.E. (Information Officer)

Writing in my notebook in 1944 whilst interned in Germany, I said this:

"I believe that these appointments were sound and as, in Ilag VII, I sit writing this, I am confirmed in that belief when I remember that none of the appointees have been removed except those who, still shouldering the heavy responsibilities which I placed on their shoulders, have been stricken by the hand of death. So passed on from this earthly sphere those good comrades in misfortune, Aylmer Mackworth Drake, who had become President of the Glasshouse Utilisation Board, and Stamford Raffles, Information Officer."

Now, in 1967, there remain only Leale, Falla and me. On my return to Guernsey in 1945, I heard of all the grave problems and deficiencies with which all of them had had to cope, very greatly surpassing any which had arisen in my time; of Sir Abraham Lainé's dogged courage in fighting the Germans for more food, of Dr. Symons struggling with them undauntedly against the requisition of hospitals and his fights against the imposed reductions of rations, etc., of Falla's magnificent efforts (what a way he had with the Germans: he wasn't even a member of our States when I appointed him but I knew my man) and of Leale's constant, patient, dogged efforts the whole time and in all respects on behalf of his fellow Islanders. How very justified I was in writing what I wrote.

At the time of the appointment of the Controlling Committee, Leale was in temporary disfavour with his fellow islanders. It was unfortunate and quite unjustified. It happened thus: one morning, after a conference with the Bank managers, I was engaged in drafting an Ordinance designed to put an end to the run on the banks which had reached alarming proportions. The Bailiff had arranged for an almost immediate sitting of the Royal Court to consider and, I hoped, pass the Ordinance. The Sea Transport Officer arrived and was ushered in and, almost simultaneously, Leale came into my office. The Transport Officer told us that there was panic at the harbour, 'that he knew panic when he saw it' and that, if nothing were done speedily, women and children would find themselves in the water as the crowd surged for the ships. My presence in the Court in a few minutes to explain and support the draft Ordinance was essential and I asked Leale to go to the harbour and ascertain the position and to endeavour to do what was appropriate in the circumstances. After Court I saw him again and he told me he had addressed the part of the crowd he could reach urging common sense and had suggested that those playing a vital part in the island's economy should return to their homes. He told me, too, and knowing how unruffled he always was, I am satisfied he spoke the truth, that the Transport Officer's report was a gross exaggeration of the situation. To those who afterwards blamed him for influencing them to stay, I would suggest that it is no easy thing to be sent on a mission based on totally false assumptions and to assess the correct situation on arrival and when the crowd is so large that only part of it could hear what he said. I am more than satisfied that he acted prudently and wisely in all the circumstances and that no responsibility for any error or judgement rests on his shoulders.

Part Two

FOREWORD

The events described in the following chapters occurred nearly a quarter of a century ago. It is inevitable, therefore, that inaccuracies due to lapses of memory or to the colouring of recollections may have crept in. Except while imprisoned in Paris and interned in Germany, I kept no diary, partly, I suspect, from laziness but mainly because it seemed inadvisable to do so.

It is possible that distance has lent enchantment to the view. Any readers I may acquire will in all likelihood attribute to this the favourable light in which I regard a number of German officers with whom I came in contact. I am certain, however, that I have not exaggerated their good qualities. I do not know how it came about but the fact remains that the great majority of the Germans with whom I encountered (and, because of the continental custom, I shook hands with many more enemy subjects during the war than I have throughout the rest of my life with people of my own nationality) were honourable, humane men. I encountered some swine but many less than I would have expected.

As head of the local administration in Guernsey when the German occupation started, I was determined to out-Job Job himself and that my administration should act as a buffer between the occupying forces and the civilian population. Now a buffer, to be effective, must above all else be resilient. It must give when the pressure would otherwise be irresistible and it must always come back in readiness to resist other and lesser impacts. That I lasted in office only from the beginning of July 1940 until early in the following November is sufficient evidence of my failure but that failure arose, I like to think, at least in part to circumstances quite beyond my control.

It sounds terribly pretentious to say so but I attempted initially, so far as I could, to run the German occupation for them in so far as it touched the civil population. I recognise now, of course, that this was a fatuous thing to do but, at the beginning, the German occupying force was so small and I was in such close touch with the commander and his staff that it did not seem to me to be impossible. As that force grew to the dimensions of a whole division or more, my successors were confronted with much tougher tasks.

Without any real power, I decided that my only weapon was to appear utterly honest and reliable and absolutely frank. For some reason or other, the Germans with whom I came in contact appeared to like me and I was amused to hear that they referred to me as "the big Englishman who says the most terrible things with a smile on his face".

I was of course aware that my motives might well be regarded with grave suspicion by many of my own people, particularly those with loads of time on their hands in which to brood over their troubles which were many and various. In the midst of my many anxieties in the early days of the German occupation, I was therefore greatly touched when one day the venerable and much loved Père Bourde de la Rogerie, Rector of Notre Dame du Rosaire, said to me: "Monsieur Sherwill, si ce n'était pas pour vous, nous serions désesperés". Exaggerated, of course, but very comforting.

It shook me to the core, though, when placed under arrest for assisting espionage to be told by the German Secret Military Police that they were shocked by my conduct because they had thought I was their man. I denied with oaths that I had ever "been their man" but my stock with the Germans slumped severely for they realised what, it seems, they had not previously detected, that behind the facade of honesty and frankness, there lurked a reserve of guile to be deployed when the necessity arose on behalf of my fellow countrymen. And so I became unstuck. Later, interned in Germany and elected British Camp Senior, I used precisely the same methods but gave an appropriate warning. At my first interview with the Sonderführer in charge of camp administration, he said to me: "Mr. Sherwill, can we behave as gentlemen to each other? I will never lie to you but I will sometimes have to refuse to answer your questions." To this I replied: "You can depend on me to be absolutely frank with you except in two respects (1) where my country's interests are concerned: this, interned as I am, is unlikely to arise: and (2) where the life or safety of any of my countrymen is concerned. In either case, I will, if necessary, lie and lie". He said the equivalent of "Good enough" and to that pact he and I adhered scrupulously.

We Guernseymen are lucky. The team I was able to assemble, some of them senior to me both in age and experience, were indescribably loyal and helpful to me personally and served their fellow islanders with the utmost devotion throughout Guernsey's darkest hour, and for years in conditions of near starvation after I had been removed from the scene. The two German Kommandants I knew (some of the later ones were of a different calibre), Oberste Lanz and Major Bandelow were good, honest soldiers and easy to deal with. They were obviously respected and held in affection by their troops. Our internment camp was commanded by Oberste Köchenberger, a great character who did his utmost for us and with whom not only I but many other internees have exchanged greetings at the New Year ever since.

1

THE GERMANS ARRIVE

Background To The Production Of The German Orders

On Friday, June 28th, 1940, a rumour spread that at 6 p.m. I would speak to the people outside the offices of the Guernsey Press Company in Smith Street. The first I knew of it was when, at about 6.15, a messenger came to the room in Elizabeth College, where I was working, to find out why I hadn't turned up. I rushed down and did my best to reassure the large crowd which had assembled and to answer the questions put to me. I then returned to my office and soon afterwards Markbreiter of the Home Office rang me on the telephone. I cannot now remember what the conversation was about. Just as we were ringing off, I heard the sound of aeroplanes and the stuttering of machine guns from the direction of St. Sampsons. (They must have been machine gunning the little steamship "Courier" bound from Alderney to Guernsey with a cargo of pigs rounded up in Alderney by our people after the total evacuation of that Island.) I remember saying to Markbreiter: "Here they come" and held the receiver up to the open window so that he, too, might hear.

The machine gunning of our lifeboat, of the usual distinctive build, and clearly marked on her deck with a large red cross, resulted in one of the crew (the coxswain's son) being killed outright. The long lines of the tomato-laden lorries at the harbour awaiting their turn to unload into the waiting ship were machined gunned and bombed very severely. Bombs were dropped elsewhere in the island doing considerable damage and there was much indiscriminate machine gunning. The raid started just before 6.45 p.m. and one bomb hit the harbour weighbridge and stopped its clock at that time. 27 men and 4 women lost their lives and 38 men and 9 women received serious injuries. Curiously enough, the mailboat "Isle of Sark", which fired on the planes with her machine-gun - the only such weapon in Guernsey at that time - and the other ships in harbour escaped unscathed. Four British planes, in formation, made a swoop over the island within about an hour of the end of the raid. It was most reassuring.

Some days later I tackled Dr. Maass - of whom more later - about the raid. He said that the German airmen had mistaken the tomato lorries for lorries carrying war munitions. I then asked him, even if such a mistake had been made, how he accounted for the machine-gunning of the plainly marked lifeboat. He replied, I remember, "There are lunatics in the armed forces of all nations".

Nothing happened on the Saturday but on Sunday, the 30th, at about noon, two German planes arrived over our airport. One landed while the other remained in the air. A Luftwaffe officer found the airport terminal building deserted and broke open a door. He left in a great hurry as British planes approached and left his revolver behind. It was brought to me and, that night, I handed it over to the officer commanding the German force which had later landed.

I remained at home near the telephone and at, I think about 7 p.m. Mr. Pierre de Putron, in charge of Air Raid Precautions, rang me up to say that several German troop carriers were flying down our West Coast. This time there was no firing and no bombs were dropped. So quickly was the invasion of Guernsey conducted that many people, not living near the airport, were unaware that the island had been occupied until their daily paper arrived the next day and they read the first set of German orders.

About half an hour later, a young German Luftwaffe officer, still in flying kit and driven by our Police Sergeant Harper, arrived at my house. He spoke English. Now, because of the bombing on the Friday, my wife and I had put our two small boys to sleep in the hall of our house. We imagined that the arches were of solid granite; alterations after the war disclosed that they were of lath and plaster. I went out by the side door and intercepted him and said: "Will you please come in by the side door?" Instantly suspicious, he said : "And why?" I told him our young children were asleep in the front hall and he said "I would not dream of disturbing your children". He asked me to accompany him to the Royal Hotel. His demeanour had greatly re-assured me and I was not in the least alarmed as to what might happen in the near future. On arrival at the Royal, where a number of our officials had already gathered, at whose request I had and still have no idea, the Luftwaffe Captain in command made it clear that he required the attendance of "the chief man of the island". The Bailiff (Mr. Victor G. Carey) who had also been authorised by the British Government to assume the civil powers of British Lieutenant

Governor (the major General who had held that position had been withdrawn to avoid him being made a prisoner-of-war), was telephoned to and the German officer previously mentioned and I went to his home at St. Martin's to fetch him. On the way up St. Julian's Avenue, the officer offered me and I accepted, a German cigarette. It seemed to me to be the strangest and most peaceful invasion of all times.

Returning, I found the Captain sitting in a chair in the hotel lounge with a junior officer seated on his left with a rifle between his knees. He was not overbearing but he treated me with scant courtesy. For myself, I was nervous, apprehensive and generally ill-at-ease. I asked him if I might smoke. He said: "Of course". From time to time, military messengers arrived and reported (presumably on how occupation matters were proceeding).

I remember he asked me what arms we had. Someone - I think it was the Bailiff - said we had none and had been totally demilitarised. He spoke without knowledge of the fact that, intensely worried by earlier confusion at the harbour caused by last minute attempts by the crowd to board ships bound for England, and the risk that women and children might be swept into the water, I had asked Colonel Freddie Brousson, the Government Secretary, to arrange for twelve service rifles and bayonets (but no ammunition) belonging to the Royal Guernsey Militia to be kept back when the rest were sent away. I intended handing them to our police and I calculated that the sight of cold steel in the hands of stalwart police officers would prevent, or if necessary, quell any such disorder. I therefore intervened and said "We have twelve rifles and bayonets". Col. Brousson had arrived by this time and he said: "There aren't any bayonets". I said "Yes, there are, there are twelve". Col Brousson then admitted he'd forgotten to keep any bayonets.

Then came the question : "How much aviation fuel have you?" I replied: "About 70,000 gallons". He looked pleased. I then told him that it was useless to him in that the R.A.F., before they left, had doctored it with tar, sugar etc. He merely said "I expected as much". (We left the petrol for weeks and, by putting in an outlet higher up in it, saved the bulk of it for civilian use.)

He spoke some English and understood more. Finally he, verbally, issued a series of orders in German. They were interpreted to me by

Mr. Isler, a German speaking Swiss national. The German officer had obviously been briefed. I put various questions for the purposes of clarification. My only contribution was to obtain the concession about the consumption of spirits that the order did not apply to stocks in private houses. He then said: "Put all that into good English". I then went into a huddle with Mr. Isler and, so far as I can now remember, Louis Guillemette went away and typed out copies and arranged for their delivery to the Editors of our newspapers. By now, however, I was very, very tired and rather depressed as I thought of the long weary months of enemy occupation which lay ahead of us and of the entirely different life which we, cut off from England, would have to lead. It was a very weary President of the Controlling Committee who crawled into bed that night.

On the Monday morning, unable to settle to work and, indeed, having nothing useful to do, I went down to the Royal Hotel to smell out the ground. No one took the slightest notice of me and I went into the ballroom, the floor of which was strewn, in some places in heaps, with fire-arms and the like impedimenta handed in, in accordance with the German orders published only a few hours before. When we were demilitarised not long before, the insular government had, by notice in the newspapers, called for the handing in of weapons. The response, I reflected sardonically, had been a mere trickle. Now, it was a flood.

Even the R.N.L.I. pistols for firing maroons to call out the lifeboat were tendered but this seemed to me ridiculous and a German Officer confirmed my view.

I was summoned there again on the following day (Tuesday) to meet the new Kommandant. When I arrived, I was told and could see for myself that he was having a meal in the dining-room. So I waited in the hall. Then I was approached by an elderly officer in the uniform of a Kapitan in the German Navy who asked me what I wanted. I told him and he said "Come and sit with me". I did and he told me that he was formerly the Commodore of the Hamburg-America Line and that his name was Koch. He said "This is a dreadful war. I have so many friends in England." He went on to say that I looked worried and I told him that I was dreadfully worried. How was I going to feed the people of the island in the coming winter? He said: "My dear fellow, there's not the slightest reason for you to worry. This war will be over in six weeks and I could, here and now, tell you the exact date in August when it will finish." Dr. Albrecht Lanz, an infantryman in

Major's uniform, then emerged from the dining-room and my conversation with Koch was never renewed. He died from a heart attack or was killed during a British air raid on Cherbourg, where he was stationed, not very long afterwards.

I now met Dr. Lanz for the first time. He was accompanied by Dr. Maass, who was not his Adjutant (Ober-Leutnant Mittelmüller functioned in that capacity) and I can only describe him as a sort of aide interpreter. Lanz was very shabby and I got the impression of a man who was very battle-weary. He was extremely taciturn and my first impressions of him were unfavourable. Maass was younger and of a completely different type. Lanz spoke no English. Maass spoke it fluently. I afterwards learned from him that he had been a prisoner of war of ours in the First World War and that he had taken a degree in Tropical Medicine at Liverpool University. I learned later that, although now in German field-grey, he was a wartime Naval surgeon and, later still and never from him, that he had been a medical missionary. I formed an instinctive liking for him on the spot and never had cause to change my opinion. (Many months after he had left Guernsey, he came back while on leave. I was holding a meeting with all the Constables of the Island when, this time in naval uniform, he knocked and poked his head into the room. I remember saying: "If I were doing my stuff properly, I should be saying: 'here's this cursed enemy again'; as it is, all I can say is: "I'm delighted to see you". He came in and had a short chat and asked how things were going.)

His presence at that time was a godsend. I thought so then and I think so now.

Now, between the Sunday midnight and the time of my meeting Dr. Lanz, I had had time to collect my thoughts, had jotted down some notes and had, to some extent at least, recovered my equanimity. Lanz, Maass and I went back into the dining room and sat down at a corner table still, I remember, covered with a white cloth. Lanz appeared deadly tired. He said a few polite words but without the least sparkle and these were translated to me by Maass. I had put my decorations of the First World War in my pocket and I now pulled them out and laid them on the table in front of Maass, saying to Maass as I did so: "Please tell Dr. Lanz that I, too, have been a soldier. I bitterly regret that I am one no longer. As there isn't a rifle left in the island, I realise I must obey orders. As a former soldier I know how to do this". Lanz picked up my medals and at least went through the motion of examining them carefully and then gravely handed them back to me. He then proceeded to 'dictate' his orders, speaking in German to Maass and the latter passing on to me in English what Lanz had said. Unlike the officer of two nights before, he was most hesitant and we went ahead quite slowly. I ascribed this to mental weariness, in keeping with his appearance. In *Appendix A* I have set out the orders of June 30th and Lanz's of July 2nd. The latter consisted of seventeen paragraphs but they were not dictated in that order nor at the same time.

At the end of it, I arranged the paragraphs in what I thought was some sort of reasonable order having regard to their relative importance and then submitted them to Maass who approved them and, I think, added the words: THE GERMAN COMMANDANT, Dr. Lanz.

One curious thing about the initial and the second sets of German orders, reproduced more or less in extenso in all the books about the occupation is that no one has ever expressed surprise that a non-English speaking Kommandant, within hours of his arrival, should be concerning himself with such things as Prayers for the British Royal Family and giving permission for the British National Anthem to be listened to on the wireless. He seems remarkably informed, too, about some of our legislation requiring the sanction of His Britannic Majesty in Council and even breaks up such legislation into laws, Ordinances, Regulations and Orders. A remarkably well-informed and percipient man! It is all accepted as the most natural thing in the world.

Para. (1) was pure Lanz as was (2), with a little titivation by me. (3) was pure Sherwill. Separated as we now were from His Majesty in privy Council, we were powerless to make any new laws or to repeal or amend existing ones, so I used the Kommandant to raise the British Civil Lieutenant Governor (the Bailiff) to the 'throne' instead. We were, in this respect, once more in working order. The expert in Public International Law may raise his eyebrows and say that this was a mere wartime expedient. So it was as were many other things I did. I was aware, however, of the legislative troubles of the French in occupied France during the Franco-Prussian War of 1870 and of the expedient eventually resorted to by the French of heading legislation 'Au Nom du Peuple Français'. Anyhow, it worked throughout the occupation and was never questioned by the British Government when hostilities ceased. (4) was to safeguard Sark so that orders published in Guernsey and unknown officially in Sark should not bite on its inhabitants. This also was pure Sherwill, as was much of para (5). (6) was pure Lanz.

Now, when we had reached somewhere about here, Lanz was called to the telephone and returned, saying that he had to fly to Jersey in an hour's time and would I go up to the airport where we would continue. I drove there and Maass arrived within a minute or so. I must have been back to normal by now for, having met Maass for the first time only about two hours earlier, as we walked up and down awaiting Lanz, I remember telling him that I had been in the van of those who had pressed for our new airport and had fought those who had considered it a wicked waste of good agricultural land. What a bloody fool I had been. Could I have foreseen the use to which it was now being put, I would have moved heaven and earth to prevent a sod of it being turned. Maass did not even sympathise; he only laughed. Then Lanz arrived and, inside the terminal building, we resumed our work. (11) was pure Lanz. (12) arose out of my query: could not the consumption of spirits in private houses permitted under Sunday's order be permitted also in clubs to which only members and not the public were admitted. The answer was: "Nein". (13) this was probably me; I cannot now be certain. (14) was mostly Lanz and (15), (16) and (17) were wholly his. We are left with paras. (7) to (10) inclusive. I had had a chance to meditate upon what our people would dearly love to have to sustain them in their ordeal and I first put to him the matter of Divine Worship in Churches and Chapels. He granted it, immediately. He was bound to by International Law. Then, tongue in cheek, I tried out Prayers for the British Royal Family and for the British Empire. To my delight, Lanz granted this, too, but he added the end part: 'Such assemblies shall not be made the vehicle for any propaganda or utterances against the honour or interest of or offensive to the German Government or Forces'. These were undoubtedly my words but they were an attempt to reflect faithfully what Lanz, through Maass, conveyed to me. I then put to him the subject matter of (8) which went through at once. Then I put to him the matter of the British National Anthem. The reply was that it was not to be played or sung without the written permission of the German Kommandant. I did not know, nor do I still, whether he was entitled to take the line he did but I think he was. I then said that there was one further matter which I had got to have cleared up, namely, the use by our people of their wireless sets. (I dreaded putting it for fear of an adverse decision and, on that account, left it to the last). Lanz said: "If I leave you your sets, you will most certainly listen to the English news and there is really nothing I can do to stop you. So I must either take them away altogether or else let you keep them. For the moment, I give you complete freedom but I warn you that, later, it may be necessary to alter this". Then, as we were packing up, it occurred to me that our National Anthem would be heard over the wireless daily and, with a set at full blast, would be overheard by the Germans with, as a result, prosecutions for a breach of para. 9. I explained this to Lanz and procured the relaxation of that para. 'as regards private houses in respect of a British Broadcasting programme therein'. I felt that I had done as well as could reasonably be expected and drove back to acquaint my Controlling committee of the good news.

2

EARLY DAYS OF THE OCCUPATION

I have always regretted that I did not keep a detailed diary from the date of the German occupation until I was arrested and flown to Paris and to prison. Probably I was too harassed to do so and was merely living from day to day. For the dates of the events narrated, I am indebted to others who did but for all other details I have to depend on memory which, I hope and believe, is not playing me false.

I remember receiving a visit from a German Leutnant (Sub-Lieutenant) connected with the German Press who told me that he was 79 and the oldest Leutnant in the German Army. I took up with him the matter of Red Cross messages and told him how worried our people in England must be about us. I prepared and gave him a letter which I asked should be dropped over England by parachute. *(A copy of this letter is reproduced in Appendix C)*. He said that the war would be over long before such a service could be organised. Obsessed by the thought of famine in the coming winter and the complete absence of all shipping and with no prospect of any (the Germans admitted that they had no knowledge of any being available and actually told me that when our Mr. R.O. Falla went to France to try to organise purchases of essential commodities, his first task should be to search the west coast of France for a suitable ship, the French having been extremely thorough in sabotaging every ship in port before the Germans arrived), I approached Lanz again and again about a plan which I propounded to him. It was this: If he would let me go to England, I would give him my solemn word of honour that, on arrival there, I would divulge nothing except our urgent need of a ship. Whether successful or not in getting one, I would return with the utmost despatch. I proposed (I did not tell Lanz this) to get Mr. E.A. Dorey, a well-known and highly skilled local yachtsman of the highest integrity, to take me across channel in his semi-fast motor-boat. On arrival I would go directly to the Home Office, where I was well known, and beg my friends there to get the Ministry of Shipping to let me have the S.S. 'New Fawn', a slow but capacious cargo vessel which had traded between Guernsey and Alderney and Sark. If possible, I would fill her with the most essential goods for which the States of Guernsey would one day pay. Lanz did not turn my request down flat; in fact, I couldn't get an answer from him for some days. Finally, the only answer I could get from him was that it was much too dangerous and with that I had to be content. In retrospect, I recognise that it was an impossible proposition and that, had I reached England, it would have been turned down flat. I was still, however, thinking that the British Government would do almost anything which would help to make life possible during the German occupation for the British subjects temporarily separated from the English mainland.

Then, on August 1st, at my morning meeting with Maass (I went to his office each day at 11 a.m. to deal with the day-to-day routine business), he told me that arrangements had been made for me to speak a message of about 100 words into a recording machine and that the record would be played and transmitted over the German Radio. *(A copy of this message is reproduced in Appendix D)*. I asked for and obtained an assurance that it would not be doctored and went away to compose my message. It ran to many more than the allotted number of words but this was not objected to. I set out to be as informative and as reassuring as possible. Not one word nor one figure was other than the absolute truth. The reference to the German officer speaking perfect English to whom I tendered my thanks was to secure his help in seeing that the message did get transmitted. I appreciated that the message would be received in England with incredulity and wondered what I could do to make it known that it really was 'me' speaking. So, perhaps moved by love for them but also by this other reason, I sent love to my three children, Mary Rose, John and Dick. I knew John was at sea in his destroyer but, imagining that the message would be gone through with a tooth-comb, I thought it not unlikely that the Home Office would get hold of Mary Rose (on my return from Germany nearly five years later, they winkled her out of her R.A.F. Station in Yorkshire and had her with me in less than 12 hours) or Dick and closely cross-examine them or one of them. Reading it over again and again and still not satisfied, I added after Mary Rose's name the words: 'Tell Diana that her parents are well'. The Germans couldn't possibly know that Diana Raffles and my daughter had enlisted together in the W.A.A.F. many months before. Would not this at least be taken as a sort of signature tune? When the message was eventually broadcast from Bremen (I never heard it myself and this was not for want of listening) Sir Abraham Lainé, our Food Minister and a very tough, retired Indian Civil Servant, came and upbraided me bitterly, but not about the message nor about my personal message to my children (which latter he regarded as not unreasonable). What he was furious about was that, when everybody was shrieking to be allowed to send messages to their nearest and dearest, I had had the audacity to favour Mr. and Mrs. Raffles (who, by the way, knew nothing about it) to the exclusion of all others. I was too hurt to explain. I had hitherto regarded our Secret Service as almost clairvoyant but, if this was what Sir Abraham made of my finale, what would they? Well, we now know, nothing. The message was suppressed. Presumably, it was not expedient for the British public to know the truth or else I was regarded as a Quisling. Probably the latter, for after all there was a war on. It was evidently regarded with consternation in Whitehall for, when nearly five years later, I reported at the British Embassy in Brussels after being freed from internment by the American Army, I was received by the Principal Secretary, Mr. Cecil de Sausmarez, a Guernseyman, whose home was within a mile of my own, with the greatest kindness and allotted a seat in the first plane out the following morning but with a veiled acidity about my 'unfortunate' message that made me realise for the first time how badly it had been received and filled me with dismay as to the reception I might expect at the Home Office.

When I was feeling very satisfied with the way things in general were going, there occurred something which filled me with dismay and apprehension as to the future. A highly respected maiden lady of about 70 was raped in her home at pistol point by a German soldier. One Sunday evening, her lawyer, Advocate J.E.L. Martel, phoned me with the news and told me that her doctor confirmed an assault had taken place. Two soldiers, both very drunk, had entered her house. One had assaulted her and had left his pistol behind. The other, who took no part in the matter, had afterwards patted her hand in sympathy. I phoned Dr. Maass who told me to go to the lady's house together with my informant and the doctor and that he would come along right away. I phoned Mr. Martel accordingly and he was already at the house when I arrived. Maass and Mittelmüller arrived almost immediately and Maass questioned the victim. The pistol was handed to him. He said that, in view of the age of the lady, he didn't believe a word about the alleged assault. The doctor then arrived and he and Maass (himself a doctor) went into a huddle in the corner of the room and engaged in whispered conversation. Maass declared himself as convinced and he and Mittelmüller left to, as they said, turn out all the troops in the island. About three hours later, Maass phoned me to say that they had found the soldier and asked me to attend a military court of enquiry at a house near the airport at 9 a.m. the following day. They would arrange for the attendance of the victim. The enquiry was conducted with a delicacy which would not have been possible, because of our rules of procedure, had our own court being conducting committal proceedings. The soldier was not present, the victim was not required to give evidence to the officer but, in a separate room, was allowed to make a statement (no one else being present) which was taken down in shorthand by Fraulein Riderer, a German lady, formerly employed in Guernsey as a lady's companion and now stranded there and impressed into the German clerical service. At the end of the proceedings, I was told that the soldier would be taken to Cherbourg for trial and that he would undoubtedly be shot. I told the officer that, as Public Prosecutor, I asked for no greater penalty than would be inflicted by our own court. I insisted that this should go into the record and he resisted this. I insisted, however, and, after some argument, prevailed. I may have been moved slightly by compassion but I regret to say that what moved me very much more was to get proof on paper (and German paper at that) that, when I interceded, as I anticipated I would have to do many times, on behalf of my people, I was following a consistent policy which applied to British and German alike.

About ten days later, I was informed that the soldier had been court-martialed, found guilty and sentenced to be shot. Some days later, I was officially informed that he had been shot. Whether anything happened to the second soldier I never heard.

PRESIDENT OF THE CONTROLLING COMMITTEE OF THE STATES OF GUERNSEY

[The opening paragraphs of this chapter include a second rendition of A.J.S.'s memories of the arrival of the young German Officer at Havelet House on 28th June, as covered in Chapter One]

The last outgoing mailboat, the "Isle of Sark", left immediately after the air raid on the evening of the 28th June and the "New Fawn", the "Courier" and the "Isle of Alderney" left the next day. I discussed with Mr. Markbreiter over the telephone the question of communications and we reached the conclusion that to continue a mail and cargo vessel service for the time being would be tempting Providence. We had excellent telegraphic and telephonic communication with England and it was arranged that every effort would be made to maintain touch for as long as possible. Then on Sunday morning I received a message from the Police Station that a fast motor launch had arrived to take away certain key Post Office technicians and to go to Jersey for a similar purpose. I phoned to Jersey and to London and it was agreed that the launch should return to England and that, as previously arranged, we should retain the Post Office engineers responsible for keeping communications open.

Then came a message - the air raid warning had preceded it - that two German planes had landed at La Villiaze Aerodrome, while a third kept watch overhead, and that, under cover of a machine gun, the terminal building had been broken into. The planes soon left. I rang up London and reported the situation and got a message to the master of the launch still lying in St. Peter Port Harbour to put to sea at once. Nothing further happened till the evening and then at about half past six Mr. Pierre du Putron, the Air Raids Precaution Commandant, had another warning sounded and rang me up to say that four German troop carriers, in line ahead, were coming down the west coast of Guernsey. I phoned London and caught Mr. Markbreiter at the Home Office and reported the position and then we bade each other an affectionate farewell until after the war. It was a sad moment and in it I realised very poignantly what lay ahead. I tried to get through to the

Bailiff of Jersey but could not for the moment. My wife got a message through to him soon afterwards in my absence.

Now, many days before, when it appeared to us that Occupation by the German Forces was inevitable and the most likely way into Guernsey was by means of the airport, we had had a letter prepared in English and in German and this letter was in the hands of the Inspector of Police, Mr. W.R. Sculpher. It contained the information that Guernsey had been declared an open island, that it was entirely demilitarized and that the bearer had instructions to put the German Forces in touch with the British Civil Lieutenant Governor. After consultation with me, Inspector Sculpher and Police Sergeant Harper went to the Airport in the Police car while I stood by at home. I remember after dispatching the Inspector I ate a hurried meal. Soon the Police car bearing a young German Officer in flying kit arrived at my home. The officer was charming and did his utmost to put me at my ease and not to make me feel the humiliating position I was in. I understood that we were to meet the British Lieutenant Governor at the Royal Hotel where the German Officer in command of the invading forces had taken up quarters and was driven there and met the German Commandant. He wanted the Lieutenant Governor, however, who was still at home waiting a call and we drove to Le Vallon and picked up Mr. Carey and took him to the Royal Hotel. The German Officers were very courteous. The Commandant asked many questions. Besides the German Officers with him, and one or two of them sat covering him with a rifle between their knees, there were present the Lieutenant Governor, the States Supervisor, the Police Inspector, the Harbour Master, the Manager of the Telephone Department, Mr. Stamford Raffles and myself. Mr. Isler, the owner of the Hotel de Normandie, a German-speaking Swiss subject, acted as interpreter. The Editor of the "Star" joined us later. Then the Commandant dictated his Orders and these were translated by Mr. Isler. I was directed to turn them into good English and orders were given for them to appear in the "Star" and "Evening Press" the following morning. At about midnight I left for home. For want of other pasturage, we had placed all the cattle brought from Alderney to graze on the Airport and Mr. Raymond Falla, the Agricultural Officer, had been summoned and directed to remove the cattle forthwith. This proved impossible of fulfilment and the cattle were driven away at dawn. Instructions were given to the Police Inspector to round up all British soldiers the next morning with a view to their being interned in Castle Cornet. The instruments connected to the cable going to England were disconnected after an English operator had enquired as to who was at the Guernsey end of the line and the officer holding the instrument had replied, somewhat stiffly, "This is a German Officer". Guernsey was really cut off from the United Kingdom. All that we feared had actually happened. It was a very depressed Attorney General who went to bed that night. We were held for the moment by a mere handful of the German Air Force.

On the following Tuesday I was requested to attend to meet the Commandant who had arrived and to say good-bye to the Officer who first took charge. Major (Doctor) Albrecht Lanz commanded an infantry Battalion and had as his Adjutant Oberleutnant Mittelmüeller and as his Chief of Staff Dr. Maass. Dr. Lanz was every inch a soldier not very easy to get to know but absolutely straight and kindly. I grew to like him very much and I believe he was adored by his men. Oberleutnant Mittelmüeller and I got on very well and became friendly. He spoke no English and I knew no German but we both spoke French so French became the language of our communications. Dr. Maass was a very remarkable man. He had been a prisoner of the English in the 1914-18 War, held a degree in Tropical Medicine of Liverpool University and spoke English amazingly well. His cheery face was a tonic in those depressing days and there can be no question but that his presence and friendly activities helped the situation enormously. When eventually he left to take up another job, we really missed him. He was an enemy but oh! such a pleasant one.

Having been introduced to Dr. Lanz, who had previously paid a courtesy visit to the British Lieutenant Governor and had received a return visit from the latter, Dr. Lanz dictated a series of Orders and directed me to edit them. I put various matters to him as requiring a decision and these were clarified in the Orders which I drafted and submitted to him that afternoon at the Airport and which, with only minor amendments, were approved by him and published on the following day.

Dr. Lanz expressed his desire for a suitable house to be provided for him as Commandant and decided, after inspecting it, to take over Government House in Queen's Road. The German Flag was hoisted where, before, the Union Jack had flown, over a building which to so many of us in Guernsey had been the scene of many a garden party and dinner. It had been here that the people of Guernsey had had the honour of meeting the Prince of Wales (later King Edward VIII) on the occasion of his visit in 1935.

The task confronting the Controlling Committee was a formidable one. The civilian population remaining was estimated at 24,000. This, as it afterwards turned out, was a very good estimate for a census held in the month of July,1940 showed a population of 23,981, of which 20,127 were of the age of 19 years or older and 3,854 were under 19 years.

Now Guernsey had been adapted to produce vast quantities of tomatoes but the hundreds of miles of glasshouses which had affected her inland beauty had also deprived her of much agricultural land. She had ceased, for all practical purposes, to grow cereals, her herd of cattle would not suffice to produce milk and butter for the people remaining and where was she to get such things as coal, diesel oil, petrol, paraffin, to name only a few of the things she was obliged to import or to go without.

For the short period between the evacuation and the air raid, the tomato export trade, which had been suspended during the evacuation, was got going again but when the Occupation came it was estimated that one half only of the crop had been exported, that this half had not done more than pay the expenses attendant on the 1940 crop and that tomatoes were ripening at the rate of about 2,000 tons a week. Guernsey certainly could not eat a tenth of these and here we were without a market for them. We couldn't even preserve them for we hadn't a factory or any of the other requisites for the purpose. In Guernsey, too, a great number of the tomato growers work on bank overdrafts secured by "obligation" registered at the Greffe on their growing estates. The guillotine which severed communications with England hit these and all growers very heavily indeed. It meant that the majority were without means of livelihood and were quite unable to keep on the very considerable staff that a modern tomato growing property requires. Something had to be done and done swiftly or we should have the bulk of our workpeople unemployed. The Controlling Committee took over as employees of the States of Guernsey all employees and their employers willing to be taken over together with the growing property on which they worked, the latter without liability for rent or other encumbrance. Now it has to be remembered that most married men engaged in the industry had a wife or children, or both, evacuated to England, and an undertaking had been given to the Home

Office that the Guernsey exchequer would to the extent of its ability meet the cost of maintaining our evacuees during the remainder of the war.

A schedule of wages was prepared whereunder married men without dependants in Guernsey were classified as single men. A sharp distinction was made between single men, married men (wife not in Guernsey) and married men with wife and other dependants in Guernsey. The scale of pay for female labour was adjusted appropriately along the same lines. The step taken put a tremendous burden on the States but we were convinced of the absolute necessity of taking it.

Before the Occupation we had speculated upon the policy likely to be adopted by the invaders and had wondered whether the English banknotes in the Island (probably some £50,000 worth) and the silver and possibly the bronze coinage would be seized. We had plates prepared for printing notes of a number of denominations but the Germans directed that "business should proceed as usual" and we never used them.

In Guernsey there were a great number of persons whose incomes were wholly derived from the United Kingdom, the Empire or elsewhere outside Guernsey. Many residents, prominent and otherwise, depended on Government pensions for their support, the wives of servicemen looked to their separation allowances paid them weekly through the Post Office. Many people deeply rooted in Guernsey had businesses there which ceased to pay.

Now in reviewing the matter with representatives of the "Big Five" and the Guernsey Savings Bank, the position appeared to the Committee to be as follows:- All moneys standing to the credit of persons remaining in Guernsey were frozen in that these moneys being notionally in London at the headquarters of the Banks were affected by the provisions of the Trading with the Enemy Act, 1939. In any case the moneys couldn't be remitted to Guernsey and even if the local branches could pay their customers they had no means of acquainting their Head Offices of the transactions entered into. Further, on instructions from London all securities (including the securities held by the States of Guernsey for the account of sinking funds and otherwise) had been forwarded to the head offices of the banks by their local branches. In any case there could be no hope of any remittance of interest and dividends on our investments outside Guernsey until after the war. Comparatively large amounts were outstanding, too, in respect of returns due to growers for tomatoes shipped in the last fortnight before the Occupation. There were other complications but I will not worry the reader with these.

In the days following the evacuation, Mr. Stamford Raffles had been busy with publicity matters (he used among other things to broadcast from the Press Office in Smith Street where the management had with great kindness provided us with the use of the necessary apparatus) but that had eased off and the Controlling Committee entrusted him with the task of interviewing persons needing advances on account of their frozen income or on the security of their frozen assets or somewhat chilly Government realty. Mr. Raffles did this job admirably and much anxiety and real suffering was spared a host of self-respecting people who, in many cases after a lifetime of industry, found themselves literally penniless. Mr. Rafffles communicated his findings to the appropriate Bank or to the Post Office (which, and its staff was, by arrangement with the British Government, taken over by the States of Guernsey) the States guaranteeing the Bank or Post Office against loss.

With incomes falling, the Controlling Committee with regret felt compelled to apply drastic cuts to the salaries of the Guernsey Civil Service, every salary being cut by one half of so much thereof as exceeded £100. Such was the loyalty of the staff and its understanding of the crisis that, notwithstanding that in many cases grave hardship resulted, not one murmur arose or, if it did, it was not audible.

In October 1938, a Committee for the Control of Essential Commodities had been set up by the States under the very able presidency of Sir Abraham Lainé K.C.I.E., Jurat of the Royal Court and who became a member of the Controlling Committee.

Sir Abraham Lainé, a member of a family much honoured in Guernsey, had spent his life in the Indian Civil Service and had greatly distinguished himself therein. At the time of his retirement in 1935 he was the Acting Governor of Assam.

Now it is remarkable that no matter how eminent a Guernseyman may become beyond the shores of the island that gave him birth, he invariably returns to Guernsey on relinquishing office and then instead of quietly living out his days in leisure and peace, he offers himself or is seized and offered by his admirers as a sacrifice upon the altar of civic duty to his native Isle. As with so many other notable Guernseymen, so with Sir Abraham Lainé. He became a Jurat in February, 1938 and never did a man better justify his title to that office.

He had working with him, on the Committee for the Control of Essential Commodities, some doughty veterans, Mr. F.T. Hill-Cottingham, Mr. J. Griffiths, Dr. A.N. Symons (who became responsible for Island Health Services) and others and had a magnificent Secretary in Mr. J.H. Loveridge who knew the answer to every question.

Under this Committee's leadership, considerable reserves of wheat and flour and general groceries had been acquired and at the time of the Occupation there was flour and wheat to last the civil population until about the end of November and chilled meat in the Cold Storage Plants sufficient only until early September. So there we were, with vast quantities of tomatoes the bulk of which could not be put to use despite free supplies to all and unlimited feeding of the fruit to cattle and pigs, with bread assured until the end of November and meat (on a very reduced ration) for not many more weeks. We had had an excellent early potato crop and there were prospects of a good main crop. I asked Dr. Lanz if we might root out the tomato crop with a view to planting other crops vitally necessary to the life and health of our people. He gave permission for half the crop to be destroyed (and this was done) but directed that the other half be properly tended with a view to the fruit being exported to France. Apparently, he expected shipping would be available for the purpose but it did not materialise and only a comparatively small quantity of tomatoes was exported by sea and air. When Mr. Drake was appointed to take charge of Horticulture it had been hoped that perhaps we might not be invaded after all but when our communications with England were cut and our tomato exports came to an abrupt end it was realised that our glasshouses had to be utilised as adjuncts for the production of basic foods. Accordingly Mr. Raymond Falla was asked to assume responsibility for all food production and Mr. Drake, whose ability and penetration were too well known for us to allow him to leave the Committee, remained as a member without portfolio and undertook under Mr. Falla the Chairmanship of the Glasshouse Utilisation Board (or GUB as it became known to the irreverent). Mr. Falla formed another Board styled the Potato Board under the chairmanship of Mr. Wilfred J. Bird and this Board took charge eventually of the storing and sale not only of potatoes but of all other vegetables.

But there were other worries: we were advised by Major Barritt Hills, the Manager and Engineer of the States Electricity Department, that his Department's supply of Diesel Oil and Paraffin could only suffice to provide electricity and to drive the pumping plant of the States Water Department (driven either directly by diesel oil or paraffin or by electricity) until about the end of February, 1941. Mr. R.G. Luxon, the Manager of Guernsey Gas Light Company Limited informed us that his stocks of gas coal would only last until the end of November or thereabouts. Sir Abraham Lainé's forecast as to the house coal position was that it would be exhausted by the first half of November, 1940. We ascertained that the only suitable fuel for the great majority of our bakers' ovens was coke. And where was coke coming from if the gasworks closed down? But then - consoling thought - if there is no flour we shan't need bakers' ovens.

But what about the petrol and paraffin situation? Two stores existed, one at the Castle Walk, St. Peter Port Harbour and the other at Bulwer Avenue, St. Sampson's. Shortly before the evacuation by the Military the Royal Air Force had taken a much increased interest in Guernsey. We had had night-flying practice by flying boats over St. Peter Port and the Little Russell and the Airport had become a flying school, hutments and hangars having been erected for this purpose. With this increased activity came the requisitioning of part of the storage capacity of the petrol dump at the Castle Walk and here, at the time of the German Occupation, were approximately 30,000 gallons of aviation spirit rendered useless, so we were given to understand, by the admixture of sugar, paint and tar. In addition, there were here some 50,000 gallons of "Pool" spirit and at Bulwer Avenue some 62,000 gallons of "Pool" petrol and some 70,000 gallons of paraffin. Stocks of lubricating oil and grease were reasonably adequate.

Petrol had been drastically rationed for some time and under the general supervision of the ubiquitous Committee for the control of Essential Commodities, Mr. Wilfred Frampton, the States Accountant, then Mr. Burlingham and, later, Mr. Herbert G. Stephenson had been successively appointed to the post rather, as I thought, grandiloquently styled "Controller of Petroleum Supplies". It seemed an unhealthy job for both Mr. Burlingham and Mr. Stephenson had been compelled to relinquish it for health reasons. Then Mr. A.C. Richings, a Guernseyman who had spent most of his life in the banking world in South America, was appointed to the post and was functioning when Major Lanz arrived to take command in Guernsey. Directions were given by Major Lanz that all motor buses for civilian use were to be discontinued as was also the use of all motor vehicles other than those which were absolutely essential for the continuance of the economic life of the Island and Mr. Richings was given the invidious task of putting those directions into operation. The Royal Hotel was a hive of activity. It was the German Headquarters for the time being (soon afterwards the "Insel Kommandantur" was installed at the Channel Islands Hotel a few doors away) and there the Controller of Petroleum Supplies functioned importuned by all and sundry whose activities formed, or were claimed to form, part of the economic life of the Island and there also came hundreds of people bearing rifles, shot-guns, revolvers, pistols, bayonets, swords, daggers and other weapons in response to the German Order that these be given up. A similar order had been given by the Guernsey Authorities at the time of demilitarisation. There had been a good response to this but the response to the German order was better.

We didn't know it at the time, but discovered later, that the foreign matters poured into the aviation spirit, in sinking to the bottom of the tanks, would leave the spirit comparatively undamaged and useable and the position as regards petrol, taking into account the greatly reduced use of motor vehicles, notwithstanding the considerable use thereof by the German Forces, was that we had supplies likely to last till the end of March, 1941. As regards paraffin there were some 70,000 gallons. The Manager of the Electricity Department claimed for a share of this to keep his generating plant and the waterworks pumping plant going for as long as possible. Without electricity there could be no cold storage, the water service would come to an end, the sewers would go unflushed or would have to be flushed to a limited degree in some sort of way, and a great part of the glasshouses, whose crops depend so largely upon constant watering to make good the evaporation which takes place, would be rendered unproductive. No wonder that the Controlling Committee's meetings were lengthy and sometimes inconclusive. Often the question before them was: "How, in relation to this particular non-recurring asset, can we obtain the most good for the greater number?". We allocated 30,000 gallons of paraffin for the generation of electricity and the pumping of water.

We allocated 2,000 tons of house coal to the Gas Company for gas and coke production being advised that this was the most economical use to which it could be put. This allocation of house coal was cancelled, however, because the German Commandant disapproved of it and thought it was more needed for use as house coal. The balance of the paraffin - with the exception of an insignificant quantity allotted for use for trade purposes and of a larger quantity destined for use in agricultural implements - was allocated to persons whose only means of illumination was a paraffin lamp and there are many such in the country districts of Guernsey.

We had a certain amount of Anthracite Coal - of which Guernsey is a large importer for horticultural purposes - and later we ordered the admixture of a proportion of anthracite with all house coal sold. Further, in all households where at least one room could be heated by a coal or wood fire, every gas and electric fire and radiator was cut off and sealed, and other gas or electrically heated water heaters were rendered unusable. By notices, too, the public were enjoined to exercise the greatest economy in the use of all fuel and water. It is not one's normal experience to find the Manager of a Public Utility Undertaking gloating over the reduced sales of the commodity to which it relates. Yet I was never able to determine who was the most self-satisfied as he reported the week's fall in production and consumption, the Manager of the Electricity Department or of the Gas Company or of the Water Department or who the most depressed if his consumers let him down by using more than in the previous week.

Mr. G. Heggs, the Assistant Engineer to the States, had had experience of water engineering and, the Manager of the States Water Department having left the Island during the evacuation, Mr. Heggs took charge of the engineering side of it. He evolved a scheme which, by utilising sundry steam boilers and adapting them, would provide pumping facilities for a limited water supply for the Island and which would provide a fairly adequate supply for an area largely covered with glasshouses. Mr. Drake's Board (GUB) reviewed the Island distribution of water pumping windmills and arranged for the transference of many of them to properties which they would serve with greater effect, the object being to supply wind power where water was to be had for the pumping and a water service from the mains when it was not.

Here we were then when the German Occupation started:

We had bread till the end of November, meat for not many more weeks and thereafter would have to depend on our own production which we knew to be totally inadequate for our needs, groceries for probably the whole winter, coal and gas till the end of November, electricity until the end of March, paraffin (at the rate of half a gallon a week for users of paraffin lamps) till the end of February, petrol till the end of March. We were very short of horses, harness and horse vehicles for practically the whole of our road transport had, for years, been performed by motor vehicles.

There were times when the minds of some of us went back to a meeting with the members of the medical profession in Guernsey on Sunday June 23rd 1940 when they unanimously recommended the total evacuation of the Island as being the only reasonable proposition in the circumstances. I knew at the time of the meeting that this was impracticable but I promised to raise it again with the Home Office. (I had done so previously) and I sent my dear friend Dr. W.J. Montague to the Home Office bearing a letter setting out the position and obtained a promise (subsequently honoured) that he would have access to the Under Secretary himself.

The German garrison increased fairly rapidly, arriving in troop-carrying planes and it has to be remembered that in the early days of the Occupation that garrison lived entirely upon our reserves. For some weeks no vessel entered Guernsey harbour.

For years we had depended on large imports of butter, margarine and cooking fats and had imported large quantities of horse and cattle fodder and pig and poultry foods and as for our flour, well we had imported the whole of it. The prospect could not be termed a bright one but it is doubtful if the bulk of the population realised how dreadfully serious the situation really was.

One Sunday morning (I believe it was on 14th July, 1940) I chanced to be looking out of my bedroom window facing the direction of Alderney when I thought I saw the smoke of a steamer. I got my telescope to bear on the object and to my amazement and delight saw a real steamer belching forth real smoke, travelling at what I guessed to be about ten knots about midway between Alderney and Guernsey and quite obviously bound for the latter Island. I had not been so excited for a long time. It was the s.s. "Holland" a tender formerly stationed, I believe, at Boulogne and she had come to inaugurate a new service between the Channel Islands and the Continent. Soon afterwards the harbour tug "Duke of Normandy" the property of the States of Jersey and previously used for servicing buoys and beacons, was pressed into service to run a Guernsey-Jersey passenger and cargo service. She was a good little ship with twin engines but much too small for the job as anyone who had rounded the Corbière in a gale of wind will be the first to admit. Later we were to have the "Diamant", "Adolph Le Prince" and "Normand" but for some time the "Holland" and the "Duke of Normandy" and occasionally a river barge were the only ships entering St. Peter Port Harbour. The cranes had been put out of action at the time of the air raid through the fracture of a cable but this had long since been repaired.

It has to be remembered that we in Guernsey were entirely ignorant of the position in occupied France. We knew, of course, the extent of the area occupied but we did not know and had no means of knowing the extent of the devastation thereof or whether, as was stated on the English wireless, a famine threatened. In the dire extremity to which, it seemed, we should be reduced before the end of the winter, would it be possible to procure even small quantities of essential requirements? No one knew. Dr. Maass assured us, however, that cereals were not wanting either in France or Germany.

Perhaps the thing which hit us most in Guernsey was our inability to communicate with our children and other loved ones in England. At that time (the bombing of England had not yet begun in earnest) we felt reasonably satisfied as to their safety but felt that they would be desperately anxious about us. A few days after the "Holland" arrived I had given a letter (written in triplicate) to a visiting German Officer with a view to it being dropped on England. It referred to an abortive British raid, asked for a steamer to be despatched to Guernsey and gave news of the Island. Whether or not it was ever dropped I do not know. *(A copy of it will be found in Appendix C.)* I also made a record, at the invitation of the German Authorities, which was broadcast from Bremen, I believe although I didn't hear it personally, about a fortnight later. I hoped it would get to the ears of some, at least, of our evacuees. Local opinion concerning this recording differed considerably, according to letters I received, some thinking it magnificent while others considered it utterly useless. *(This message is reproduced in Appendix D.)*

On July 15th Dr. Maass, looking unusually severe, had visited me at Elizabeth College on a grave mission. He told me that during the previous night the local inhabitants had built a stone barricade across the road on the town side of Doyle's Column, St. Martin's, and that a Bren Magazine had been found nearby. He told me he feared there would be serious trouble and asked that the matter be investigated. I felt convinced that this was no rising by the local inhabitants and told him so and asked for patience for a couple of hours while we investigated. I got into touch with the Police Inspector who went to the spot. Down in Petit Port Bay there were found rifles, machine guns, steel helmets, uniforms and equipment and it became clear that a British landing party had been at work. It was ascertained later that some of them had been seen and, for some obscure reason, they had cut the telephone wires of, I think it was, nineteen subscribers. The whole of the facts were reported to the German Commandant who directed that the Police and Special Constables should commence a search the following morning at dawn for members remaining ashore of the raiding party.

None of them was found by the search party but two British soldiers were taken prisoners by the German troops at Les Marchez, Forest and, some weeks later, two British officers connected with the raid surrendered at the Insel Kommandantur. The mother of one and the sister of the other were subsequently ordered to proceed to France and to reside at least 15 kilometres from the coast for the duration of the war, for having aided these officers and not reporting the matter to the German Authorities. They lived in a hotel at St. Lo where, though very bored and unhappy at being severed from their husbands, homes and relatives, they were tolerably comfortable.

The Controlling Committee had been taking some pretty big decisions and spending States' money like water and it was felt that it was highly desirable that the States should be convened and be given an opportunity of assenting to or dissenting from what had been done. Further the meeting which had created the Controlling Committee had, in law, been a nullity and the Committee itself was in the same position. Accordingly the Bailiff convened a meeting of the States in time honoured manner and placed before them a resolution which would, if approved, regularise the position and which gave the States the opportunity, if it disapproved of the acts done in its name by the Controlling Committee, of showing that Committee and its President the door in double quick time. The German Commandant expressed his desire to attend and came accompanied by Dr. Maass. He occupied the seat normally used by the Lieutenant Governor at States' Meetings and Dr. Maass sat behind where the Government Secretary usually sat. They showed great respect to the President and the Assembly and stayed for nearly an hour. I reviewed the position at some length and the States unanimously confirmed the resolution of their previous meeting and approved what had since been done by the Committee. They directed that the report should be placed on record. (*A copy of it will be found in Appendix E.)*

So far as legislation is concerned, it has to be remembered that the States together with His Majesty in Council form the legislative body for the Island of Guernsey, the States petitioning His Majesty to sanction a prepared text and His Majesty sanctioning it by and with the advice of His Privy Council. But we were cut off from His Majesty and His Privy Council. It is true that the Bailiff had been given the civil powers of the Lieutenant Governor but, on analysis, it appeared that those powers were non existent. There were obvious limits to the powers of the Court of Chief Pleas to legislate by way of Ordinance. Were we to be unable to tax ourselves and to enact legislation for which Privy Council sanction would ordinarily be necessary? Something had to be done and I hit upon the device of getting the German Commandant in his Orders to direct that the approval of the British Lieutenant Governor of any legislative measure of the States ordinarily requiring the sanction of His Majesty in Council should, during the German Occupation, have the effect of validating such measure. The power thus conferred upon the Lieutenant Governor was exercised for the first time as regards the Sales Tax law which Jurat Leale introduced in the States on 19th August, 1940 and which the States passed. Strangely enough, the sales tax appeared to be one of the most popular (or perhaps I should say, the least unpopular) tax ever imposed in Guernsey.

We had been officially informed that the cost of the supplies to the German Troops, the wages of personnel employed by them, the cost of the vehicles used by them and of the drivers and the cost of and the furnishing of the premises used by the "Army of Occupation" all fell to be borne by the States. They were very pleasant about it and said they had no wish to bankrupt the Island but, the garrison having increased very considerably, it appeared to us that the cost of the

Occupation might amount to about 1,000,000 Reichmarks (or say, £100,000) per annum. It was a heavy burden in view of the chaos into which the Island finances had been plunged.

In the middle of August, 1940, there arrived Dr. Reffler, Dr. Brosch and Herr Moor whose functions were detailed in a note dated August 16, 1940, from the German Feldkommandantur:-

K.V.R. Dr. Reffler

Manager of the Sub-office, intercourse with Feldkommandatur in Jersey, with the local military authorities and with the States of Guernsey, also agriculture and nutrition.

K.V.A. Dr. Brosch

Dr. Reffler's right hand, general administration, finance, taxes, police matters as far as the German military authorities will not attend to these, Foreigners, Press, Film.

Sdf. Moor

Industrial economy, Fishing, Traffic, administration of coal and petrol and similar stuffs, electricity, gas and water works, labour and social matters, price stop.

They formed the local branch (Nebenstelle) of Feldkommandantur No. 515 which was commanded by Colonel Schumacher and had its headquarters in Jersey.

These three gentlemen were kind and helpful and we got on excellently with them although we could not always see eye to eye with them. It had been realised by the German Authorities in Jersey as well as in Guernsey that the food and fuel position would become desperate if imports from the Continent were not forthcoming. Dr. Symons had started excavations for peat at the Race Course belonging to Mr. S.J.C. Duquemin situate at La Grande Mare, Vazon and large quantities were being got out and stacked for drying. Dr. Symons had also started a salt and brine making plant at the harbour where a limited quantity of salt and brine could be produced in sunny weather. Other experiments in the same direction were being made on his instructions at the premises of the Guernsey Railway Company and the Guernsey Brewery Company. The Controlling Committee had also secured the services of Mr. H. Lloyd de Putron of Caledonia Nursery, the most knowledgeable person on trees in the Island, to undertake the supervision of the tree-felling operations which were instituted. Tools and Equipment were provided and gangs of men were formed and under Mr. de Putron's supervision trees that were, or might soon become, dangerous or unsightly were brought down, cut up into suitable lengths and carried to various depots to be further cut into logs for fuel. This work went on for many months; it provided much fuel for the cold weather and work for many who would otherwise have been unemployed. I think it can be said that as a result of Mr. de Putron's loving care, for that is what it amounted to, not a tree which ought to be left standing was brought low.

But what about bread and meat. The Germans were now supplying themselves with meat from France and were importing a limited quantity of rye flour and bread. Our own reserves of meat were almost exhausted, the lack of poultry foods had resulted in the wholesale killing off of a great number of poultry so that eggs were becoming scarcer and scarcer and the outlook as regards the feeding of our milch cows and the fattening of pigs was very dark.

Then came the directions from Dr. Reffler that we must find a representative to become a member of a purchasing Committee with a German president and one other Jersey member and with headquarters in Granville. We found it a supremely difficult matter to choose the Guernsey representative. He must speak French fluently, he must be persona grata with the Germans, he must be a really competent business man, he must be able to adapt himself to French methods of business, he must be a keen buyer, possess abundant energy, he must have such knowledge as would enable him to purchase wheat or meat, dead or on the hoof, or flour, or wireless batteries without being had too badly. Where was this paragon to be found. The only man who appeared to possess, even faintly, the qualities needed for this venture was Mr. Raymond Falla, the member of the Controlling Committee responsible for Agriculture. We could ill spare him but we could find no one else having the capacity necessary and willing to go and he was willing to try his luck. We sent him with our blessing. At first nothing happened and then there came a regular (and adequate in all the circumstances) supply of meat, masses of agricultural seeds (of which we had practically none and were in desperate need), a thousand tons of flour, a hundred and twenty-five tons of sugar, and small quantities of many other essential commodities. The German Authorities sent us a cargo of coal at the beginning of November and altogether we began to face the winter with new courage.

When, on the 14th October, 1940, Mr. Falla returned to Guernsey the Controlling Committee passed the following Resolution:-

Extract from the Minutes of the Meeting of the Controlling Committee of the States of Guernsey held on the 16th October, 1940.

This Meeting of the Controlling Committee of the States of Guernsey, specially convened to welcome Mr. R.O. Falla, Agricultural Officer, on his return from his purchasing mission in France and to hear his report thereon, places on record its deep appreciation of his unremitting and highly successful labours on behalf of the inhabitants of his native Island. Without the qualities possessed by Mr. Falla to such a remarkable degree, namely: great tact and savoir faire, indomitable determination, a profound knowledge of the Island's basic requirements, and business ability of a very high order, coupled with almost unlimited physical endurance, the remarkable results achieved in securing seeds, foods and feeding stuffs and a variety of other goods would have been impossible.

Further, the extensive character of his journeyings in Occupied France has enabled him to estimate the possibilities in regard to further supplies; information which will be of great service.

The Committee desires also to express its sincere thanks to Mr. W.G. Hubert, who accompanied Mr. Falla during the early part of his mission and rendered him then and since such valuable help.

Further, the Committee places on record its deep appreciation of the fact that Mr. P.A. Mahy, at a time of life when he might, with every justification, have sought to be excused from such strenuous undertaking, volunteered to fill temporarily the post of Purchasing Commissioner in France, and is now doing so with great success.

> In order that the fellow islanders of these three gentlemen may be aware of the conspicuously meritorious nature of the services rendered by them, it is decided to forward a copy of this minute to the Bailiff with a view to such publicity being given to it as he deems proper.
>
> Lastly, the Committee desires to place on record its keen appreciation of the invaluable assistance afforded to its representatives in France by the Officers attached to the German Feldkommandanturs in Granville, Jersey and Guernsey, and by the Insular Authorities in Jersey.

Mr. W.G. Hubert had been particularly careful in checking in the supplies sent by Mr. Falla and treated it as a labour of love to serve his Island. Mr. P.A. Mahy, the doughty leader in the first Alderney expedition had set out again to serve his Island "in foreign parts".

As previously stated, Guernsey had been accustomed to import a great deal of the butter, margarine and cooking fats that it consumed and, even with the much smaller population which now had to be catered for, it was clear that the local herd was insufficient to provide milk and butter. As from the Occupation, it was only a matter of time before putting into operation a scheme for the collection of all milk and the separation of all but that needed as whole milk for children, expectant and nursing mothers and invalids. Actually the Feldkommandantur put forward the scheme that was finally adopted but there was a difference over the matter between the German and the Guernsey Authorities. However regrettable it might be, with the exceptions mentioned, only separated milk was available (at all events during the winter) for the population. Children up to two years of age were entitled to up to two pints of whole milk, children from two to fourteen years had a pint and the quantity for expectant and nursing mothers and invalids could in appropriate circumstances exceed two pints. When the Order instituting the Scheme was made, we had in cold storage a reserve of national butter and of French butter but our local production was considerably below the local consumption and was steadily falling as winter reduced the cows' yield of milk.

Provision was made for the free distribution at the elementary schools of half a pint of whole milk to each child desirous of drinking it there and for the free distribution to children under school age in many circumstances of a similar quantity. It was perhaps inadequate but after very careful consideration it was found that a more generous and comprehensive scheme would in all probability give rise to much fraud and might confer little benefit upon the children it was designed to help. The States Dairy undertook the distribution of this school milk and in fact the whole of the milk supply of the island so perhaps a word or two of explanation as to how it came into being and a few facts concerning it may not be out of place.

Although Guernsey is the home of one of the most valued breeds of milch cattle in the world, it must not be thought that the Guernsey farmer had during the period between the 1914-18 War and the 1939 War lived in the lap of luxury for nothing could be further from the truth. Good as is the Guernsey cow in regard to the quality of her milk - I personally am unimpressed with her performance as regards quantity but then you can't have everything in this life - neither she nor any other cow can be controlled like a soda fountain so as to emit the right quantity at the right time and in order that a farmer may be able to supply his customers with their milk requirements in the depth of winter - when incidentally, the cost of milk production is much heavier than in summer - he must have such a number of cows as will, in the flush period, say April to June, produce much more milk than their owner can dispose of for consumption in liquid form. The surplus must be turned into butter. Now in earlier days, it mattered little to the Guernsey farmer whether he sold his milk as milk or as butter for the net return to him in either case was roughly the same. I do not suggest that there was a handsome profit but at all events there was no loss. But the cost of production had increased very considerably, rents had risen under the impact of the ever continuing demand for land for glasshouse purposes, the wages of farm workers had practically doubled by reason of the competition of the glasshouse industry for labour at a wage which the farmer could not or could only ill afford, the cost of hay, straw and all the other commodities forming the raw material for the production of milk had all risen considerably, while, on the other hand, the American market for the disposal of stock at tantalisingly high figures had long been closed and the sales to English buyers at only very moderate prices had not proved a satisfactory set-off against such closure. Meanwhile the price of milk for consumption as liquid had risen almost in proportion to the rise in the farmer's expenses while the price of Guernsey butter remained at substantially the figure at which it was sold before the 1914-18 tornado. On every pot (half-gallon) of milk churned into butter then, the farmer made a loss which, taking the industry by and large, was probably as great as, or greater than the meagre profit on the milk consumed in liquid form. With a view to remedying this state of affairs Mr. Robert Chilcott of the firm of R.E. Chilcott and Sons Ltd., a well-known firm of butchers and farmers in Guernsey, had started a Dairy at The Grove, St. Martin's and, not to be outdone, the Guernsey farmers had opened another dairy at Belmont Road, St. Peter Port, under the name of the "Guernsey Farmers Co-operative Dairy". Now the Grove Dairy was able to sell for liquid consumption a greater proportion of its purchases than was the Co-operative Dairy with the inevitable result that the price for milk paid by the latter was well below that paid by the former. Much misunderstanding existed among the farmers and, in particular, the Co-operative Dairy Management was greatly criticised and blamed for a situation which it was beyond its power to remedy. Fantastic remedies, such as the prohibition of the importation of preserved milk and of butter and margarine were suggested but how could the States of Guernsey justify to the working man who, when blessed with a family, has all his work to do to make both ends meet and whose wife, in order adequately to feed and clothe her man, her children and herself (I deliberately put them in that order) has to be a cross between an angel and Diogenes, a policy which would deprive him of English butter at one shilling and eight pence per lb. or margarine (containing, or so the advertisements said, rather more nourishing properties, weight for weight, than butter) at 8d per lb. while enabling him to obtain Guernsey butter, admittedly excellent and oh! so attractive to the (Guernsey) eye at a price which under the drive of demand, in the absence of substitutes, might well have risen to four shillings per lb. It could not be done. At the same time the Guernsey farmer was getting very restive. Farming entails hard work and long hours, it entails Sunday labour and never gives its devotees a real let up. Farm labour, too, was scanty. Only the enthusiast or the man who couldn't get a job elsewhere stuck to farming. Was it any wonder that, with only bankruptcy staring them in the face, Guernsey farmers were gradually turning their attention more and more in other directions. There were few properties in Guernsey run purely as farms; rather was it the case of growing and a little farming being carried on concurrently but the little was becoming less. And then the States were asked to interest themselves in the matter and they set up a Committee to report on it. Eventually, though very reluctantly, the

States took over both dairies and amalgamated them in the Grove
premises, of part of which they took a temporary lease, and the States
Dairy came into being. The States were a little dubious about their
adopted child and were not at all sure quite how they were to provide
for its development and it seemed at times that this state of mind was
that of the Committee to which the administration of the Dairy was
entrusted. Anyhow the States allotted a subsidy of £5,000 to enable
the farmers supplying the diary to receive a better return and the price
payable to them ranged form $8^1/_2$d to $9^1/_4$d per pot (as against $5^1/_4$d at
one time paid by the Co-operative Dairy). Later, as a result of
representations made by the farmers to the effect that prices of feeding
stuffs had again risen (and this was undoubtedly the case) a further
increase in the subsidy was made and the price of milk to the public
was raised.

When, in July, 1940, the Milk and Butter Scheme, which resulted from
the severance of communications with England, came into being, the
wholesale price payable by the States Dairy to farmers was 11d per
pot, while the retail price of milk was $3^1/_2$ per pint (fetched) and 4d per
pint (delivered). It will be apparent that farmers able to sell for liquid
consumption direct to the consumers the whole of their production
were making a greater margin of profit than their brother farmers
whose only outlet for their milk was the States Dairy. This statement
needs some qualification for the producer-retailer has troubles of his
own to contend with which the dairy supplier has not to contend with
but, as an approximation, it is correct.

The Dairy Committee had long disliked the existence of two sets of
farmers, the one making more profit (or less) than the other. The
producer retailer disliked the Dairy and, for some reason or another,
regarded it as competing unfairly with him. Without putting it too
strongly, the average producer retailer lost no opportunity of belittling
the Dairy and the Dairy resented this attitude and were, I think,
justified in resenting it.

Now had come the glorious opportunity of putting all milk producers
on an equal footing and of selling Guernsey butter at a price nearer its
cost of production. Both apparently very sound objectives.

But the Controlling Committee did not take that view. They insisted
on holding down the price of butter so that the wind might be
tempered to the shorn lamb. And they did not see any reason for

compelling producer retailers who had an asset in the business which they were running, often the result of years of hard work in all weathers and who had cost the States nothing. But, as regards the last, circumstances were too strong for the Controlling Committee for the Feldkommandantur, which controlled (through the Controller of Petroleum Supplies) the licensing of motor vehicles and the issue of petrol, directed a drastic reduction in the number of motor vehicles engaged in the delivery of milk and, a hastily sent-out questionnaire revealing that the great majority of producer retailers could not continue their milk rounds by other means, as from 13th October, 1940, all milk had to be taken to collecting depots set up by the States Dairy Committee who became responsible for the handling (though not the actual delivery to consumers) of the whole milk supply of the Island. In accordance with the Biblical exhortation that "Thou shalt not muzzle the ox that treadeth out the corn" farmers, members of their families and of their resident staffs were entitled to a ration of half-a-pint of whole milk. They were the only able-bodied adults who were but no one begrudged it to them. At the same time, the wholesale price of milk was fixed at 11d per pot (One shilling and ten pence per gallon) and a certain amount of free labour was allowed to farmers to enable them to perform necessary work which would otherwise have been beyond their power to do. *(In Appendix F will be found the Orders relating to Milk and Milk Products to which or to whose contents reference has been made in this chapter.)*

I had appointed Deputy R.H. Johns to take charge of the Department which I had termed Labour, Unemployment and Re-employment. I made my choice very deliberately. Richard Johns had been a Deputy for St. Sampson's and the Vale for many years. There was no one, I think, living in that part of the Island who was more liked and respected. A shrewd business man, with one of the kindliest dispositions imaginable, he was a star turn among the Methodist local preachers and an astonishingly good debater in the States whose poise put most of us to shame. I realised the difficulties of the task I was confronting him with. I was not wrong in believing he would tackle and make a success of it. He sought the collaboration of a friend of his, the Reverend Philip Romeril, the Methodist parson in charge of St. Sampson's. Romeril was an inspiration in those early days when all seemed chaotic. Courageous, cheerful, hard-working, full of organising ability and of ideas, he nearly killed himself with work and did his parson's work besides. How he managed it I do not know.

Many a time in July 1940 did I thank God for his presence and cheerfulness. Later, too, Mr. Johns added Deputy Wilfred Corbet, an old friend of his and mine, to his immediate entourage. He, too, was from the North end of the Island, a devout Methodist and leader of adolescent thought and a skilled musician, there is no kinder man on earth. One could be certain that the halt and the maimed and the struggling would not have a deaf ear turned to their requests for assistance whilst this trio was in control of the Department, while the robust common sense of their chief would, and did, prevent the Department being made the sport of knaves.

I now relate a minor but rather extraordinary incident which occurred before my fall from German grace. It must surely be the only occasion on record when a British legal official has been asked to advise a foreign government whether or not his country was really at war with it. The questioner was Dr. Brosch of the Feldkommandantur.

I never knew why he asked but can only suppose that it may have been connected with food rationing and the slightly better supplies available, under Germany orders, to neutrals including the one or two citizens of the Irish Free State in Guernsey. It raised possibilities and I am pretty confident that I could, with a multiplicity of words, have concocted an opinion supporting our absolute neutrality which it would have been very difficult for the Germans to unravel. I am glad to say, however, that hardening my heart at the temporary expense of my fellow islanders, I replied within the hour that when His Majesty the King of England declares war, he declares it not only on behalf of the United Kingdom but also on behalf of the Channel Islands. In these circumstances, Guernsey must be deemed to be at war with the German Reich.

Fortunately, search in the files has produced a copy of this unique epistle and here it is:-

    In reply to Dr. Brosch's questions:-

    Acts of Parliament, in relation to the Channel
    Islands, can be divided into two categories –

    Those which contain a specific declaration to the
    effect that they apply to the Channel Islands.

    Those which empower His Majesty the King to apply
    them to the Channel Islands by Order in Council

with such modifications and adaptation as he may deem expedient.

Both categories are transmitted to Jersey and Guernsey accompanied by an Order in Council directing their registration.

As regards category (a), the Islands are not consulted and no representations by the Island Authorities to the Privy Council are of any avail in that His Majesty is himself bound by the terms of the Act.

As regards category (b), consultation (by correspondence or personal interview, but usually by correspondence) takes place between the Home Office and the Island Authorities as to the modifications and adaptations of the Act which are necessary in order that the Act may be fully operative in the Channel Islands, and, when these modifications and adaptations are settled, the Act is transmitted accompanied by an Order in Council setting forth such modifications and adaptations and directing that the Act shall be registered and that it shall have effect as modified and adapted.

The English view is that transmission of an Act of Parliament with the appropriate Order in Council directing its registration suffices as a sufficient promulgation in the Channel Islands and that the failure of the Royal Court to register it in no way affects its validity therein but merely deprives the inhabitants of the knowledge of an Act legally binding on them.

His Majesty the King has power to declare war and to make peace, acting on the advice of his responsible Ministers. A declaration of war by His Majesty undoubtedly binds the people of Guernsey and is effective therein.

No Act of Parliament was necessary on the occasion of the declaration of the present war in that the power to declare war resides not in Parliament but in the Sovereign. Usually declarations of war are announced to the nation

```
by  means  of  a  Royal  Proclamation.   I  can  find  no
trace  in  our  Records  of  such  a  Proclamation
having  been  transmitted  to  Guernsey  but  a
Proclamation  dated  the  3rd  September,  1939
specifying  the  Articles  to  be  treated  as
Contraband  of  War  which  was  transmitted  and  was
registered  on  our  Records  on  the  13th  September,
1939  contains  the  following  recital  -
```

```
"Whereas  a  state  of  war  exists  between  Us"  (that
is  to  say:  His  Britannic  Majesty)  "on  the  one
hand  and  Germany  on  the  Other".
```

```
11.9.40.
```

For upwards of more than a century, Guernsey had had two Poor Law Institutions termed locally "Hospitals", one situate at the foot of Hirzel Street, St. Peter Port, and the other lying just off the main road leading from the Castel Church to L'Aumône. The former served as casual ward, workhouse and hospital and lunatic asylum for the inhabitants of St. Peter Port, the latter served the same purposes - and was also utilised as an extension of the Children's Home, for housing the babies in the care of that Institution which was overcrowded - for the inhabitants of the remaining nine parishes. Besides those two institutions there existed of course other hospitals and nursing establishments of which the principal was the Victoria Hospital situate at Amherst founded in 1888 mainly as the result of the efforts of Dr. Ernest L. Robinson and the Lady Ozanne Maternity Home in Cordier Hill, the latter named in honour of Lady Ozanne (the Widow of Sir Edward Chepmell Ozanne K.B.E. a former well-loved Bailiff) who had done so much to bring into being an efficient maternity service. Originally parochially built, the two Poor Law Institutions had come under the control of the States in 1925 or thereabouts and each had its "Hospital Committee", the poor law services as a whole being under the general supervision and control of a Central Poor Law Board presided over by Mr. Henri Daniel Ollivier, M.B.E., another staunch Methodist full of character and personality who had given the bulk of his spare time for many years to the care of the sick and the needy, and had acquired a really vast mass of knowledge concerning the Poor Law as it operated here and in England. In 1936, however, the States were not altogether satisfied that changes reflecting more modern opinions might not with advantage be made in our Poor Law system and set up a Committee of Investigation. In Guernsey it should be stated, if it is not already apparent from what I have written, a Committee is set up by the States without much difficulty. It does not by any means follow, however, that the Committee's report, no matter how skilfully prepared, will be adopted. When this particular Committee's report was presented, however, the States approved its contents and I think that I was the only critic of some of its proposals. In effect, it substituted the expression "Public Assistance" in all contexts which had previously contained the words "Poor Law" and set up a series of Boards and one Committee. Mr. Ollivier was unanimously elected to preside over the new States Public Assistance Authority. He had, by a lifetime of service to the community, deserved well of Guernsey and Guernsey desired to add this honour to that recently conferred upon him by His Majesty the King. The two "Public Assistance" Institutions, the Town and Country Hospitals, henceforth came under the control of one Committee. Later the States built an up-to-date mental hospital at Le Vauquiedor (The Valley which is of gold), St. Andrew's and refusing to attach to it any word referring to mental disease or its treatment called it "Le Vauquiedor Hospital". One never knows what there may or may not be in a name, probably not as much as one is sometimes inclined to think but one hopes at all events that a sojourn in the Valley which is of gold may bring gladness and light to many a poor sufferer where before there was only misery and darkness. It will certainly not be the fault of Dr. W.R. McGlashan, the Medical Superintendent, the Matron and her Staff and the States Mental Health Services Committee if it fails to do so. The matter of a modern mental hospital had lain heavily on the conscience of the States for many years in consequence of the very unfavourable reports by experts on the suitability of the buildings attached to the Town and Country Hospitals and the Bailiff of Guernsey (Mr. Victor G. Carey) used every effort to bring about better conditions and it was not a little due to his prudence that the spacious and well laid out hospital for the treatment of mental disorder (with 110 beds) exists in Guernsey today. On the 6th March, 1940, the new Hospital was licensed for use by the Royal Court and shortly afterwards the task of transferring patients there began.

Now, in November, 1936, the States had set up yet another Committee initially presided over by Mr. G.A. Carey to study and report upon the matter of Air Raid Precautions. There were, I think three schools of thought, that which had the decided idea that in no circumstances whatsoever was there any need of air raid precautions in Guernsey, one that viewed the matter of such precautions as being of the very greatest importance and urgency, and the third frankly indifferent but willing to spend a limited sum of money on this "latest States' toy". Mr. Pierre de Putron, who had been a member of this Committee from its inception, became its president in December, 1937. He had spent many years in the Nigerian Political Service and his outstanding quality was thoroughness. Whatever the job given to him, and he was (and is) a glutton for work, it could be depended upon that he would do it efficiently and well. He had been an inspiration on the Aerodrome Committee but nothing he had done surpassed his handling of Air Raid Precautions and, very largely due to him, we had in Guernsey a first-rate organisation, first-rate personnel and first-rate equipment. Of course he was helped in all this by experts not least of whom were the Doctors. Anyhow, on the outbreak of war the Country Hospital patients were evacuated, some to the Town Hospital and some to their homes, and within forty-eight hours there was in being ready at any moment to receive 200 patients, an emergency air raid precautions hospital complete to the last detail. It was, I fear, an object of ridicule to many until the night of June 28th 1940 and then if ever anything justified its existence, the Emergency Hospital did, for to it were brought the poor maimed, broken bodies of the victims of the air raid, collected and given first aid by the gallant Air Raid Wardens, Special Constables, Ambulance Drivers and Nurses and tended throughout that ghastly night by the Doctors of Guernsey working in relays until dawn and thereafter nursed back to health and strength by the staff in the Emergency Hospital which it was confidently protested would never be used. The simile used by Mr. Pierre du Putron on one occasion in the States was an apt one. He said he had always regarded the Air Raids Precautions Organisation in the light of a fire insurance policy; all the better if the event insured against never occurred. A little later the States elected Mr. de Putron to the office of Juré Justicier in a three cornered fight with two other strong candidates.

When the Germans occupied Guernsey it appeared unlikely that there would be much more serious bombing of that Island - except possibly in the neighbourhood of the Aerodrome and its defences - and this area was to a great extent evacuated by the civilian population following upon a bombing attack by a British plane which damaged some houses and broke thousands of panes of glass on greenhouses in the neighbourhood.

Dr. Symons, the Director of Medical Services on the Controlling Committee, interested himself in the Emergency Hospital. The Hospital Administration proposed (and, in fact, installed) by the Air Raids Precautions Committee had been rejected by the States and the Hospital Committee of the Public Assistance Authority had been directed to resume control. When the Occupation occurred, it became apparent that the Victoria Hospital and the Lady Ozanne Maternity Home could not continue as separate organisations for lack of funds and other reasons and Dr. Symons succeeded in merging these institutions and the other nursing homes in one hospital with the Emergency Hospital. The merging of the staffs was not easy and human beings, especially of the fair sex, being what they are, the going was not always of the very best. Still the welfare of the patients did not suffer except that the Controlling Committee received repeated complaints about the food which, it was alleged, was insufficient in quantity and unattractively cooked and served. Dr. W.B. (Bill) Fox, from the occupation onwards, slept at the hospital every night and acted as Night Surgeon for the difficulties of night travel were such as to discourage the doctors from venturing forth. In November, 1940, Dr. Symons presented to the States a masterly report which the States adopted and the Country Hospital was given a new Constitution completely divorcing it from Public Assistance Control for the duration.

A Committee - yet another one - presided over by the late Jurat Dan F. Aubert had been studying the question of the erection of a really modern Island Hospital when war broke out and put an end temporarily to such a development. Until this again becomes a possibility the Emergency Hospital will doubtless serve all Island purposes particularly in view of the diminution in the population.

On the 6th September, 1940, eight men and a boat succeeded in leaving Guernsey. We learned afterwards by radio that after a long and perilous journey they reached Southern Ireland.

From the time of the Occupation, fishing had been controlled. There was a limit beyond which it was forbidden to go and German armed guards were usually placed in each boat or patrol boats manned by German troops were sent out to escort the fishing boats. Judge French's "Ranger", which had been towed down to Guernsey by the "White Heather", was at one time used for this purpose. From time to time fishing was prohibited for a few days and in fog and misty weather boats were not allowed to go to the fishing grounds. These restrictions could only result in a great diminution in the quantity of fish caught at a time when the Island could do with every ounce of food of this description. The Casquets Banks and the Schole Bank, usually fished from Alderney and which provided Guernsey with a constant supply of turbot, ray, conger, mackerel and whiting each in due season, were out of bounds and so, to a great extent were the waters to the western end and southern end of Guernsey where are to be found the best crabs, lobsters and crayfish. After the British raid on the night of the 14th-15th July, 1940, the whole of the south coast and part of the east coast had been mined and access to the beaches in those regions was forbidden and was in fact impossible. Fishing went on, however, from St. Peter Port, St. Sampson's, Bordeaux harbour, Grand Havre, Perelle and Rocquaine but, unable as the fishermen were to work the tides as usual, for fishing was absolutely forbidden at night, it is doubtful if their reward was worth their labour. Still they provided what they could and, at times, the picturesque Fish Market in St. Peter Port, so well known to English visitors, made a brave display. The Sark fishermen were not greatly interfered with and some of their catches were brought to Guernsey and were very welcome.

But after the departure of the eight men in a boat, fishing was brought to an abrupt end. It was a selfish, unthinking act of the people concerned and could only result in retribution. The Controlling Committee knew nothing of the impending departure of the boat in question and disapproved strongly when it learned what had happened. I feared others might emulate the example of the eight and published a notice which I hoped would be effective in discouraging them. I also gave instructions for the watching by the Police of the bays and harbours. Some of us did appreciate that the occupying force could not tolerate such getaways for by means of them military information of consequence might be conveyed. But no one anticipated what in fact happened. An order emanating from the German Naval Authority in control of the region embracing the Channel Islands directed that, in Jersey and Guernsey, fishing should only take place from St. Helier's and St. Peter Port respectively and, consequent upon this, a local order of the Feldkommandantur directed that all boats of every description should be hauled up and later that they should be brought to St. Peter Port. With great difficulty in some cases, for some boats had to be brought overland, the order was complied with and the boats of the Island were placed under the control of the Harbour Master.

On the night of 23rd-24th September, 1940, a British plane had dropped leaflets in a number of places in Guernsey. My attention was drawn to this by the German Authorities and I was told that people finding these leaflets were expected to deliver them up at the Insel Kommandantur. Under a German order promulgated earlier the communication of any publication not authorised by the German authorities was an offence heavily punishable by fine or imprisonment or both and I was greatly worried lest the very natural temptation for our people to read and pass on copies of the pamphlets (remember we had had no word or news from England where so many of our nearest and dearest were, except by radio, since the end of June) might not lead them into serious difficulties and I published a notice clarifying the position. I remember I received at least one anonymous letter in connection with this action of mine which urged me to play the man and assured me that my behaviour would in due course be reported to the British Government by the writer. Presumably the sender of the missive would have approved if I had urged people to read and pass on the leaflet and if dozens of harmless, well-meaning people had gone to jail for lengthy periods.

We had taken a census of Guernsey and Sark in July, 1940, for we were anxious to learn the exact composition of the population, foreseeing, as we did, some tough problems consequential upon the changed conditions in which we were living. It could, for instance, be anticipated that as stocks disappeared many shops would be compelled to close down, throwing on the labour market a mass of their employees while, on the other hand, with the much increased need for the local production of every kind of food we were capable of providing ourselves with and the likelihood, or should I say, certainty, of motor traffic coming to an abrupt end in the spring and the insufficiency of horses, carts and bicycles and bicycle accessories, there would have to be a movement back to the land and it seemed that much of our transport would have to be done by man power. The problem of fitting women into appropriate niches of industry was likely to be the most difficult of all, for the diminution in the means of the well to do was throwing domestic staffs out of employment and these were neither fitted nor very willing to do the rougher, heavier tasks that alone seemed to be likely to offer.

Then on 15th October, 1940, the German authorities required all persons being on a British Reserve of Officers or having relatives serving in the British Forces or being on a Reserve of Officers to register and the Controlling Committee carried out this regulation.

For some time, it had been apparent that every adult and adolescent civilian would be required to carry an identity card and in October 1940 the Registration and Identification of Persons Order, 1940, a measure agreed upon but in reality dictated by the German Authorities was made by the Controlling Committee.

The Census particulars proved very useful in connection with the rationing of Clothing and Footwear which was carried out under the general supervision of the Committee for the Control of Essential Commodities by Mr. W.D.M. Lovell (of Lovell and Co. Ltd.) who was styled the Controller of Clothing and Footwear Rationing. The rationing scheme and the ration card was practically identical with the German system, being based on the points method. It was certainly very ingenious. It was not forced upon us initially. It was greatly criticised and I fear not without some reason for unless one started off with a good stock of clothes, underwear and footwear, the number of articles available within a given time against the production of coupons appeared lamentably inadequate, particularly in the case of children whose ability to wear out clothing and boots and shoes is so well developed. It really came to this: in most cases the goods were in the shops and the wherewithal to buy them in would-be customers' pockets, but the coupons so limited the range of purchases that goods and money largely stayed where they were instead of changing hands to the benefit if not of all at all events of most.

At about this time, John Leale and I and some assistants met two German officers of a commission sent to Guernsey to requisition all motor cars available (many would have been useless after a long period of disuse; they were sold, most of them, at advantageous prices and brought in millions of French Francs wherewith to purchase much needed essential commodities and, given the option of being paid in German Occupation Marks or French Francs, we elected the latter as being the better bet.) Our haggling concluded, tea was brought to us and the German officers were offered and accepted a cup each. The senior of them had, I remember, a withered left hand but an exceedingly able brain. With John Leale and me on the one side of the Principal of Elizabeth College's dining-room table and the German officers on the other, I made some idle remark or other about something being the truth. To my astonishment, the German took me up with the words: "Truth; what is truth?" Though fortified by strong tea, Leale's theological training, the German's philosophical bent and my own less tutored but incorrigible bump of curiosity, we failed, I regret to say, to elucidate the mystery. They took their leave and I made to escort them to the door for I was quite happy at the replenishment in the near future of our denuded coffers. The philosophical German refused, however, to allow me to do so, saying: "There is no need for you to see me out."

Now in July, the British Government no doubt anxious to learn how we in Guernsey were getting on, sent in a young officer in plain clothes to find out. He came and stayed with his parents and left again. I was quite unaware of the fact that he was in Guernsey until some time after his departure when I was told.

The news worried me greatly. I had a boy of my own in the Service, a great hulking fellow bigger and stronger than myself despite the fact that he was only seventeen and lots of other people in Guernsey were similarly placed. Was this the first of a series of such visits and, if it was, how would the matter end. To say that I was distressed as to the possibilities is to put it mildly. I hoped, however, that the matter was at an end.

4

The Unusual Case Of Mr. H.H. Collins

In *"Guernsey under German Rule"*, Mr. Ralph Durand correctly described this case as "the trial of a man for an offence that was not illegal at the time when it was alleged to have been committed". He went on to suggest that this unusual feature should give it a prominent place in the history of Guernsey jurisprudence. So far as I know, it is unique. Mr. Ridgway, then H.M. Solicitor General, prosecuted but only at my request. I take full responsibility both for the prosecution and for the drafting of the Ordinance which made it possible. The latter was certainly rushed through the Royal Court but not "at the instigation of the German authorities". Its purpose and the reason for making it retrospective in operation were to avoid Mr. Collins being brought before a German military court and being given, possibly, a stiff sentence of imprisonment. I make no apologies for substituting expedience for orthodoxy in this case.

On July 30th, 1940, I went down to the Kommandantur at the Channel Islands Hotel as usual - I went there most mornings at 11 a.m. to get approval of orders and directions being issued by the Controlling Committee - to find Dr. Maass and Oberleutnant Mittelmüller buckling on their belts and about to go out. I remember saying: "You look very fierce this morning; what's up?" Maass replied: "We're going out to arrest Mr. Collins of Le Riche's Stores; he's been guilty of propaganda against the German Army" and away they went, leaving me standing. I heard later from the Police Station that Mr. Collins had been arrested and lodged in prison.

Now, Mr. Collins was a man of sterling worth much respected by his fellows and known to me personally for many years. He was also, to my knowledge, a very sick man at the time and I feared that imprisonment by the Germans might well accelerate his death. I went back to the Kommandantur early in the afternoon to try to secure his release, at least until his trial. I failed in this with Maass and Mittelmüller but insisted that it be referred to the Kommandant, Dr. Lanz. With great reluctance, they went to consult him and returned with this reply: "Dr. Lanz says that it is not because Mr. Sherwill says that Mr. Collins is innocent that he is". Mitttelmüller then told me - he had little English and I less German and we always conversed in French - that his people were willing that Mr. Collins should be tried by the Royal Court. I jumped at the idea but my problem was that there was no enactment in force in Guernsey enabling a prosecution to be brought for uttering words likely to cause a deterioration of relations between the occupying forces and civilian population. I discussed this with Mittelmüller and he drew my attention to paragraph 7 of the German Kommandant's Orders of July 2nd permitting assemblies in churches and chapels for Divine Worship and which terminated with the words: "Such assemblies shall not be made the vehicle for any propaganda or utterances against the honour or interests of or offensive to the German Government or Forces". I told him that I certainly couldn't convince myself let alone a court of law that Le Riche's Stores constituted a place of worship or that its customers were an assembly within the meaning of that paragraph. He replied that, if we couldn't deal with the matter, they certainly could and that they would be much more severe in their punishment.

I could see only one way out of my dilemma and said to him: "What I propose to do offends against a cardinal principle of criminal law as we administer it. I am going to ask the Royal Court to pass an Ordinance making an offence of any behaviour by a civilian likely to cause deterioration in the relations between the occupying forces and the civilian population and this with retrospective effect back to the date of the German occupation. You will appreciate the unorthodoxy of this" (he was a graduate in law of Jena University) "to bring the Ordinance into force will require the Kommandant's approval. Will this approval be forthcoming?" Mittelmüller replied that it would and that he was completely indifferent to my departure from orthodoxy.

I went to the Bailiff and told him all about the matter and asked him to convene a Full Court for the next morning to consider the Ordinance which I was about to draft. I then visited Mr. Collins in prison and told him what I was doing and asked him whether, if the Court passed the Ordinance, he would like his trial expedited or whether, as he was entitled to do, he would insist on 48 hours notice of it. He was most anxious to get it over and waived any notice at all. I drafted the Ordinance and had copies prepared for the Court's use. The Court met the next morning at 11 a.m. and I explained the matter to them in detail in private. All of us were anxious to save Mr. Collins and the Court, in public session, passed the Ordinance without comment.

At 3 p.m. the same day, Mr. Collins was tried before Mr. Quertier Le Pelley, the Acting Police Court Magistrate.

Now the facts appeared to be as follows:-

An assistant, C., at Le Riche's Stores who spoke fluent German and was, I have been told, the son of a German mother, had the habit, when a German soldier came into the shop, of leaving the customer to whom he was attending and offering his services to the soldier as an interpreter. Mr. Collins had noted this and had told him not to do this but to continue dealing with the customer he himself was serving and then, and only then, to turn his attention to the next customer, be he Guernsey or German.

C. had talked to some German or other about this and it appears that he had even said that Mr. Collins had told him not to speak German. As against this latter allegation, which Mr. Collins emphatically denied, it was proved that Collins had actually purchased a German-English, English-German dictionary and had placed it in the shop for the use of all the assistants.

C. was very confused in giving his evidence, which was completely uncorroborated, and he actually admitted that he may have misunderstood what Mr. Collins had said. He appeared extremely unhappy in the witness-box and no one sought to make him feel otherwise.

The Acting Magistrate found, very properly, that there was no reliable evidence to support the charge and dismissed the case against Mr. Collins who behaved throughout with great dignity and composure. I listened to the proceedings but took no part in them.

Mittelmüller had directed me to report the result to him as soon as possible. The usual shorthand note was taken and I asked the stenographer to expedite the transcript so that I could take it with me to the Kommandantur. Armed with it, I went there at 7 p.m. expecting real fireworks when they learned that Mr. Collins had been acquitted. There were none. To my surprise, all that Mittelmüller said was: "I expected as much".

I came across C. again in Ilag VII, Laufen. He had been deported for internment several months before I was. He was clearly in great favour with the German Camp Office and could get out of camp, I believe, whenever he wished to. Whether he kept that office informed of happenings in the camp I do not know but I have no reason to suspect that he passed on any information of importance. When, in 1943, six Guernsey internees and five Jersey ones left camp on repatriation on medical grounds, they were accompanied to the islands by one of our medical orderlies and by six of our internees as porters of their luggage. The German office suggested C. as one of the porters and I raised no objection because C.'s knowledge of German was likely to be of considerable assistance to the party in their journey. I was most anxious to have my portable typewriter brought from Guernsey for use in the camp office and asked C. to call at my home and bring it back with him. This he did.

To me, C. was an enigma. He did not appear to be anti-British and truth compels me to say that he was, basically, a kind, obliging person. It seemed that he couldn't resist currying favour with anyone in authority for the moment and that he loved to meddle.

C. had some grievance against me as Camp Senior during the latter part of our internment (I have completely forgotten its nature) and had spoken to the German Sonderführer about it. The latter raised it with me and I remember saying: "You think a lot of C. but I'll tell you something. When the Russians arrive, I'll guarantee that, within a week, C. will be sporting the biggest Russian arm-badge procurable."

The Russians didn't reach us but the Americans did. Some days later, an American officer called at the camp to talk to me on some matter or other. He was accompanied by what was apparently an American solder in full military uniform. To my astonishment, for I was unaware that he had left the camp, I saw that it was C., now attached to the American Army as an interpreter in German. My prediction had not been so inaccurate after all; C. was running completely true to form.

5

THE NICOLLE AND SYMES AFFAIR

During the time Dr. Lanz was commanding the German troops in Guernsey, I met him only rarely. My impression was that he was completely straightforward but of an unusually taciturn nature. He was not a person who inspired affection but I respected his integrity. He spoke little or no English. On one occasion, when the Controlling Committee were reviewing the likely food position for the coming winter, I asked him if he would indicate what, in his opinion, would be the maximum number of troops we should take into account and he replied that he thought it unlikely that the island garrison would ever exceed five hundred.

In August or early September, 1940, he was promoted from Major to Lieut. Colonel and was decorated with the Ritter Cross or the Iron Cross and was transferred to the Eastern Front where, not long after, he was killed.

On the eve of his departure I had a message that he wished to call on me to say goodbye and it was arranged that he would call on me on a Sunday morning at 11 o'clock. He duly arrived, accompanied by an interpreter.

He was extremely well turned out (usually he wore the shabbiest of uniforms) and was wearing his new decoration, on which I remember congratulating him. He was in a much more cheerful frame of mind than was usual. After some general conversation, I told him that I had done all in my power to avoid difficulties between the occupying forces and the civilian population during the period of his command. "Did he appreciate that it was not because of lack of loyalty to my own country but because I was convinced that, during an enemy occupation, this was the only way of securing the greatest possible measure of liberty and normality for the people of the Island?" He replied – through the interpreter – that he had never had any doubt as to where my loyalty lay or that I was doing what I was in the interests of my own people.

When he arrived in Guernsey on July 1st. he was accompanied by his adjutant (Oberleutnant Mittlemüller) and by a Dr. Maass who wore military uniform without badges of rank. Maass had been a prisoner of ours during the first world war, he had a Diploma of Tropical Medicine of Liverpool University, he had, I believe, been a medical missionary and he was then a Surgeon in the German Navy. He spoke perfect English and was a most charming person. I never discovered what his true function in Guernsey was. It was far more than that of an interpreter and I suppose he can best be described as in charge of civil affairs. He was highly capable and most considerate and it was largely due to him and to the influence he wielded that conditions in the early days of the occupation were as good as they were and indeed very much better than we had expected. We were indeed lucky that a man with his knowledge of English and of England was there at that time.

A day or so before he left, he told me one morning: "Your troubles are now about to begin, the Civil Service is arriving to-morrow".

The next day Dr. Reffler (later killed in Italy), Dr. Brosch and Herr Moor arrived and installed themselves at Grange Lodge which became the Guernsey branch of the Channel Islands Feldkommandantur or Civil Affairs Command. From then on, my visits to the Military Kommandantur virtually ceased but visits to the Feldkommandantur were almost a daily occurrence. I hardly ever dealt with Moor but, at first, usually with Reffler and, later, almost daily with Brosch. Both were invariably courteous and Brosch, particularly, was a kind, likeable person. When years after the war, I went to Munich to receive back the drums of the Royal Guernsey Light Infantry, I enquired of Prince von Oettingen, who had been head of the Feldkommandantur in Guernsey after Reffler left, as to what had happened to Brosch and he told me that, utterly down and out, he had come to him for help. He had helped him with money and then Brosch had disappeared and it was his belief that, unable to obtain employment, he had committed suicide.

And then at Grange Lodge was little Unteroffizier Krafft, always kind, patient and courteous, even when his home town was bombed almost to destruction and he was without news as to whether his wife and small boy were alive or dead. They survived and I met him and them years afterwards and was grieved later to hear that he had died of cancer of the brain.

When Dr. Lanz left Guernsey, he was succeeded as Military Kommandant by Major Bandelow, a completely different type of man. He asked me to meet him at the Kommandantur and he had laid on a very young German soldier who had apparently expressed himself as competent to act as interpreter. The boy was hopeless at the job and the usual German officer would almost certainly have torn a strip off him and sent him away humiliated. Not so Bandelow; he was kindness itself to the lad and eased him out of the situation with great understanding. I was most impressed and reassured as to future relations with the military.

A day or so later, the Manager of Lloyds Bank rang me up to say that a German officer had been in with the key of a strong-box in the Bank's custody belonging to the Battalion of the Royal Irish Fusiliers which had been quartered in Guernsey and Alderney and had been recalled not long before the Germans arrived. The labelled key had been found in a cupboard at Fort George and the German officer demanded to see what the box contained. It held the Regimental Trophies and the mess plate and silver of the Battalion. The officer directed that the silver should be sent to a local firm of silversmiths 'to be weighed'.

I told the Manager to hold on to it till he heard from me and I decided to see Major Bandelow at the first opportunity. That very day I was at the Feldkommandantur when he walked in. I told him of the matter and said that the contents of the strong-box were undoubtedly of very considerable intrinsic value but of very much greater sentimental value to the Regiment. I added: "I cannot believe that, you a soldier, will allow these things to be broken up and disposed of." Bandelow replied: "You are quite right; they will stay where they are. I am going on leave; on my return I will make an appointment with you and we will go and view them together. I should be most interested to see them".

He never made the appointment because, when he returned from leave, I was in prison in Paris. The strong-box remained intact until after he had relinquished his command but, later, the Germans again demanded that the contents be handed over. This time Mr. Victor Carey, the Bailiff, made the most urgent demand that they should be left intact. He was not wholly successful; the trophies were left undisturbed and were eventually restored to the Battalion but the Germans insisted that the mess cutlery should be handed over for use in their mess and I fear that the greater part of this, if not the whole, was lost to the Battalion.

Now, around this time, I had a message from Oberleutnant Schnadt, Bandelow's adjutant, that the Kommandant wanted to see me. I gathered that he thought it likely that members of the British Armed Forces still remained in the Island and that he wished to arrange a date with me by which they must surrender. A meeting was fixed for 11 a.m. the following Sunday at the Kommandant's house in Mount Durand.

Now I was most intrigued at the prospect which this opened up in relation to two British Officers whose presence in the Island was causing me great anxiety.

Some weeks before, Emile Nicolle, the Secretary to the Controlling Committee, who was on sick leave and staying in the country, came to me and told me that his son, Hubert Nicolle, and another young officer, Jimmy Symes, had been landed in civilian clothes with instructions to reconnoitre the situation. The arrangements for taking them away again had broken down and his son had contacted him and he felt bound to shelter him. Would I recall him to duty so that he would have a suitable reason for leaving the lodgings where he was staying without exciting comment?

I told him – he already realized it – that aiding espionage in wartime was a highly dangerous occupation, that by reason of extraordinary luck, I had got away with it in the case of Mulholland and Martel but that I had to remember that, as head of the Controlling Committee, my first duty lay to that Committee and to the people of Guernsey. The possible discovery by the Germans that, whilst appearing to be cooperating with them, I was aiding espionage was likely to be followed by the Committee and me being swept away and by the full rigour of direct military government being imposed. In the circumstances, whilst I fully understood that he felt compelled to shelter his son, I must refrain from any part of it. Mine was a completely unheroic attitude; I leave readers to judge for themselves whether I was right or wrong in adopting it. (*Sherwill's account of the Mulholland and Martel Affair has unfortunately been lost. Brief details of that adventure are given in Appendix G.*)

On the Sunday I attended at the appointed time to be told by the adjutant that the Kommandant had been out all night visiting picquets and was then asleep. He apologised and said the Kommandant would make another appointment. He explained what the Kommandant had in mind and said that if members of the British Armed Forces gave themselves up by the day to be appointed, they would be treated as prisoners of war and nobody who had harboured them would be punished. He went on to say that if, however, members of the Armed Forces were discovered later, the Germans would select twenty prominent civilians and shoot them.

I said: "And one of those will be me". He replied: "Oh no, Mr. Sherwill". I said: "If not, why not. I tell you that if you do this awful thing, the British will never forgive you". He then said: "Let us talk of more pleasant things. Have a cigarette". I had a cigarette and we talked for a few moments of more pleasant things.

Now, the members of the Controlling Committee knew of my appointment and knew also of Nicolle and Symes and they arranged to gather at our offices at Elizabeth College to hear the result of my interview with the Kommandant. I drove straight there and told them what in fact had happened.

I must have had a macabre sense of humour for, after telling them of the threat to shoot 20 prominent Guernseymen, I said, with my eye on Dr. Symons, a member of the Central Douzaine of St. Peter Port consisting not of twelve but of twenty Douzeniers, "I had obviously to make a gesture, so I offered Oberleutnant Schnadt the Central Douzaine". Dr. Symons's face (we all adored him) was a study until I added: "Not on your life, I didn't".

Bandelow called me to the Kommandantur the following Tuesday morning. He was his usual cheery self and uttered not one word about shooting anyone. He told me that he felt pretty sure that some soldiers had remained behind when the German occupation began or had entered the Island since. We must clear the matter up. He wished to arrange a date with me by which all such personnel must surrender. If they did, they would be treated as prisoners of war and no one who had harboured or helped them would be punished. If any did not and were subsequently discovered, they and those who had helped them would have to take the consequences. After, all there was a war going on. He was going on leave and he would get his second-in-command to arrange with me the actual date for the surrender.

Weeks had gone by since Nicolle and Symes landed and I had lost any hope I had had that they would somehow be taken off the Island. I was aware that a number of Guernsey relatives and friends had helped them and that their presence was known to a lot of people. I feared that eventually news of it would, not through treachery but through idle talk, reach the Germans. In that case there would, almost certainly, be some executions and a number of stiff prison sentences. I kept Emille Nicolle posted with all the happenings and told him that my advice was that the two officers should surrender. Emile was very dubious as to whether the Germans would keep their word if the boys did surrender. I told him that I was sure the Kommandant would.

At my meeting with the Kommandant, I told him that if indeed there were any British soldiers in the Island I feared that his communication to me might be in such official military terms that it might not inspire confidence in those whom it might concern. Would he allow me to draft his letter to me in English and submit to him for approval a German translation of it and of my proposed reply? He readily assented and I took some trouble in preparing a slightly clumsy letter in English from him to me and an extremely suave reply. These were translated into German by Monsieur Pierre Hollard (a dear little Frenchman whose services to the Controlling Committee as a translator throughout the occupation were beyond praise) and despatched to Bandelow for approval.

He rang to say that the German was very good but not, in some cases, what he would himself have used. Nevertheless, let that pass. He did, however, need to make an insertion informing the populace that Major General von Schmettow had been appointed Commander-in-Chief in the Channel Islands and he made one other slight amendment.

I remember my reaction to the mention of General von Schmettow was that I couldn't care less. Little did I foresee that, later, he would back Bandelow to the hilt and be instrumental in saving all concerned in the Nicolle and Symes affair.

The English version of the Kommandant's letter and my reply were duly published in the newspapers. I had no means of judging the reaction of the public. I understand that some people thought I was playing into the Germans' hands and were highly critical of me. That is quite understandable to me. *(The English version of these letters, and the subsequent Notice, are reproduced in Appendix H).*

Now, although besides Nicolle and Symes, there were some five or six other British soldiers in the island, I was quite unaware of this. What I was hoping was that Nicolle and Symes and those concerned about their safety would receive such assurance from the letters that Nicolle and Symes would, in fact, surrender. For this was in doubt to the very last. They were most stout-hearted and anxious to take advantage of any opportunity of getting away from the Island. Emile Nicolle, anxious as he very naturally was for his son's safety, was dubious as to whether the Germans would honour the undertaking given. I advised him that, in my view, much as I regretted the surrender of the two officers, it was in the general interest of islanders as a whole that it should take place.

The Kommandant went on leave and his second-in-command got in touch with me to arrange a surrender date. He proposed 11 p.m. of Saturday, Oct. 19th., 1940 but I managed to get it extended to 6 p.m. of Monday, Oct. 21st., in the hope that a council of war would be held by all concerned on the Sunday when all would be free from their various occupations to give their undivided attention to the matter. A notice to this effect was published. On the Monday morning, Emile Nicolle told me that it had been decided that his son and Jimmy Symes would surrender that evening and, at 6 p.m. precisely, the Police Inspector rang me to say that they had. I reported the surrender to the Kommandantur and was instructed that the two officers were to be placed in the prison, temporarily. Under German rule there was nothing sinister in this and I was in no way alarmed.

Here, I should explain that when they surrendered, they were dressed in British military uniform which had been provided by Nicolle's uncle, the Guernsey Deputy Harbour Master, who secured it from a store of captured military uniform and equipment which he knew existed at the White Rock and to which, no doubt at considerable risk, he gained access. If, then, the Germans did not become aware that the two officers had entered the island in civilian clothes, there were good grounds for believing that, with a Kommandant of Bandelow's geniality and integrity, the immediate future could be regarded with considerable confidence.

I do not know what alerted the Germans to the irregular manner of their entry into the Island and I have no grounds for suspecting treachery on the part of anyone. The others who surrendered were not harassed in any way. One, I remember, was a man who had volunteered for some special service, had been accepted and attested and then sent home to await call-up. He had never donned uniform in his life. I tried very hard to get the Germans to release him. They were not unsympathetic but pointed out that, on being attested, he had in law become a combatant.

Whatever it was that did alert the Germans over Nicolle and Symes, they certainly pursued the matter with awful thoroughness and, by dint of repeated questioning, they traced all those concerned in helping them. To me, they said not one word but the rumours which reached me of what was going on caused me very great concern. During the week following the surrender, thirteen people had been picked up and lodged in jail. On the Saturday, I went to the Feldkommandantur with a view to making the most urgent representations. As soon as I got there, I realised that I, too, was under suspicion. The office staff with whom I had been in touch for months and who had, invariably, been courteous and obliging, were reluctant to have anything to do with me and I had some difficulty in securing attention. I asked to see Dr. Brosch and was shown in to his room. I got the impression of a deeply troubled man. I said: "Dr. Brosch, before he went on leave, the Kommandant gave me his word of honour that any members of the British Armed Forces who surrendered by a given date would be treated as prisoners of war and that no one who had helped them would be harmed. They surrendered by the due date and since then you have been making a whole series of arrests. Are you going to keep your word?" Dr. Brosch, not looking at me replied: "We must keep our word but it is going to be very difficult and only the Führer can decide". This answer chilled me to the marrow; if indeed it was true that the Führer was being consulted, then I had no expectation of a favourable outcome.

I met my old friend, Major Jack Falla, by chance that afternoon and he asked: "Well, how's it going?" I replied: "Very, very badly indeed. My number is up. I give myself a week." I remember him saying: "Oh, surely it's not as bad as that?" and my reply: "Well, wait and see!"

The next day, Sunday, my wife and I had just finished lunch when I saw an officer and a soldier arrive. I said to her: "This is it." I let them in and took them to our big drawing-room. I had a heavy cold and the room was icy. I suggested to my visitors that we should move to a smaller room and knowing that a fire was laid ready for lighting in another room, I called out to my wife: "Be a dear and put a match to the fire in the sitting room." Like a flash the two pushed past me; they obviously suspected the burning of incriminating papers. Reassured by the contents of the grate, they calmed down.

The soldier, speaking English with an American accent, did all the talking; the officer posed as neither speaking nor understanding English. I am sure that he understood everything that was said but he never spoke to me direct. I have no longer the faintest recollection of what was said. Then an officer, clearly with Japanese blood in him, arrived and was left to guard me. I tried to engage him in conversation but all he did was put his finger to his lips.

After an hour or so, he was relieved by a corporal. He said: "You will laugh when I tell you my name; it is 'Geese'". He had been a merchant in Liverpool and spoke English fluently. He was kind and considerate but asked me not to reveal that he had talked to me.

Between 5 and 6 p.m. he was relieved by a man in plain clothes, undoubtedly belonging to the Secret Military Police. His English was excellent. He told me that it had been ascertained that I was implicated in the espionage carried out by Nicolle and Symes and asked me what I had to say. I replied that I was saying absolutely nothing. Eventually he said: "But this is nonsense; do you not realize the terribly dangerous position you are in?" I again said that I would say nothing. He then told me that they knew everything about the case and, in particular, that Colonel Brousson and I were the joint heads of the espionage service in Guernsey. This shook me for not only was it absolutely untrue but, to the best of my belief, Col. Brousson knew nothing about the two officers and had certainly not lent them any aid. And then fantasy took a hand and I had what almost amounted to a vision of Queenie Guillemette with her eyes swollen from weeping. Had Louis, her husband, my private secretary, been picked up too? Col. Brousson, although I didn't know it, was under house arrest at this time. It occurred to me that if the Germans' suspicions were as wild as they appeared to be, it would be best that I should try, so far as possible, to eliminate those who were innocent. So I told the German that, since they believed they knew everything, if he would tell me what they knew, I would quite honestly tell him what was true and what was false. He said: "I can't do that" and I replied that, in that case, I would remain completely silent. The temptation to get from me corroboration of what he knew or suspected was too much and he began to open out. I told him I was not, never had been and never would be a spy and I was sure the same applied to Col. Brousson. He said: "I can prove the contrary about Col. Brousson from what he himself published in your newspaper just before we arrived." I said: "Nonsense, what did he publish?" And he produced a 'Press' containing an announcement signed by Colonel Brousson to the effect that he had been appointed Liaison Officer between Guernsey and the Home Office. I asked him if he really believed that a spy would announce his avocation as publicly and told him – which was true – that I had never seen the announcement, having been so deluged with work at the time as not to have time even to scan the newspapers. I told him how Colonel Brousson, the Government Secretary, had been left completely in the air when the Lieutenant-Governor was recalled, that his wife and family having evacuated, he had sought a passage to England in Capt. Clark's yacht, had reported to the Home Office and been promptly told to return. No doubt, either on instructions or of his own initiative, he had published the notice to give himself some status in the new situation. In any case, I was certain that he was the last man in the world to engage in espionage. I must have convinced the German that I was speaking the truth for (as I learned later) after leaving me, he went to Brousson's house and released him from arrest. The interview went on for some time but as, in fact, I knew virtually nothing of Nicolle's and Symes' movements in the island or who had, or had not helped them, there was little to be got from all the questioning.

Then my wife was allowed in and, furious with what was going on, she gave the German such a piece of her mind that I tried to stop her, saying: "If you go on like this, you'll only be doing me harm" and the German, intimidated, begged me to assure her that he'd treated me fairly. He told her that she was free to go to bed but that I would remain in the sitting-room under close arrest. Then the American speaking soldier and two young officers arrived. The Germans manhandled a couch (for me) and two easy chairs into the room and the officers went into a corner, turned their backs and loaded their revolvers.

Before the others left, I asked if the rule of silence still applied. The soldier questioned the officers and said: "The matter does not arise, neither of these officers speaks a word of English. The three of us settled down for what I expected to be a night of silence. After a long spell of this I enquired whether either of them spoke French. Both did and seemed as relieved to talk as I was.

One was a regular soldier, quite content with the war. As he explained: war meant casualties and casualties meant promotion. The other was an architect from Cologne. He detested the war: all he asked was to get back to his drawing board as quickly as possible. I named them: 'Monsieur Destruction and Monsieur Construction' Ja! Ja they said and were delighted at the joke. Strange to say, we spent quite a cheerful night together.

They were to be relieved, I understood, at 8 a.m. but, as nothing happened, we offered them breakfast, which they refused and I had mine. I asked if I might get a bath and they said that they would be only too happy that I should but that they had strict orders not to let me out of their sight and that I must remain where I was.

Just after 1 p.m. the American speaking soldier returned and announced that I was free to go back to the Controlling Committee whenever I liked. I was astonished at the news and asked: "Does this mean that the whole matter is at an end?" He replied that he had not said that but that, for the moment, I was free to go where I liked.

I had a hurried lunch and went to my office in Elizabeth College where I found all the Committee assembled and concocting plans which they hoped would lead to my release.

6

I WINTER IN PARIS (NOV. – DEC., 1940)

The initial draft of this Chapter and the Diary *(to be found in Appendix I)* were written in Cell No. 38 of the Cherche Midi Prison in the Quartier Latin in Paris in November and December, 1940, where I was lodged by the Germans when they discovered that I was implicated as regards the espionage activities of those very stout soldiers, Lieutenants Hubert Nicolle M.C. and Jimmy Symes M.C. We, in the prison, were suffering intensely from cold, a near starvation diet and much anxiety. It looked as though the two officers and at least some of those who had helped them would be shot and that the rest of us would spend the remainder of the war - or much longer if Hitler won - in captivity in appalling conditions. I had managed, when searched, to secrete a memorandum tablet and, in this, I wrote unendingly. My supply of stationery being so limited, I committed my recollections to paper in such small writing that it is only with a magnifying glass that I can now decipher them at all. Much of what I wrote is tinged with emotion which is, I suppose, understandable. It was done by way of occupational therapy and not with a view to publication. Even ten years ago, I would not have dreamed of exposing my secret thoughts to the public gaze in that I would have been ashamed - if that be the correct word - to do so. Now, with not that much time left, I am relatively indifferent to those impostors, public praise and blame. It is, no doubt, due to the advent of senility.

I kept a diary during my winter 'vacation' lasting from November 7th to December 31st, 1940, and spent in the Hotel des Ambassadeurs, Boulevard Haussmann, Paris (twenty-four hours) and the two larger establishments under German management: La Prison de Versailles (six days) and La Prison du Cherche Midi situated in Le Quartier Latin, Paris (forty-five days) and, finally in a tiny hotel under French management in Granville (thirty-six hours). With some hesitation - because it is, in some respects, so very personal and at times sad - I have decided to include it in the appendix. It is precisely as I wrote it except that, in all, I have inserted seven words to aid the sense and, in two or three instances, adjusted the punctuation. No doubt, the emotions portrayed are already well known to serious students of penal reform but an account of them may, perhaps, be read and do good

154

sometime, somewhere. I have, by good fortune, always possessed a sense of fun often emerging, quite unexpectedly, at awkward moments. One such moment occurred while I was sitting in the Junkers troop-carrier awaiting take-off from the Guernsey Airport. I told my captors that I was a shocking air passenger and that I was likely to make an awful mess of their spotless aircraft. One of those standing around was the young Luftwaffe officer in command of our airport: he, taking me seriously, actually ran the hundred or so yards to the terminal building and returned with a fire bucket which was placed at my side. (Many weeks later when I returned to Guernsey and reported to my old Controlling Committee, I informed them that the bucket would be found to be missing at the conclusion of hostilities and suggested that my account should be debited accordingly. They graciously waived their claim.)

Then, still wishing to make a nuisance of myself, I told the sympathetic Germans that it was not right that I, a non-combatant, should be placed in such peril. As sure as fate, we were about to be shot down by a Spitfire. They sought to reassure me and explained that, by night, a British plane might intrude into German airspace but that, by day, such a thing was most unlikely. I listened gravely and then told them that I would give anything to have a Union Jack in my possession. They asked me why and I replied that, as the Spitfire approached, I would wave it at the window, the British pilot would spot it and sheer off and that their plane would be saved, they would be saved, and even more important, I would be saved. It would be an act meriting the award of the Iron Cross. It is quite untrue that Germans have no sense of humour. They showed intense appreciation of my own heavy brand.

The journey to Paris was uneventful. The Spitfire let me down or, rather, up. To say that I was surprised at the palatial quarters allotted me at the Hotel des Ambassadeurs would be an understatement. In times of peace, I should not, for financial reasons, have dreamt of occupying anything so grand. I was even more surprised when I was taken down to dinner. As Mette and I entered the vast dining room, I was astonished at the array and apparel of those already seated. Elderly officers smothered in decorations, one with two Iron Crosses (it was explained to me, though not by him, that one was a Reich decoration and the other conferred by one of the kingdoms into which Germany was formerly divided), some with brightly coloured trousers

(Staff). It certainly surprised me to see so many naval officers of high rank in the heart of Paris. As we entered, Dr. Mette halted and did a magnificent Hitler salute. I felt I must do something and so did my best Buckingham Palace style head bob, painfully learnt for the purposes of some pre-war Royal visit to Guernsey. The startled look on the faces of the great nearest me and the whisperings at least informed me that my politeness had not gone unnoticed. I remember asking Dr. Mette during dinner whether he had an overwhelming desire to do me in. Surprised, he denied any such wish and enquired why I asked. I could only say that I didn't really know.

The next morning, I was offered a walk and elected to go to the Madeleine to look at the pigeons. It was explained to me that I was the only Englishman under 65 'at large' in Paris. This did not comfort me. In my second entry in my diary, I refer to Dr. Mette as 'an interpreter' for he had, in answer to my question: 'What do the letters G.F.M. on your shoulder straps stand for?' told me this. After a good lunch, I was sitting with Mette and another soldier with similar markings when Mette was called to the telephone. He had previously told me, in an attempt to satisfy my insatiable curiosity, that his friend was an expert in Scandinavian languages so, to make conversation during Mette's absence, I asked his friend which it was he spoke, Norwegian, Swedish or Danish. Looking intensely surprised, he said that he spoke none of these. It now dawned on me that I was being 'taken for a ride' and should exercise caution. Later, I learned that the letters meant in English: Secret Field Police.

I was taken for a really long walk in the afternoon and was allowed into a book-shop where I purchased a French masterpiece on the heroic defence of Verdun in the First World War, a book I found a godsend - and wept over - in prison later.

As, after dinner that night, in the same exalted company, I yawned and closed this book and was about to say that, if Mette didn't mind, I would go to bed, there walked in a tall German officer whose uniform was of a slightly lighter hue than the others I had seen. He said something to Mette, who told me that we were moving on and must pack. I asked: 'Are we going to another hotel?' and Mette replied: 'I hope so'. Evidently, we were not. We got into a car with the tall officer and drove out of Paris. After some time, I insisted that I had a right to be told where I was being taken. Mette consulted the officer and then told me: 'I regret to inform you that you are under arrest'.

From then on, I kept my mouth resolutely shut. We arrived at a prison which I later found to be Versailles and I was left standing in a corridor with an Englishman (?) and a Frenchman, the officer going into a near-by room and telephoning in my hearing. I heard him speak of 'espionage' (pronouncing it in German fashion) several times. Meanwhile, the Englishman approached me without let or hindrance and, as I thought, too effusively. He wanted to know what I was accused of and, to me, seemed to speak a strange brand of English. Believing him to be an agent provocateur (I was highly suspicious by this time for I had demanded of the officer before he left me to telephone that he should tell me what I was accused of and he had told me that he had no instructions on the matter) I brushed him off quite ruthlessly. From the strange brands of English I heard much later in my internment camp, I think it highly probably that the Englishman I was so rude to was quite genuine and merely (like me) in sore need of comfort.

My first night in clink was, naturally, in appalling contrast with my surroundings of the night before. It is adequately dealt with in my diary. The next few days were very difficult ones. For the first - and last - time in my life - so far - I understood the meaning of the phrase 'the balance of his mind was disturbed'. I swung - without evident reason - from hilarity to deep depression and back again. I told myself, aloud, when at the top of the swing: 'Don't be a bloody fool, you're for the high jump' and, when in the depths: 'Cheer up, old chap, things are never so bad as they seem when they first happen' (Lord Haig, during First World War). Gradually, by this means and by working hard cleaning my filthy lavatory, I achieved equilibrium.

I asked for exercise; I really wanted company. I was allowed to walk alone in a tiny triangular yard. The gale of the night before had stripped the sycamores of their leaves. I picked up three and used two as plates and one - beautiful and multi-coloured - as an ornament. At my request, instead of my food being brought to my cell, I was allowed to walk along the corridor to the kitchen to collect it. Once, getting my coffee, I said to the kind little German soldier: 'Kein Zucher?'. He said; 'Ja! Ja!' and, diving under his bed, pulled out a carton and dropped six lumps into my coffee before I could stop him. On returning to my cell, I tried, unsuccessfully, to retrieve some of them for another occasion.

After one false alarm, I was driven away at 6 p.m. on November 15th in a four-seater car. On the front seat by the side of the driver, knelt an armed guard facing the back seat containing me and the little French girl (she would have been about 17) who had been in the cell adjoining mine. Neither of us knew where we were going but she told me she thought they were taking her to her aunt's. They were not; they were taking us both to the Cherche Midi Prison. She said she had no idea why she had been arrested and I never learnt what became of her. Arriving, we were taken into the guardroom where I lit a cigarette at which 'Nicht Rauchen' was roared at me. I hastily complied. Conditions here were very tough, the toughest I have ever encountered. I was pushed into Cell No. 38 on the top floor. It was pitch dark and I had to feel around to find my bearings. In doing so I fell over a slop-pail. At Versailles, the food was ample and quite good and there was central heating. Here, the food was exiguous and the whole place, for the first twelve days, freezing cold. When stoves were lighted - in the corridors - life was slightly more bearable but never comfortable; it was a very cold winter. The cell doors were tight fitting and the only heat came in through the trap over each door which, while guards were on duty, was required to be kept closed. I have spent hundreds of hours standing on my stool, itself standing on my table, with my head touching the ceiling so as to get the benefit of the rather warmer air in the upper half of the cell.

On my first morning, I had to go down to the 'salle' on the ground floor to hand in my belongings. Accompanying me on the journey was a small and quite inoffensive Frenchman and, in charge of the operation, was a gigantic German Feldwebel, an absolute brute. We were not moving fast enough for his liking and he shouted the German equivalent of 'Jump to it'. The Frenchman, in front, and I both thought he said: 'Halt' and did so. Furious, he seized the Frenchman by the scruff of the neck and hurled him down the stairs. The poor fellow went down and slithered on his face through the door at the bottom and on to a gravelled patch outside. A more kindly bespectacled soldier ran and got water and a towel and did some first aid. I was not touched but I have no doubt that, had I been in front, I would have been the victim of this brutal assault. There was no one to whom one could appeal. I never saw that sergeant again but I have often heard him rushing along our corridor swearing at the top of his voice and, with a long rod, slamming closed with appalling force the trap doors that we, to get just a little warmth, had been so imprudent to open.

Sunday was the worst day of all. The guards went off duty at noon and we were just abandoned. One Sunday afternoon, when I judged it was about 5 p.m., I asked the man in the cell opposite who could see the prison clock if that was the time. He looked and replied that it was twenty minutes to two.

We were atrociously fed, except on Christmas Day. Sunday was worst in this respect. At 9 a.m. (double summer time) we received a small mug of unsweetened mock coffee. At 10.30, a big ladleful of soup, then the hard rations to last till 4.30 p.m. the following day were issued: a very small ration of very hard German rye bread, a small spoonful of margarine or lard - occasionally of butter - a tiny piece of sausage or a desertspoonful of potted meat or - not and - of ham and, if neither of these was available, one held out one's hand and about a dozen sultanas were placed in one's palm. On such a diet one grew noticeably weaker.

Our straw mattresses had been in use for so long that the straw was in inch lengths and, consequently, as hard as the boards on which they rested. After some weeks, we were allowed out one afternoon to refill them with clean straw. It was the first time I had seen the sun for weeks and I remember the thrill I got from seeing the coloured lichen on some logs waiting to be cut up as fuel for the stoves. We each had two very old and thin blankets.

What of the hundreds of other poor devils in similar plight to my own? From time to time - each morning on rising, we were sent down, in batches, to empty our covered slop-pails and refill our water jugs - I caught sight of many elderly and apparently eminent Frenchmen, some of whom had the miniature ribbon of the Légion d'Honneur in their buttonholes, all of them looking the picture of abject misery. Of my own people, I never saw but two: Emile Nicolle, the father of one of the two British Officers who had been the unwitting cause of our imprisonment and who, the fate of his boy being then anybody's guess and his wife also being a prisoner in some other part of our grim prison, was always cheerful and certain that, despite all the odds, there would be a happy issue out of all our afflictions: and Bill Allen, groundsman at Elizabeth College Playing Fields, who had sheltered the two officers in the pavilion there and was thus implicated. He was not so cheerful. My cell was at one end of a corridor and Bill Allen's at the other: Nicolle was housed about half-way along another corridor running (opposite Bill Allen's cell) at right angles to ours. At night, when the guards were off, the French inmates of the cells round about us would call: 'Silence pour les anglais' and I could relay messages via Allen to Nicolle and he could thus reply.

Our Guernsey party consisted of sixteen persons including the two British Officers. I had been flown to Paris last of all. The others had been taken in a small Jersey tug from Guernsey to Granville in a howling gale. Among them were six ladies of whom two, for some reason or other, had been dropped off at Caen and were in prison there, the other four being with the rest of us in the Cherche Midi.

I only saw the faces of at most three of my immediate neighbours during the whole of my incarceration. Naturally, I formed mental pictures of the people to whom the voices with which I became so familiar belonged. When I was released and walked along throwing in to them some small and very stale pieces of bread and saying good-bye, I was astounded to find how completely false were those pictures. For instance, Roditti, whom I had pictured as dark, clean-shaven and sharp-featured, I found to sport a very full and ragged ginger beard and moustache.

Let me tell you something about just three of them.

There was Julien, a Belgian, disheartened and morose, the owner of a motorbus, running an authorised service between Paris and Brussels. He had been stopped at a roadblock and found to have two Jews (husband and wife) in his vehicle, their papers, according to him, in perfect order. Everybody in the bus had been turfed out, the bus had been impounded and he himself had been arrested and had lain in the Cherche Midi for months. How many times have I not heard him say, in that mournful voice of his, in reply to a question - as to what offence he had committed - from one or other of our 'new boys': 'J'avais deux Juifs dans ma voiture'. He was eventually given one month's imprisonment and, having already served much longer, was released whilst I was still there. He never expected to see his bus again - I wonder if he did.

Then there was an intensely interesting character, whose name I never learned, in the cell next to Julien's. There is also an extremely sinister note in my diary under the date 14.12.40. Saturday. 'Nothing happened except that No. 36 left for an unknown destination'.

In various instalments, he had told me his story. At the time of the German occupation of the northern half of France, he was a member of the French Deuxième Bureau which I understand approximated to our M.I.5. He had been living with a French girl in Paris and entertained much affection for her. He went over the zonal boundary leaving her behind, she being in no way implicated in his activities. After a time, having found a suitable apartment, he wrote asking her to join him and enclosing the fare. Unconscious of the fact that she was being shadowed by the German Secret Police, she went to the station and purchased a ticket at the 'guichet' for the station nearest the boundary. She turned away to board her train, was seized and taken back to the 'guichet' where she was made to hand back her ticket and received back the money she had paid for it. She was then freed. She, thoroughly alarmed, did not dare write her lover saying what had happened. He, getting no news of her, decided, after many weeks, to go back to Paris and find out what had happened to her. He did and was picked up by the Secret Police as he got off the train. He had been in the Cherche Midi ever since. We often talked about his fate. He was certain, he told me, that he would face a firing squad. He was quite resigned and very brave. Late at night, on the Saturday mentioned in my diary, they came for him and I was intensely sad. And that is all I know.

There was never a vacant cell and no sooner had my poor friend vacated his than it was reoccupied by a man named Roditti. He told me that his family were Spanish Jews who had been driven from Spain in the time of Ferdinand and Isabella. They had found refuge in Turkey and now lived in Constantinople. For centuries, they had been Turkish nationals yet, so strongly does habit persist, they still spoke the Spanish of the time of Ferdinand and Isabella in their everyday family conversations.

He told me that, during the First World War, his father was in business and Turkish Consul in Brussels and that he had been instructed to make representations on behalf of the Turkish Government to General von Bissing, German Governor-General of Belgium, for the reprieve of the death sentence passed on our Nurse Cavell. He went on to tell me that no German sufficiently influential could be found to make a recommendation to that effect to Berlin and this, not because of detestation of the 'crimes' she had committed, but because her haughty demeanour and calculated cold contempt for Germans and all things German had enraged them against her. I have no means of knowing whether this is true but it is certainly what he told me.

On Sunday 29.12.40. we Guernsey civilians were released and were told that the two British officers would be treated as prisoners of war. They were and, in the fullness of time, were repatriated. We had no inkling of how it had come about. I thought that perhaps the very lengthy statement I had put in and to which I refer later in this Chapter had had some effect. Learning the whole truth much later, I doubt if it had any. This final outcome, which fulfilled the promises made by Bandelow in his letter dated 11th October, redounds very greatly to the honour not only of the German High Command but also of the more junior officers in command in both Jersey and Guernsey.

My diary up to that date is very neatly and legibly written. The entry for that day is barely legible for I wrote most of it in the bus on the way to Granville.

I had heard rumours the night before that our Guernseywomen had left for an unknown destination. It was untrue; they had merely been moved to another part of the prison. Why, then, before 'reveille' that morning, was I up and dressed and my bed made and my suit-case ready to be clicked shut when Feldwebel Fach (not the brute but a nice fellow) came to my cell, unlocked it and leaving the door open, said to me 'anglais partir tout de suite' in execrable French. I do not know, but I was. *(His youngest son, in Guernsey, appears to have had a similar premonition, as recounted by Sherwill in Appendix J, "A Case of Telepathy?".)*

All our things were restored to us, a pail of sweetened coffee was made for us, lashings of bread and butter and tins of pork-meat were handed to us and a bus was summoned to take us to the coast. In charge of us was a giant of a German Sergeant-Major of Feld Polizei wearing a huge metal plaque slung from his neck denoting that he was on duty. With him was a lance corporal and a private soldier drove the bus. We were told we could stop where we pleased. There was only one restriction we must obey; we must not obtain nor consume any spirits.

Now, a very sad thing had happened on December 23rd. Mr. L.M. Symes, the father of the other British Officer, had been found dead in a cell with his wrist slashed by a safety razor blade. I know it has been said that the Germans did this but I honestly believe this to be untrue. The following, to the best of my knowledge and belief, is what happened. A day or so previously Mr. Symes had complained to the Germans that his cell was lousy and inspection had proved this to be correct. Accordingly, he had been removed from it so that it might be de-loused and, there being no other cell available, Mr. Symes, but not by way of punishment, had been placed in the punishment cell, which differed from the others in having no wooden bed and straw mattress but a concrete block instead. To sleep on that with only thin blankets was, undoubtedly, a grave hardship. Presumably, at the end of his tether through anxiety as to the fate of his officer son, who might quite likely be shot as a spy, worry about his prisoner wife and worry about himself, this final indignity caused his nerve to snap. This terrible tragedy shocked me intensely for, only a couple of days previously, Mr. Symes had been the bread orderly, that is to say, he dragged the huge bag containing our rations of bread along the corridor for distribution at each individual cell. I had seen and spoken to him and I then noticed nothing abnormal in his condition.

Poor Mrs. Symes; in what a turmoil of mixed emotions she must have been. Widowed, released from prison, her son saved from probable death. She was wonderfully brave and even joked with us as we drove through the countryside. We were in a jocular mood and yet, conscious of what she was feeling beneath the brave face she was showing the world, again and again a ribald joke would be cut off half-way as the joker caught sight of her tense face.

Our first stop was at Dreux. I had 500 French francs, - thoughtfully provided for me by the Germans against the equivalent in Guernsey money for my 'few days stay in Paris' - and the others drew on me. We went into a 'pâtisserie' and bought a lot of unwholesome delicacies. My purchase was a huge 'Baba au Rhum'. We then adjourned to the nearest hotel restaurant. One of us (not me) suggested that some 'eau de vie' would do us all good. I consulted our giant Oberfeldwebel, who joined in the feast, as to whether the prohibition concerning spirits included 'eau de vie' and, with a huge grin, he assured me that it did not. Eau de vie was therefore served and served again. I have never been privileged to contribute to any medical journal but I now make a pronouncement worthy of inclusion in all of them. Having undergone famine conditions for many weeks, do not, when rescue comes, start off with rum baba and brandy or, as the Germans so often told me during the early weeks of the occupation of Guernsey as to what would happen to me if I didn't do something they wanted done, the consequences will be very disagreeable. I was not so ill, however, that I could not get back to duty. Before leaving Guernsey I had been asked by the relatives of an elderly man suffering acutely from heart trouble to try to procure for him some 'Coramine' as stocks in Guernsey were exhausted. I now got the hotelier to get a chemist to open up his shop and was able to purchase the few phials of it that he had in stock. At Granville, the next day, I did the round of every chemist and obtained from each as much as he was willing to sell me, not much but, in the aggregate, quite a lot. To my relief, the invalid was still alive when I got back to Guernsey and I hope that his life was prolonged.

The momentary indisposition of our party passed and from Dreux to Granville, the ladies of our party were kept fully occupied cutting bread and making sandwiches of which we, the men, - as was our right - disposed of them.

Of course, from time to time we had to stop the bus. After reconnoitring, we did so whenever there were two haystacks, one on the right of the road and the other on the left. Our German driver became quite expert in stopping the bus precisely halfway between them. Then it was merely a matter of 'Ladies to the right, gentlemen to the left' or, to avoid monotony, vice verse. Indeed, before we reached Granville, we had formed an 'Old Cherche Midi-ans Association' complete with sign and countersign, or rather, call and counter-call. The first was 'Seaux et Brocs' (Slop-pails and Water Jugs) (pronounced 'Soesaybro') in remembrance of the time-honoured call each morning at Cherche Midi (Col. Dreyfus must, during his long incarceration there, have heard it daily) and the answer was 'Haystacks' in honour of god knows what. How unspeakably vulgar. No doubt but in our excited state we thought it very funny.

Meanwhile, a fast German staff car was speeding to Caen to pick up Mrs. Frank Nicolle and Mrs. Marriette and restore them to their respective husbands.

It arrived at Granville almost as soon as we did. The Hotel Pellerin, very tiny, had been requisitioned for our comfort and a meal was awaiting us. It included sauté potatoes. One of us (I omit his name, since he is now dead, though not because of that) had five helpings; they did not agree with him. The young German staff officer who had retrieved the two missing ladies was charming; he was also 'hochgeboren', being entitled to be addressed as 'Ritter'. We would, that night, have gladly supped with the devil himself: he not being available, we invited the officer to preside at our meal and this he did with the utmost cheerfulness.

The huge Oberfeldwebel, the lance corporal and the private also joined us at table and they were allotted the rooms in the attic for the night. After dinner, they went into the town to refresh themselves. Successful in this, they returned at about midnight and, careful not to disturb our rest, removed their heavy field boots at the foot of the stairs and crept up in their stockinged feet. Unfortunately, at the very top, one dropped a boot and, trying to recover it, let fall the other. The noise as they hit each stair to the very bottom disturbed most of our party but it had no effect on me.

The following morning, bright and early, we were driven to the harbour where a very fat German major told us that a tempest was raging and that it would be imprudent to embark us that day. I could detect no breath of wind and suspected that the Germans had tired of well-doing as regards us. The next day, however, we were put aboard the 'Holland' en route for Jersey and Guernsey. It was a flat calm with pouring rain so, clearly, there had been no 'tempest'.

With a day to spend in Granville, I put it to the giant that the likelihood of our escaping when liberation was in sight was extremely remote and, against orders, he set us free until the evening. Believing myself to be still the President of the Guernsey Controlling Committee (I had, in fact, been dismissed by the Germans from that exalted position), I went to our 'Purchasing Commission' office in la Rue des Hirondelles to enquire the state of affairs. The French clerk received me kindly (our Guernsey agents were away on their various black market and other missions) and I was horrified when he showed me between fifteen and sixteen millions of French francs, more money than I had ever previously seen at one time, heaped in an ordinary French softwood armoire, the lock of which I, not being trained thereto, could easily have burgled in five minutes. On return to Guernsey, I sent over my rather outsize office safe as a more suitable receptacle. Then I called on Monsieur and Madame Mauduit, whose only son had been killed in the German bombing raid on the Guernsey harbour on the

28th June. They had befriended our purchasing agents and they now befriended me.

The next morning, we sailed for Guernsey. The sea was so calm that it seemed impossible that anyone could be seasick. The Oberfeldwebel, however, achieved the impossible for he was a stout fellow; it seemed that his stomach was his Achilles heel. I thought he would have died; evidently, the night before had something to do with his near-fatal illness.

Arriving in Jersey harbour, I pointed out to the Military officer on duty for the voyage that the ladies were drenched to the skin; could I go into St. Helier and fetch some sandwiches and, above all, a hot drink? He agreed and 'phoned the harbour guard to let me through. Arriving at the weighbridge, I made contact with the friendly Jersey policeman on duty there with several Germans and was allowed to telephone to Alexander (now Lord) Coutanche, the Bailiff of Jersey, who was at home. He told me to go to the Royal Court and he would be with me in a few minutes. On my way, I called in at Gaudin's Restaurant and ordered sandwiches and a pail of coffee and then spotted Charles Duret Aubin and Cecil Harrison (Attorney General and Solicitor General) having lunch and had a chat. They were relieved to see me in spite of the fact that I belonged to Guernsey and told me that the rumour in Jersey was that my party and I had long since been 'fusillés' and our bodies disposed of. This, I explained, was untrue. Then on to the Bailiff's for a long chat. Gaudin's insisted on giving me all the slightly cracked cups in their establishment to be thrown overboard after use and a basket in which to carry them and the sandwiches. This and the pail I was to keep. I had not gone ten yards when a lorry materialised from nowhere and I was driven back to the ship in style. Never, since the cataclysm which separated Jersey and Guernsey for ever, had a Guernseyman received such V.I.P. treatment in Jersey. It was, it was explained to me, because I was looking very ill. At the quayside just before the 'Holland' sailed for Guernsey, a tragic parting took place. I had promised the friendly giant, restored and able to stand, that in token of my gratitude for all his kindness, I would, on arrival in Guernsey - which I gave him to understand, as infinitely superior to Jersey so far as its amenities went - take him to the Royal Hotel and treat him to the largest and most expensive drink he could think of. Now, although I am fairly tall, communication between us was difficult in that my head was about on a level with his elbow:

nevertheless, he heard and understood. Then he was told by a superior that, once we cleared the pier heads, the need to see that none of us absconded would disappear and that he should return instead to Paris. He did not actually cry with disappointment but had he not been in the presence of the enemy, he might well have done so. *(Set out in Appendix K will be found a letter, written in 1950, by one of the German soldiers who accompanied the Guernsey party.)*

With remarkable thoroughness, the Guernsey Germans had kept our Controlling Committee acquainted all day with the movements of our ship and, on our arrival, the whole of the Controlling Committee were on the quay, each complete with car and Dr. A.N. Symons drove me to my home. There, re-united with my wife and two small sons, I read in the newspaper the official German proclamation concerning those of us who had just returned. It said that our guilt had been proved conclusively but that, in spite of 'aggravating circumstances', the two officers would be excused the death penalty and treated as prisoners of war; the rest, except me, would not have to serve up to fifteen years penal servitude so richly deserved by them: so far as I was concerned, I had made declarations contrary to the best of my knowledge and had acted against my 'appointed duty of information'. I had therefore been guilty of favouring the above and acting disloyally towards the Inselkommandant. The penalty was imprisonment up to one year. I was 'forgiven' but released from my office as "further co-operation with the German authorities is no longer possible". Believe it or not, I was terribly disappointed; it was a complete anticlimax. Here had I, for weeks, been bracing myself to face a firing squad with a smile on my lips and the blasted Germans had evaluated my crime as deserving of a mere twelve months imprisonment at the most. Clearly, I had been wasting my time.

I felt better the following morning, New Year's Day, 1941. My wife and I got out her last bottle of wine and we broke into tiny fragments (it was impossible to cut it) a chunk of stale dry Cherche Midi rye bread I had brought home to show what I had been enduring. We telephoned our nearest friends and bade them come to the feast, which they did.

The next morning, I called on the Bailiff at the Royal Court to take my leave of him on my 'promotion'. He advised me to keep as far away from the Germans henceforth as the size of the island allowed. I promised to consider his advice and went straight to the

Feldkommandantur where I was received by Dr. Reffler. Was it true, I asked him, that Major Bandelow, the Inselkommandant, had moved heaven and earth to secure the release of our party, as I had heard it rumoured? He assured me that it was true. Then would he telephone to Bandelow and ask him to receive me so that I might thank him in person. He would and did and Bandelow said I was to be brought along at once.

What happened was most interesting. When I raised the matter of his efforts on our behalf Bandelow replied very modestly that he had done his utmost in the matter. On his return from leave he had learnt of what had happened and, not knowing whether I had appreciated the situation in all its bearings, he had informed his superiors that he had given me an unqualified assurance and had not specified that he included only members of the British armed forces who had come in in uniform. He told me that, at that time, he was unaware of the presence in Guernsey of any spies, and that the fact that it had since transpired that at the time of our talk I was aware of their presence and status and was in touch with them, and that I had disobeyed the order of the Judge of the German Feldkommandantur in Jersey addressed to me as Attorney General to report all offences against the German Army, had made his task most difficult. Nevertheless, he had called for a Court of Honour. This I have gathered since meant that if the Court upheld him, his military superiors must accept the obligation entered into by him and if the Court found against him, it would mean he would have to resign his commission. I told him that I regarded his action towards a number of British subjects in time of war in the circumstances in question as in the very highest traditions of chivalry and I still so regard it.

May I now retrace our 'steps' first to Granville and then to the Cherche Midi.

At Granville, during my morning walk, I suddenly saw a sight that made my heart flutter. Through a gap in the houses, I saw the Jersey flag (the red cross of St. Patrick on a white ground: I understand that it was adopted because long, long ago, a Jerseyman found in an ancient illustrated tome this particular flag with, below it, the word : 'IERSE' and concluded that this was an unusual way of spelling JERSEY) flying from the staff of the cargo ship 'Normand' which, in addition to the 'Holland', the Germans had found somewhere and appropriated for use between France and the Channel Islands. Her master was Captain

Sowden, a Master Mariner living in Jersey and trapped there by the occupation. If ever there was a stout-hearted matelot, Captain Sowden was. For a long time, he would not allow a German in uniform on his ship and, with the Germans, his name was mud, only more so. I do not know how it all ended for I was interned and you must look in a book by a Jersey author for the truth concerning all this. I now looked with joy at the Jersey flag. Never had I seen a sight so sweet even if I could have wished that she flew the Guernsey flag (the Red Cross of St. George) instead. Except during the occupation, even Jersey and Guernsey owned and registered ships always flew the Red Ensign and now, for the first time in history (and I hope the last, but please don't take this as a dig at Jersey) a Channel Island flag had attained international status.

May we now go on to the Cherche Midi and, with me, re-enter Cellule No. 38 on the top floor, through the window of which, by propping my stool on my table and standing on the former, I could just discern through the glass blackened by the soot of more than a century the words 'HOTEL LUTETIA' on a roof-top sign. I spent much of my time writing. The circumstances, if good for nothing else, taught me one thing. Everything that happens to us from a very early age is recorded and it only required the necessary stimulus to bring it to the surface. No effort on one's part can produce such a result; provide the appropriate conditions and it happens effortlessly. I cast my bucket down into the well of memory and, sometimes, it brought up some very precious things. Some of these I committed to paper. One of my principal tasks, however, was to prepare what I thought of as a brief for the defence of my companions and myself at the trial which, so it was said, was to be laid on in Paris and to be followed by findings and sentences designed 'pour encourager les autres'. I worked on this for weeks ever polishing and re-polishing. I should very much like to see it now and to find out to what extent the end product resembled the truth. Please remember that I am, by nature and by training, an advocate or nothing.

In it, I distinguished between the officers, the parents, relatives and friends, and myself. As regards the officers, I relied on the promise of the German Kommandant that they would be treated as prisoners of war. As to the others, except myself, I relied on his promise that none of them would be harmed and went on to picture them as kindly, uninstructed in the laws of war and merely filled with compassion and fear for the safety of those very dear of them. As regards myself, I pointed out that I had done my damnedest to run the civilian side in accordance with the laws of war and that I had been completely frustrated by the, to me, utterly obnoxious action of the British Government in sending in Guernsey boys for the purposes of espionage. Would I, unless mad, have had a hand in getting in Lieut. Nicolle, the son of the Secretary to my own Controlling Committee? I did not plead ignorance of the laws of war but pointed out my position: either I had to commit treason to my own country or else to commit what I understood to be called, under German military law, treason felony: in the circumstances, I could do no other than I had. Eventually, it was impossible to do any further re-polishing and I put the statement away to await the day of reckoning.

There were no arrangements for doing laundry and no hot water was available. Very occasionally a barber visited to give haircuts or a shave. I had an electric razor which worked but my nail scissors had been taken away. I washed my socks - and nothing else - in cold water and dried them, one at a time, on my electric light bulb which could only be switched on from outside the cell. One evening my sock was on the bulb when the guard went along the corridor switching out the lights. He obviously thought my light was out or that the bulb had blown and didn't even touch the switch. From then on, I always had a sock on the bulb when he came along and it always worked. There was no later inspection and I could remove the sock from the bulb and read or write.

For physical exercise, I paced my cell, four paces each way. One soon gets fed up with that. Then, to spin out the day, in the morning I undressed and washed the upper part of my body in cold water; in the afternoon I undressed and washed the lower half. This routine never varied.

On the 26th November, an American Quaker visited my cell (the Americans had not yet declared war) and arranged to take away my dirty laundry and to bring in some books, the first of which I received on Dec. 3rd. Such visits were allowed until Dec. 17th. Then there was an abrupt tightening-up of the regime; I never learned why. From then on, no visits and we, having previously gone down to the yard to empty our slop-pails and fill our water jugs just before dawn, now never left our cells for any purpose whatever. This was really tough.

On the 16th I wrote in my diary "…..there being no sausage or other delicacy to serve with our 'casse-croute', we were given a second bowl of soup this afternoon. To-day, for the first time for a month, I have had enough to eat."

On the 4th December I was visited by a German Unteroffizier Inspektor (probably Intelligence). He told me that it was wrong that I should be confined in such conditions but that they had nowhere else to put me. He said he would be questioning me on the morrow or on Friday.

On the afternoon of Friday the 6th, I was taken to an office on the ground floor and questioned by the Unteroffizier. At my right elbow as I sat in front of him were that day's Paris newspaper and two packets of French cigarettes. I recognised that this was part of the treatment but smoked innumerable cigarettes as he interrogated me. (Only days before, a Frenchman bread orderly, who had got hold of and was smoking a cigarette as he delivered our rations, had very sweetly offered me 'a puff' and I had expressed my gratitude and refused, saying (and believing): 'I shall never smoke again'. This was now conveniently forgotten. After lengthy and detailed questioning, including research into my wife's maiden name, I said that I had prepared a long statement and that perhaps, if I handed it to him, it would save a lot of his valuable time. He took it and glanced through it and said he would read it carefully. Soon after, he dismissed me and I went back to my cell clutching the newspaper and the rest of the cigarettes.

On Monday the 9th he came to see me. He said: "Yesterday afternoon was my free afternoon; I spent it translating your statement into German". He went on to tell me that he thought it set out the case very thoroughly and that he recognised that I had been in an impossible position. He was pretty confident that his superiors would understand. He had placed the statement and German translation on the top of my dossier so that, when the latter was opened, it could not be missed. He was hopeful that there would be no trial and that all of us, except the two British officers, would be released and returned to Guernsey. He was charming, friendly and sympathetic. He also told me that Field Marshall von Reichenau had passed through Paris while on leave and had been consulted about our case and had said:- "When one gives one's word, one gives one's word but I cannot decide it".

The key of my cell and a composite photo of the facade of the prison lie before me as I write this. Some years after the war, I took my two boys to Paris at Eastertime. I had previously obtained a ministerial permit to visit the prison. Outside was lovely sunshine; inside the prison the gloom was as great as in the winter in which I had been one of the occupants. After much difficulty, with the help of the concierge bearing armfuls of keys, I found my cell. The prison was in process of being demolished: already one wing was gone and offices were being built in its place. When we returned to the Directeur's office, he offered each of us a glass of wine and, I remember, I was a bit doubtful of accepting this because I had noticed how restive my boys had become in the awful gloom. I said to him: "Monsieur, I notice that you are demolishing and rebuilding and will obviously have no further use for the keys. Might I have mine as a souvenir?" He replied that, although they were rebuilding, the locks and keys, two centuries old, were of a quality that could not be obtained now and they were refitting them in the new doors. He regretted, therefore, that he could not grant my request. I said that I must forget about it and bade him au revoir. Arriving at the street door, the concierge, who had been standing by during the conversation, excused himself for a moment and, coming back, placed something heavy wrapped in a scrap of newspaper in my hand. I said: "Qu'est-ce que c'est" and he replied: "C'est le clef de votre cellule: il dit que vous ne pouvez pas l'avoir; moi, c'est moi qui suis le concierge". I thanked him heartily. It was the best piece of French insubordination I had come across. Evidently, the German occupation had been unsuccessful. As regards the photographs, before I left the Rue du Cherche Midi, I paid a French photographer to take them. Weeks elapsed and I finally wrote him rather acidly. Another long delay and then they arrived together with a letter. He had tried vainly to get a permit to photograph the prison. It was refused for security (?) reasons. He had had therefore to sneak in to do the job when the Director was at lunch. He apologised for the great delay.

For years, I tried in vain to discover the origin of the name 'Cherche Midi'. Col. Dreyfus (of the famous Dreyfus trial) had been a prisoner there for a long time but it had nothing to do with him. At last I discovered why it was so called. It had originally been a convent and the Sisters daily, at midday, dispensed soup to the many poor persons living in the neighbourhood. These would congregate in the street outside which became known as La Rue du Cherche Midi (the street where the midday meal is sought). From this, the building, when it became a prison, took its name.

Cherche Midi Prison, Paris

AJS at Laufen Internment Camp

Laufen Internment Camp: King Ambrose with bodyguard and court jester

H. Gompertz, American Camp Senior; Mr. Erik R. Berg, representative in Germany of the world's Alliance of Y.M.C.A.s; and AJS, British Camp Senior

The BIRD-CAGE, magazine produced by Laufen internees

Joly and Rollo burying a German soldier on the beach at Cobo, Guernsey

Joly, John, May (holding Mimi), and Rollo *(end of war 1945)*

AJS at the wheel of Mary Rose – sketch by Gilbert Holliday

Sir Ambrose Sherwill, Bailiff of Guernsey 1959

**Sir Ambrose and Lady Sherwill at Essex Castle, with Fort Île de Raz in the
background**

7

AN ATTEMPT AT A RATIONAL APPROACH TO CERTAIN CONTROVERSIAL ACTIONS OF MR. (LATER SIR) VICTOR G. CAREY DURING THE OCCUPATION

Some will say that, as respects Mr. Victor Carey, it were better that I let sleeping dogs lie. I have long pondered this matter and have reached the contrary view because some of those dogs, in the shape of contemporary writings, did a grave disservice to his reputation as a loyal British subject.

These things will undoubtedly be raked over by future historians of the Island and it is right that they should know the truth.

Having regard to what immediately follows, I think any unbiased reader will accept that I am unlikely to be so enamoured of the Careys as to be likely to seek to 'whitewash' one of them.

They are one of the oldest island families and their pride in their family and its doings is intense. This is justifiable for, over the centuries, their services to their Sovereign and to their Island, have been immense. In other words, they are out of the top drawer and not unaware of that fact. I, myself, came out of the bottom one. When, therefore, in 1920, it came to their knowledge that I was marrying one of them (through her deceased mother), their resentment was intense. My wife's grandfather, a kindly old family doctor, told her that she would become a social leper. My future father-in-law, the then Dean of Guernsey, (her mother's second husband and himself now remarried to another Carey) absented himself from the island to avoid officiating at our wedding. I, strangely enough, could see their point of view but my wife was furious and her rage was largely concentrated, not on her grandfather, but on her cousin Victor, himself regarded as the local head of the Carey ramification of families. At a later date, Victor's sister, the late Miss Edith Carey, an erudite local historian, so loathed me still that, at the time of the great island controversy as to whether or not we had the moral duty to make an Imperial Contribution in money, she attacked me bitterly in the columns of the Guernsey press for the part I had, as a People's Deputy in the States, played in it and accused me of being a lick-spittle whose principal object was preferment at the hands of a grateful British Government. She was rebuked a few days after in those columns by another Carey (the then Dean of Guernsey) and reminded that 'Noblesse oblige'. I was so hurt and resentful that, when soon afterwards a group of distinguished French savants (including Monsieur Edouard Henriot, then or soon afterwards Prime Minister of France) visited Guernsey and I took them to Miss Edith Carey's home to examine her collection of historical manuscripts, I remained outside during their visit to her. Now as to Mr. Victor Carey himself. He had, I understood been intended for a career in Engineering but changed course in midstream and, instead, studied at Caen University and was called to the Guernsey Bar. Could he be questioned, I am sure that he would not dissent from the view that his legal attainments were slender. Pompous, even arrogant outwardly, with the characteristic Carey irritability, beneath it all he was kind, gentle, generous, compassionate and deeply solicitous for the welfare of Guernsey and its inhabitants. He was also most receptive of advice and acutely aware of his legal limitations. I have often heard his stock joke about himself when meeting other members of the Guernsey Bar. It was: 'Like necessity, I know no law.'

I knew him well for, from my earliest days at the Bar, he was consistently kind to me. And I was his Attorney General during the five years preceding the occupation and for some nine months after it terminated.

In the early days of the occupation, I became increasingly aware of the fact that the Germans regarded me as the top man (which I was not) and that he, the Bailiff and acting British Lieutenant Governor, was becoming increasingly isolated from them. I therefore suggested that I should bring Dr. Lanz, the German Kommandant, to pay a courtesy call on him at his home (they had never met) but not, please notice, a courtesy call by him on Lanz and there was never any question of his returning Lanz's call. He was very dubious as to whether he could receive Lanz with propriety but I (rightly or wrongly and, if wrongly, I accept all the blame) prevailed on him to do so. When approached by me on the matter, Lanz agreed at once and the call was arranged for the following Sunday morning. I was to bring him along and, if my memory serves me aright, the Bailiff asked me to bring my wife. Lanz put on his best uniform and the Bailiff received him with great dignity. I feel sure that, if it did no lasting good as respects the population as a whole, it at least did no harm.

I would say, too, with more than usual emphasis, that no one suffered, as the occupation progressed, more greatly than did the Bailiff from want of food and lack of heating. During the winter of 1942-43 when I was again allowed by the Germans to act as Attorney General for a time, I was struck by his shrunken frame (he had always been a man of generous proportions) as he sat by his empty office grate huddled in a heavy rug and, at the end, his physical condition was pitiable. The usual mode of progression to the office of Bailiff was via those of Contrôle (Solicitor General) and Procureur (Attorney General) but Mr. Victor Carey had held neither of those offices. Further, as H.M. Receiver General in Guernsey for many years and, as such, responsible for receiving and accounting to Their Lords Commissioners of the Treasury in London for the many Crown Dues payable in the Island, he had felt unable to do any criminal work - a member of the Guernsey Bar is obliged to represent any person accused of an indictable offence who chooses him to defend him: he is entitled to charge a fee for this but, in ninety-nine cases out of a hundred, the accused is without the means to pay and, unless acquitted, does not, in the place where he has gone, increase his material prospects to any appreciable extent. In other words, to the advocate, it is an unprofitable chore but an extremely valuable contribution to his legal experience.

Now, with the German occupation, there was no conveyancing and virtually no work in the Courts over which the Bailiff habitually presided. With the creation of the Controlling Committee, the meetings of our States became most infrequent. The Bailiff became almost without occupation to distract his mind.

We held him in reserve, the big gun to be brought to bear on the Germans at the Feldkommandantur only when some more than usually difficult or unpleasant matter was under discussion. I come now to the controversial matters associated with Mr. Victor Carey. These are his address to the States on March 21st, 1941, following the German Bekanntmachung (notice) of the 19th March concerning a 'recent act of sabotage'; his warning in the press about the use of the 'V' sign of the 4th July, 1941, followed on the 9th July, by his offer therein of a reward of £25 for the first information leading to the conviction of anyone posting up the 'V' sign or anything of that nature; and, finally, his notice in the newspapers of August 11th, drawing attention to the German order of October 10th, 1940, which had proclaimed that the penalty for hiding or sheltering escaped prisoners of war or of enemy forces was death. In his notice, the Bailiff, most unfortunately, himself used the expression 'enemy forces' when he was referring to Allied Forces. Now, Ralph Durand, in Chapter XI of 'Guernsey under German Rule' - while highly critical of the foregoing - went to considerable lengths to explain them. Perhaps the Germans had dictated the Bailiff's speech to him. He goes on, after drawing attention to the clumsy wording in some of the notices, to suggest that these and other notices appearing over the Bailiff's signature were drafted by the Germans and put before him for signature. Ralph Durand, not content with this, then goes on: "This theory suggests another. It may be that the German authorities - believing that we might more contentedly heed advice from our leading officials than direct orders from themselves - inspired many of the public utterances of the Bailiff and the successive Presidents (I here insert 'which included Mr. Sherwill') of the Controlling Committee. The Woods, in 'Islands in Danger' suggest that the Bailiff may have been guided, as regards the £25 Reward notice, by the advice of G.J.P. Ridgway, the Solicitor General, a sick man who died not very long afterwards. A friend of Ridgway's wrote them: 'I knew him as an extremely astute lawyer .... here was a bit of cunning that worked well to quieten the Germans. It is exactly the sort of thing he would have done and chuckled over.'"

I read once that history is bunk and after reading the foregoing, I am more than ever persuaded that some of it, - that based on inferences - is. I knew Ridgway for over thirty years and was well acquainted with his drafting. He was very able, very courageous and a skilled draftsman. I discern no sign of his drafting in this. As regards the Germans dictating or drafting the notices, I happen to know that they, themselves, were surprised at the appearance of the reward notice. Victor Carey, when he came to the office of Bailiff was most slenderly equipped for the post. As Attorney General, I have listened to many a summing-up of his in a criminal case. I do not know what effect it had on the prisoner in the dock but I do know that it terrified me. His drafting abilities were very mediocre and his clerk, Louis Guillemette (appointed States Supervisor (Chief of the Guernsey Civil Service) after his outstanding work during the occupation and still occupying that post) and I, jointly and/or severally must have rescued him on scores of occasions from predicaments in his drafting of his forewords in the Billets d'État issued by him when convoking Meetings of the States. I think he was quite unaware of this for he never mentioned the matter and, so excellent were our relations always, I think he would, had he realised it, have expressed his gratitude.

To sum up, I cannot accept that he was made to issue any notice by the Germans or that they prepared notices and put them before him for signature. They certainly never did to me and, in the early days, I was very much more closely in touch with them than he ever was. I am convinced that the true explanation is as follows. He had, month after month and year after year of the occupation, no work to occupy his mind and nothing to do but worry and he worried himself sick, not about himself - that would be quite out of character - but about Guernsey and its people. He deplored - as did we all - the stupid things like painting up 'V' signs and he believed that his speeches and the notices over his signature - that of the acting Lieutenant Governor and Judicial Head of the Island - would deter people from doing foolish things and incurring condign punishment and would serve to warn them that the Germans would exact the extreme penalty in certain cases. That he was clumsy and did not appreciate the effect of his words on his island people I grant you; that he was ever in thought, word or deed, consciously disloyal, I refuse absolutely to accept. Had I ever done so, I would not willingly have served under him as Attorney General from my return from internment in Germany until his retirement from the office of Bailiff. The opinion, bull-dozed out of me by the Permanent Under Secretary of State at the Home Office in June, 1945, was the truth, crudely expressed though it was at a moment when I was quite unprepared for his question. To-day, more than twenty years later, I remain of the same opinion.

I have been very frank in this chapter and what I have said may still give pain to those whom he loved and who loved him. I much hope that it will not and, in particular, I would tell his grandson,[9] now a young member of the Guernsey Bar, that I, old and withered, follow his career with interest and predict a great career for him in it and beyond.

---

[9] Sherwill's prediction has come true. Following a distinguished career, Mr. (Later Sir) de Vic G. Carey was appointed to the Bailiwick's supreme office in 1999.

8

A GUEST OF HITLER'S REICH

In 1940, I was Attorney General in Guernsey and, together with the then Bailiff, the Solicitor-General and the other Crown officials, was instructed to remain in Guernsey and to do my best for the civilian population during the occupation by the German Forces which was then imminent. Had I continued only as Attorney General, it seems probable that some of the rather strange experiences which befell me would not have happened.

I was concerned lest our system of government by committee should prove too cumbersome in the conditions to which we were likely to be subjected and it seemed to me that we should devise some simplified system whereby we might cope swiftly and effectively with any situation that arose. It never occurred to me that I should be the leader for I was a Crown official and, in my view, the leader should be someone who was already in office by the election of the people of the Island. One man, in my view, stood head and shoulders above the others, namely Jurat John Leale (now Sir John Leale). He had a firm grasp of finance and economics and of administration generally whereas my experience was in the different and narrower field of law.

It came to me as a complete surprise when, late one morning, John Leale came to see me and told me that he had called together the other Presidents of States Committees and, with their assent, had already asked the Bailiff to summon an emergency Meeting of the States for that very afternoon and that it was the intention of those he had consulted that, at that Meeting, my name would be put forward as President of a Controlling Committee with power to appoint the members of that Committee. I was reluctant that this should be but John Leale put the matter so forcefully that before he left he had obtained my assent.

The Meeting was held and I was elected with one dissentient vote. I had great respect for the views of the dissentient and, because of this and also because it seemed to me better, in the days ahead, to have him with me rather than against me, I included him in the Controlling Committee in charge of Public Relations. He worked very hard for us until his untimely death, following a grave illness, only a few months later.

If I were to be asked how best I served Guernsey during the unhappy time of the German occupation, the answer is very simple. It was in the calibre of the men I was able to appoint to form the Controlling Committee who served their fellow Islanders so valiantly. As instances: John Leale in charge of Finance; Sir Abraham Lainé in charge of Food Rationing; Aylmer Drake in charge of Horticulture; Raymond Falla in charge of Agriculture; Dr. Symons in charge of Health; Dick Johns of Labour etc.

My departure to prison in Paris and, on my return, the German refusal to allow me to hold any office and then my deportation to Germany, made no difference. Thanks to the Controlling Committee, the affairs of the Island continued to run as efficiently as was possible in the circumstances of the great and growing shortages of most essentials of life.

The Controlling Committee was given something short of plenary powers to run the Island and the States were only called at rare intervals to deal with the most important topics and with taxation. Each member had a specific department and gathered around him the most expert and able subordinates he could find.

The Committee met regularly as a sort of Cabinet and decided the various issues involved and worked as a team.

When the Germans first arrived, they were certain of early complete victory. Officers bought lengths of suiting. They were going to have them made up in Savile Row in London. On July 2, 1940, I was summoned to meet the new Kommandant and, while awaiting him, was invited to sit with an elderly officer of the German Navy, Kapitan Koch. He said that I looked worried and I told him that I was dreadfully worried. How was I going to feed the people of the island in the coming winter? He replied:- "My dear fellow, there's not the slightest reason for you to worry. The war will be over in six weeks and I could, here and now, tell you the exact date in August when it will finish".

Now, the British Government started sending in young Guernseymen serving in the Armed Forces to reconnoitre the position and report back. They were completely untrained in espionage and were sent in in civilian clothes so that, if caught, they were subject to be shot as spies under the Laws of War. Some got back safely but it was inevitable, sooner or later, that some would be trapped. By stealing, from the Germans, British uniforms which they had captured, I was able, with help, to put two British officers who had landed as civilians into uniform and thus secure that they were treated as prisoners of war and not as spies. Later, two other officers in similar circumstances were supplied with uniforms, though not by me personally although I was kept informed about them. Unfortunately, the Germans got to know about them not, I think, by any act of treachery but because of loose talk, and a devil of a row blew up and the whole of the facts came out. All those who had helped them were popped in gaol in Guernsey, I was placed under house arrest with two officers who would not let me out of their sight and we were eventually sent to the Cherche Midi Prison in Paris, to await trial.

Now the German Commander in Guernsey, a straightforward and, indeed, genial soldier, had undertaken that, for a limited time, any members of the British Armed Forces who might still be in Guernsey would be treated as prisoners of war if they gave themselves up and that no one who had harboured them would be harmed.

It was a Heaven sent opportunity to save the lives of the two officers in question and they gave themselves up on that understanding. What the German Commandant did not know when he gave his undertaking was that British officers had infiltrated in civilian clothes. Nevertheless, when eventually he learned the truth, he stood by his word and claimed that his honour was at stake. It would take too long to tell the whole story. Suffice it that the Commander in Chief of the Channel Islands stood by him and managed to secure that the two officers should be treated as prisoners of war and that all the rest of us should be released. If he had not, it is unlikely that I should now be writing these words.

Our incarceration in the Cherche Midi Prison (it was the one in which Capt. Dreyfus had been imprisoned before being sent to the Île des Diables) was a very grim experience. Semi-starvation and solitary confinement and the intense cold of the last months of 1940 brought us very low. I, of course, knew nothing of the efforts made on our behalf. To appreciate our situation, it has to be remembered that Germany was everywhere victorious, the Americans were not yet in the War, the invasion of England seemed still probable and the War likely to go on for years, long after my companions and I had died in prison from malnutrition or had been bumped off. It was with some relief that we reached St. Peter Port Harbour once more.

Needless to say, after this I was not persona grata to the Germans and it was only in August, 1942, when the Solicitor General died, that they allowed me to return to the job of Attorney General again.

Then, in February, 1943, some two hundred of us from Guernsey and a rather smaller contingent from Jersey were deported. There had been an earlier deportation towards the end of the previous year of those not born in the Channel Islands. This time, it appeared that those selected were potential trouble makers and officers of the first World War who might be expected to be leaders in case of trouble. After a most unpleasant trip to St. Malo, where we awaited the arrival of the people from Jersey, we entrained and proceeded in a leisurely, but not too uncomfortable, manner through France and Germany and eventually reached a village called Laufen, on the German-Austrian border. At the start of the journey there had been quite a number of women in the party but these were dropped somewhere south of Paris and were taken to a camp at Compiègne where they were kept for many months until they and their husbands, who were with us, were united at Biberach. At Laufen, we joined those who had previously been deported from the Channel Islands. They were by then reasonably well settled in but they had had a very bad time at Dorsten in N.W. Germany, where accommodation and conditions generally had been very bad. Our Lager was a very large schloss or castle which had started life as the country residence of the Prince Archbishops of Salzburg and had then been successively a cavalry barracks, then a prisoner of war camp and now a civilian internment camp. It lay in very picturesque surroundings on the edge of the River Salzach and just across the river lay the little Austrian village where the famous Obendorff carol 'Silent Night, Holy Night' was written and set to music and performed for the first time in the little Church of St. Nicholas. That church had been swept away in the floods of, I think, 1896. (I should explain that the shallow river Salzach, which made a hairpin bend around the village of Laufen, received the melting snow waters of that part of the Bavarian Alps and that, in the spring and in times of torrential rain, - and it was a very rainy district, - would rise as much as twenty feet in a single night.) On the mound of ruins of the old church, the Austrians had built a chapel with stained glass windows commemorating the village priest and schoolmaster who had written and composed the tune of the carol. Although I had no right to go across the bridge into Austria (my pass only allowed me to visit British workers on farms etc. on the German side of the bridge), I sometimes, when feeling really browned off, went across and borrowed the key of the chapel from the village shop opposite it and went in and luxuriated in the peace of mind it seemed to give.

Now, when my party arrived at Laufen, Mr. Frank Stroobant, the Wholesale Merchant of Guernsey whom many of you probably know, was the British Camp Senior who had been elected as such by the British internees. He did his job extremely well and I, for one, was content to settle in as an ordinary internee doing his best to combat the boredom which was inevitable in such a shut-in existence. We were, of course, surrounded by barbed wire with sentries permanently posted. Being herded together seems to bring out the best and the worst in human nature and grievances against those in authority crop up all the time. Towards the end of June, 1943, there was an acute temporary shortage of Red Cross parcels and cigarettes and, as the date of the arrival of the next consignment was anybody's guess, Mr. Stroobant decided, very wisely, to cut the issue of cigarettes from 50 weekly to 25. It was a most prudent thing to do in the circumstances. But many of our internees thought otherwise and made such a song and dance about it, that Stroobant, fed up with the continual fault finding, resigned. I was asked to stand for election to succeed him and although I made it plain that I supported him and would have taken exactly the same action in his place, I was elected. Fortunately, new consignments arrived and the situation eased. But, on many subsequent occasions, trouble blew up, even the same trouble, but the only thing to do was to try to do the right thing in the circumstances and let the trouble makers go hang. We had an Advisory Council elected by the head of each room, himself elected by his room mates and whenever a difficult decision had to be taken, I took it with the advice of the Advisory Council.

Now, in our castle, there were really two internment camps each in separate quarters: The British in one part and the American in another, each with its own Camp Senior. Now, you mustn't take the words 'British' and 'American' too literally. Most of our people were British subjects either from the Channel Islands or else picked up all over Europe, including a large contingent from Italy and another from

Greece, hardly any of them speaking any English but, as the children and grandchildren of Britishers who had settled in those countries and had married Italian or Greek girls, in possession of British passports. Then I had an Egyptian Jew, a Persian, and a native of Bethlehem and his two sons born in Berlin of a Viennese mother. One poor chap, who had been picked up in, I think, Czechoslovakia, was mentally deranged and caused me no end of trouble when, one morning, when called down to the German office for something or other, he snatched a picture of Hitler off the wall and threw it on the floor and jumped on it. Believe it or not, the German Commandant was quite annoyed but eventually accepted my explanation that the chap was mad. Perhaps he was saner than the rest of us.

We were about 530 on the British side and on the American side there was approximately the same number. They were, however, a very motley lot and, when the American Army eventually overran our Camp, narrowly beating the Russians to it, and an American Consul General arrived to screen them, there were, how many do you think, United States citizens? Exactly 17. The rest were mostly Poles, the majority Polish Jews, having in their possession Passports de Protection which they had purchased from the Legations of Costa Rica, Honduras, Panama, etc. etc. Anyhow, it had saved their lives.

In charge of the Camp was a very decent German Colonel, a very pleasant Security Captain who had spent years in America, a Sonderführer who had been educated at Midhurst in Sussex and a dear old German military doctor who really did his best for the sick. The troops who guarded us were mostly very badly wounded soldiers quite unfit for the front line. The German Sergeant Major, Ertl, was a good soldier who put up with a great deal more than any English N.C.O. would have stood. You will be surprised when I tell you that during all the time I was interned, I never saw or heard of a German finger being laid on a single British subject. Knowing what went on in other camps and particularly in the concentration camps, you may well think and you would be right in thinking that we were exceptionally lucky.

The food supplied by the Germans was poor and extremely monotonous but, except for rare intervals, we were well supplied with Red Cross parcels and we were certainly very much better off as regards food than the people we had left behind in the Channel Islands. In the last weeks of the war, when German transport was almost completely disrupted, we expected to have to tighten our belts, for our stock of Red Cross parcels was getting very low and then, to our amazement, two wagon loads of parcels arrived at our village station. Later, the American Tank Company that occupied our village had outrun its supplies and was very short of food and, for some days, I was able to supply them with stuff from our Red Cross stores. When supplies reached them, they were most generous to us giving us cases of eggs, quantities of pastry flour and, if you please, sacks of crushed ice for which we could find no use whatever.

Now, the Swedish Y.M.C.A. were most generous to us and supplied us with masses of books, so that we built up quite a good library, sports and games equipment, drawing and painting materials and a host of other things. And we had an excellent Education Committee and lots of people able to teach a wide variety of subjects. You could take a course in modern Greek or in Italian, or in navigation, or aeroplane construction and lots of other subjects. The camp chores had to be done but with so many people available, they were done on a rota system, except for the camp cooks, who carried on for months at a time. The Poles on the American side did not think much of our British cooking and eventually volunteered to take over the kitchen and we were only too happy to let them, although we had grave reason to suspect that they gave the better parts of the very scruffy meat supplied to us to a little colony of Polish girls who worked in a leather factory in the village.

From time to time, something outstanding would occur and, instead of a drab recital of our day to day existence, it would be more interesting to concentrate on these.

The Stolen Petrol

One Sunday afternoon, the German Security Captain sent for me and told me that an American Jew and his wife, interned at Liebenau, were due for immediate release on repatriation to the U.S.A. as part of an exchange scheme. Their child was in a children's home in the Bavarian foothills and he had orders to retrieve the child and convey it to its parents. The time available in which to do this was excessively short. What did I advise? Now, I don't know to this day why he had consulted me. The child was not even a British subject. I said "It's simple, send your motor ambulance". He said "I've no petrol". I said "Borrow some from the Burgomeister, he must have a reserve". He said "He has but he won't let me have any unless I guarantee to return it; where am I to get petrol?" He went on to tell me that the only plan he could think of was to lash a stretcher between two bicycles and send two soldiers to get the child. We totted up the distance and I said "I doubt if they can do it in the time". Then I had a flash of what I thought to be inspiration. The Representative of the Swedish Y.M.C.A. was due to visit our camp in two days time. He had worked near miracles before on our behalf and I reckoned that he would come to my aid. So I said "Look, while we're talking, precious time is passing. Borrow the petrol from the Burgomeister and I'll replace it". He said "But where will you get petrol?" It was a reasonable enough question. If he couldn't, how on earth could I? I said "I always keep my word". Believe it or not, he borrowed the petrol, sent off the ambulance and the child was restored to its parents.

The next day, I had a letter from the Y.M.C.A. man to say that all his plans had been upset, he had been called back to Sweden and he would have to postpone his visit for at least three months. You can imagine my dilemma. I then remembered that one of our internees, Edgar Guille of Guernsey worked in a local garage. I got hold of him and asked if he could get hold of any petrol. He said his German boss was a stickler for the regulations and all he could do would be to steal a little at a time from the quantity they were allowed for washing engine parts under repair. I said "Will you start stealing this very day and let me know how you get on".

Meanwhile the Burgomeister bothered the Security Captain and the latter kept on at me. I assured him it was only a matter of him being a little patient. He wasn't very impressed but he knew, and I knew, that he couldn't reveal that he had been such a fool as to take my word for it. He would have been a laughing stock.

Many weeks went by and, then, one day, Guille sent me a message that he had amassed the petrol. I went out on my pass, which enabled me to visit the British workers, and reconnoitred to see that the German garage owner was safely off the premises. Then I collected two full jerrycans of petrol and lugged them back to camp. The guards on the gate were a little surprised but let me through with my petrol when I told them it was for the Security Captain. I went to his office and deposited my cans on his office floor. He was delighted but most astonished. He said "But Mr. Sherwill, how did you get it?" I said "It was no part of our bargain that I should tell you that; all I promised was that I would restore the petrol". He gasped a bit but nothing more was said. A child had been rescued from unhappiness and restored to its parents and it seemed to me that, in the circumstances, participation in the crime of larceny was unlikely to be held too strongly against me at the Judgement Day.

The Hostages

You have almost certainly heard of the highly placed British personages that Hitler ordered to be conveyed into the area in the Bavarian hills which was called the Hohenzollern Redoubt in which, it seems, he had proposed to make his last stand against the advancing British, American and Russian troops. The drive by the Americans through the heart of Germany capsized any plans he had as regards this. But I came into touch with them to my intense surprise. Whether Hitler was proposing to use them to try to ensure his own personal safety or not, I have never been able to learn.

One Sunday (things always seemed to happen on a Sunday) there were rumours in our camp that a convoy of French Officer Prisoners of War of high rank were on the point of arriving and in the early evening, a convoy of buses arrived.

The Camp Commandant sent for me and told me that a number of British Officer Prisoners of War had arrived and that they were providing them with a meal but had no drinks to give them. Could I provide them with coffee? I said I could and, the Red Cross stores being locked and one of the two keys being in the possession of a German N.C.O. absent over the weekend, I set about gathering supplies from our various rooms and got the cooks to heat water. The Commandant said I could go in with the coffee and, so far as he was concerned, he had no objections to my chatting to our visitors. They would be leaving after their meal for Tittmoning, a schloss about twenty kilometres away, also under his command, where a large number of Dutch officers were held as prisoners of war.

I found that all the officers had come from Colditz, the super-security P.O.W. camp mostly occupied by persistent would-be escapers. I found them very apprehensive at their probable fate and of the opinion that there was some obscure political motive for their removal from their fellows at Colditz.

Among the party were Viscount Lascelles, now Lord Harewood, the Master of Elphinstone, a cousin of Queen Elizabeth the Queen Mother,

Giles Romilly, Lady Churchill's nephew and young Winant, the son of the then American Ambassador to London. The names of the others now escape me. But with them were General Bor-Komorowski, who led the famous Warsaw revolt in which the appalling battles in the sewers of that city took place, and the whole of his headquarters staff. He was a most cultured man, speaking perfect French.

I promised to do anything I could to get news of the party to the ears of the Protecting Power i.e. Switzerland. The Swiss visited our camp from time to time and I could only await an opportunity for the Germans would certainly not let any letter from me to the Swiss, containing a reference to the party, to leave the camp. From memory, I don't think I was able to get any news of the party to anyone who could protect them.

We were horribly disturbed about them. And then, a most extraordinary thing happened. Sixteen of the party disappeared from their quarters in Tittmoning. The only clue was a rope dangling from a window but it appeared unlikely that they had escaped that way. I understand that our Sgt. Major Ertl, who was rushed off with the Commandant to investigate, swore they couldn't have.

Every inch of Tittmoning Castle was searched. It was even more mediaeval than Laufen with enormous chimneys the size of a small room. After probing everywhere, fifteen were found in a disused chimney where they had secreted themselves with a small supply of food and it turned out that Giles Rommilly and a Dutch officer had escaped. These got clean away and eventually made contact with the advancing American Army. I have never discovered what purpose was sought to be achieved by the others secreting themselves as they did. It seemed completely mad. I have visited Tittmoning since the war and was shown the outside of the chimney (then bricked up) in question and the guide was well acquainted with the story.

Then orders came to our Germans from above that an officers' camp was to be created in the centre of our internment camp and passages were bricked up and masses of wire erected and the whole party were brought to Laufen. There were the strictest orders that we were to make no attempt to communicate with the officers but within about an hour we were in communication and we were able to supply them with cigarettes and tobacco with the German's consent.

About two or three weeks later a rumour reached me that the hostages were being moved the following morning for an unknown destination. I was intensely disturbed and finally decided to beard the Luftwaffe Captain who was in charge of the guard over them. I went to his office that afternoon and told him I knew what was on foot and asked him to tell me where he was taking them. I expected him to kick me out of the room but he didn't. I got the impression that he was very concerned himself about the whole matter. He said to me: you have obviously got hold of information which you ought not to have but I will not lie to you. We are leaving to-morrow but it is as much as my head is worth to tell you where we are going. I can see that you are greatly concerned about these officers. I will tell you this: I have my orders from my general not to let any of these officers fall into the hands of the S.S. or the S.A. and I give my word that I and my men will die to the last man before that happens. He was obviously sincere and I was slightly relieved. But whether these fellows were eventually going to have a very sticky end on Hitler's orders was another matter. As you know, they were found safe and well, when Germany finally collapsed, at a place called St. Johann.

The Camp Is Searched By The Bavarian Criminal Police

On or about the 12th March, 1945, our Camp Guards, headed by Oberfeldwebel Ertl, made a systematic search of every room in the camp. They also searched the vast chimneys in our schloss. They collected basketsful of prohibited articles including stills for making alcohol out of Red Cross raisins. One room, in particular, had a bedside lamp to every bed and, as our electric circuits were so overloaded that fuses blew nearly every night, these lamps were taken away.

In the German office, it was clear that they were in a dither but I could get no indication from them of what was afoot.

Then the Sonderführer sent for me and said: "We know you have a wireless set because of the things some of your people write in their letters home, things that they couldn't have possibly known unless they heard them on the B.B.C. We've searched but we haven't been able to find it. You have a wireless, haven't you?" I said: "I wouldn't know." "No", he said, "I understand you can't tell me. Well something is going to happen - I can't tell you what - but if a wireless set should be found, it will probably mean that the Commandant and I and the others will be removed and replaced by the S.S. Would you like that?" I said: "Heavens, no." "Well", he said, "I very strongly advise you to hand me your wireless." "Well", I said, "if I should find we have one and hand it to you, what will you do with it?" He said: "I'll lock it in that cupboard and hand it back when it's safe to do so." I said: "You give me your word on that?" And he replied: "I do."

I went back and had a conference with Frank Stroobant who was responsible for running the set and he saw the chaps who worked with him and, eventually, they handed it over to me on the basis that I would go out of camp on my pass, and place it in a secret hide-out. I could not tell them I was going to hand it to the Germans for they would never have believed that we would get it back. I arranged to meet the Sonderführer in his office at, if I remember rightly, 1 p.m. He had warned me: Not a word to the Security Captain, he's not wicked but much too nervous to take part in this. The wireless was in a haversack and concealing it under a mackintosh over my left arm, down I went to my rendez-vous. The Sonderführer wasn't there but the Security Captain was. It was an awkward moment. The Captain was most affable and wanted to know what he could do for me and said he could attend to what it was just as well as the Sonderführer. I somehow managed to extricate myself, leaving him intensely puzzled. I went back to my room. In spite of what I thought I knew of him, had the Sonderführer tricked me? It couldn't very well be that for if he had arranged a trap for me, there would have been an armed guard waiting with the Security Captain ready to seize the wireless set and me. I was looking out of the window, very disturbed indeed, when I saw the Sonderführer return. Minutes later, the Security Captain left. I went down again. All that had happened was that the Sonderführer's wife had been a little late in giving him his lunch and his late return had held up the Security Captain's departure for his lunch. The Sonderführer had nerves of iron and he laughed heartily when he heard of my discomfiture. I handed over the set and then, mackintosh still over my shoulder, went out on my pass watched, I am sure, by the eyes of the wireless team. I stayed out for an hour and on my return announced that I had hidden the set in an extremely safe place.

Nothing more happened for a couple of days and all the information I could get in my enquiries at the German office was that what was going to happen hadn't happened yet. My wireless team began to get impatient with me but I told them they really must trust me. Clearly, they didn't.

Then, on the 17th March, 1945, it happened.

We were just finishing breakfast in our room when we saw two huge lorries drive into the convent across the road which housed our camp guards. The outer gates were closed behind the lorries but from our upstairs window we saw the lorries disgorge a large number of uniformed men. They must have been packed into the lorries like sardines. I said to my room-mates: "Chaps, this is it". It turned out it was a detachment of Bavarian Criminal Police.

Whistles blew to summon us on parade and we were made to stand with our hands crossed in front of us (it had never happened before) while the Commandant, for the benefit of the visitors, put on a fine show barking orders at us. He never did it before or afterwards.

Then we were marched away by rooms to strip and be searched. Meanwhile, our rooms were being minutely searched. They threw everything in our lockers, including a minute quantity of coal that we had saved during the winter, on to the floor. I told you that the search a few days before had produced baskets of contraband but this was nothing to what was now unearthed. Finally, having finished their job, a conference was held in the room in which, locked in a cupboard, reposed our wireless set. They then drove away.

The next day, I went down to the German office and asked if I might have our wireless set. The Sonderführer unlocked his cupboard and handed it to me. I said: "Is it just as I handed to you?" He said: "It is, but I don't mind telling you that I was very curious and have had a good look at it." It was in action again that night and, believe it or not, within the next few days, all the contraband so carefully collected was handed back to us. I must qualify that: so far as I remember they kept the bedside lights and wiring.

We were very puzzled at the whole business and the best explanation I ever had was this: One of our internees worked in the village for the local butcher and, in the village inn, under the influence of drink, had bragged that lots of firearms were concealed in our camp. I understand that quite a number of villagers were of the opinion that our Commandant was too soft with us and were only too ready to report anything indicating that we were desperate characters. The police found no firearms, for we had none, so thorough was their search that it seems to me likely that they would have found the wireless set, the possession of which was, of course, prohibited, and the finding of which would have brought considerable trouble, possibly to us but more likely to the German Camp staff.

I actually went to Berlin, under guard, on the 15th Jan. 1945, and got back to camp three days later. It is the only time I was ever there. It was an interesting but exhausting experience. It was in connection with the repatriation of sick and infirm internees and I am glad to say that it resulted in the repatriation to the Channel Islands of some two dozen of our worst cases. The damage in Berlin from our bombing was devastating but, to my astonishment, the people I saw did not appear to be in too bad fettle. Conditions, though, were such that, for the only time, I was delighted to get back to camp after my journey. I shall tell the whole story in the next Chapter.

About twenty-four hours before we were finally relieved by the American Army, the German General in command of all the P.O.W. and Internee camps in our region arrived in our camp. All his other camps had already been captured and he came to us to await capture himself. He sent for me, as British Camp Senior, and said: "It is only a matter of hours before you are liberated. Is there anything I can do to alleviate your conditions meanwhile?" Surprising as it may sound to you, I couldn't think of anything. I had actually left the room he was in when it occurred to me that it would be fine to get the B.B.C. openly and all the time on the German set in the canteen. The news purveyed to us on it had been the German news in English. So back I went and asked for it. My request was immediately granted and I went along to the canteen to check up that his order was being carried out. You can imagine my feelings when, within minutes, the B.B.C. came on and almost immediately the voice of Churchill saying "and to-morrow, our dear Channel Islands will be free".

And, believe it or not, in Guernsey, listening on a minute crystal set, one of the many that our son, Joly, had made, was my wife, who was even more thrilled than I was, to hear these words.

9

MY WINTER VACATION - TRIP TO BERLIN IN JANUARY 1945

To make this Chapter intelligible, I must go back to May, 1944. I then received a circular letter from the Protecting Power (Switzerland) advising me that a Scheme of Exchange between British and German Civilian Internees was under way. I treated it as a serious communication (I am, by nature, gullible) likely to be followed by results in the near future and, having informed the Camp (my stock as Camp Senior rose enormously for a short period but plummeted to a new low when nothing further happened), I set aside a large notice board in our main hall on which I expected to post the many further communications I would receive.

When the following January arrived and precisely nothing more had happened, my views and those of my co-internees can be imagined.

I exaggerate when I say 'precisely nothing more had happened' for two things had.

After many months I received a letter one morning to the effect that a definite exchange had been arranged between five British Indians in our camp and five Germans who had been picked up in the Yemen. Now, these Indians had been merchants in Gibraltar and just before the outbreak of war, they had taken ship to India. Unluckily, their ship had been intercepted and sunk by the "Admiral Scheer" almost in sight of Bombay. They had been taken on board the German raider and conveyed to Germany and - until they were transferred to us - had been interned at Milag Nord. The climate there and at Laufen had done nothing to raise their spirits and they suffered from deep depression at their long incarceration.

I nearly ran, therefore, to break the glad news to them.

I need not have bothered for, that same day, by a later post, came another letter from the same source intimating that the Indian - Yemeni German exchange had fallen through. This time I did not hasten to convey the news to those whom it most affected.

Anyhow, in January 1945, a visit to the Camp by Representatives of the Protecting Power was expected at any moment and the American

Camp Senior and I had decided that, when they arrived, we would take the matter up with them with the utmost vigour.

They arrived on January 15th and we did. They were most sympathetic but explained that their particular department had nothing to do with repatriation and that they had no information to give us. They said: "You should see Dr. Frei in Berlin". We replied: "A fat chance we have of seeing Dr. Frei in Berlin!" They then said: "We will go and speak to the Kommandant about it". Mr. Gompertz and I laughed and sat down to wait for them to return discomfited. On their return they told us, to our amazement, that the Kommandant had said: "If I ask my superiors, they say 'No'. Therefore I do not ask them. I give permission myself" and they told us that he would issue military railway warrants for the express to Berlin leaving Salzburg soon after 8 p.m. that evening. They themselves would lend us their Swiss Legation car to get to Salzburg from Laufen.

Around six o'clock we were standing in the outer courtyard of our "schloss" talking amiably to the Kommandant while we awaited the arrival of the car. Out of the corner of his eye he suddenly observed one of the guard coming on duty behaving sloppily and 'tore a terrible strip off him'. He at once resumed the conversation with us in the most friendly terms. He said to me, pointing to an Obergefreiter (Corporal) standing by, "You know him?". I said: "Yes, nice chap". (He was an Austrian hairdresser from Vienna). The Kommandant continued: "I send him with you not so much to guard you as to serve you. Use him as you will". I need hardly say how useful this soldier was in straightening our path for us.

There was deep snow and our car slithered its way to Salzburg where the military police took charge of us and arranged to put us in a reserved compartment before the train came into the station to pick up passengers.

Feeling it prudent to visit a certain place before embarking on the long journey (I knew my way for I had occasionally been to Salzburg to visit our sick in the hospital there) I stepped out confidently and narrowly missed a nasty fall in the dark when I suddenly discovered that a considerable length of the platform and the haven where I would be had been removed by the recent British bombing we had heard from our camp.

We got under way on time and soon realised that there was a disturbance in the corridor jammed tight with standing passengers and suit-cases - so tight in fact that I doubt if any could sit on them. The Obergefreiter investigated and told us that the passengers were incensed that their government should have provided luxurious accommodation for dirty foreigners while leaving good Germans to stand for some thirty-six hours. He had explained to them, with incredible tact, that we were very important prisoners going to Berlin on a special mission which would result in a lot of German prisoners of war being repatriated. "Ah!" said the discontented, "That was different" and they accepted the situation with the utmost grace. And then I saw standing in the corridor a poor old woman and a young woman with an infant in arms and said to the Obergefreiter, "Look, this can't go on, let them come in". They did, with much politeness, and so, too, did others including a Sergeant in the S.S. - for whom I had not bargained - and his young wife (on honeymoon, as I learned) until the compartment was packed! I felt that it might be imprudent to take exception to the Sergeant's presence (it would certainly have been impolitic for he, later, produced a bottle of wine for general consumption) and my only cause for regret was the baby who cried virtually without ceasing throughout the long journey. Without any human loving kindness whatever, I tried what effect a little Red Cross chocolate might have on the child. It worked. Hardening my heart against thoughts of what the British Red Cross would say if they could see me intent on nourishing a German baby, I popped minute pieces of chocolate into the brat's mouth throughout the journey. I realised vaguely how very bad it was for the child and could not have cared less. The silence which resulted after each application was most rewarding and I believe that, as time went on, the brat cried not out of misery but to get more of my chocolate. The mother made no attempt to restrain me. She appeared to be at the end of her tether concerning the child, and, as I was, too, she and I got on admirably.

Engrossed as I was in contemplating with approval the Christian rectitude with which I had behaved to the enemy populace in their hour of need, I gradually became conscious of the growing urgency of an early visit to the small compartment at the end of the corridor. When it could be postponed no longer, I threaded my way through the densely packed multitude in the corridor. The train was travelling at high speed and its swaying was such as to make it difficult to avoid treading on tender portions of German anatomy. I succeeded and, turning sharp left, was rendered speechless with dismay at finding my objective occupied by three young Luftwaffe officers, two seated on their suitcases and one - presumably the senior - resting on a more solid foundation. I looked at them and they looked at me and then one of them - he who sat upon the throne - said with a charming grin: "Ah! we get out for the big Englishman". Presumably the news of my love for his people had reached him and I was now to receive my reward. When I emerged from the Luftwaffe strongpoint, I bowed gravely to each of them with a 'danke schön' and they, in turn, grinned all over their faces.

Except that we stopped in cuttings on one or two occasions on account of bombing, the journey was uneventful. On arrival, we took the Underground, working faultlessly, to the Parizer Platz station and walked across to our destination, the Swiss Legation housed in what had been the American Embassy near the Brandenburger Tor. At Laufen, the Swiss had told us that, although the Legation had been badly damaged by bombing, there remained two or three guest rooms and they were sure we would be put up for the night. The concierge sitting in the open swathed in coats and mufflers, told us that our people had been over two nights before and had dropped a land mine quite close and that, as we could see for ourselves, there remained nothing habitable and he had not the slightest idea what could be done for us. Then the Air Raid Alarm blew and we were escorted along pavements strewn with shattered glass to a deep shelter. I was surprised to see how well nourished and apparently cheerful the people in it were and noted the disciplined bearing of a squad of armed police also taking shelter there. After some time the "All clear" went (there was no bombing of Berlin that night) and we emerged.

On our return to the Legation we were told that they had 'phoned the Hotel Adlon to see if we could be given a meal and had been told: "Don't send them here, we have absolutely nothing" and that for the night, if we didn't mind, they could put us up in the Legation cellars. We said we didn't mind anything and, by this time, we really didn't. After much telephoning, they announced that they had arranged for us to be given a meal at a 'Soldatenheim' (a sort of N.A.A.F.I.) about a mile away. We were conducted thither by our Obergefreiter and had an execrable meal free of charge and were then given a cup of 'real' coffee (a great luxury in Berlin at the time) by a 'grateful' German Army. I had never previously witnessed such destruction. Whole streets seemed to have been enveloped in vast fires and there was not a pane of glass intact anywhere. The next day, I was shown Dr. Goebbel's house. It had received a direct hit.

I slept soundly but when I awoke in the cellars I got the shock of my life for my bed was surrounded by German soldiers. I took an extremely dim view of my situation. I need not have worried. Apparently, there were masses of soldiers in Berlin recovering from wounds on the Eastern front and these, still on light duty, had been detailed to help the Legation staff in clearing up the mess left by the recent bombing.

After a 'café complet', I went by underground passages to the offices in the basement being used by Dr. Frei and, learning that he was frightfully busy and that I might have to wait quite a time to see him, I sat down to do so. Noon came and passed and the woman clerk in the outer office said to me in perfect English: "It may be hours before Dr. Frei can see you, why don't you go out and get something to eat?" I told her I had come hundreds of miles to see Dr. Frei and that I didn't propose to move from the office till I had done so. She then offered me a delicious apple and, getting her empathetic assurance that she could spare it, I accepted it with gratitude for it was the first one I had seen, let alone tasted, for about two years. I then said to her: "Your English is perfect; were you at school in England?" and she replied: "I was English but I married a German boy". I did not dare to ask what had happened to him lest the answer should be that he had been killed.

Eventually, I saw Dr. Frei and he told me that the repatriation delay was due to the fact that women and children were being exchanged first but that they had reached the men and that if I could there and then give him a list of twenty-four of our old and chronic sick internees, he would include them in the next repatriation party. (The 24 actually left Laufen for Jersey and Guernsey on February 26th, only six weeks later, and arrived safely.)

I was quite unprepared for such a request but sat down to do my best to prepare a list of those I thought the most urgently in need of repatriation and, on my return to Camp, I showed a copy of my list to Dr. Schichofer, our elderly German Camp Doctor. I was intensely relieved when he said, no doubt partly out of kindness: "I could not have done better myself".

The American Camp Senior and I spent a pleasant evening with the concierge (a Polish citizen formerly employed by the American Embassy) and his very rotund German wife who gave us a very good meal. They showed us a huge globe of the world in what had been the principal room in the Embassy. Standing on it with wings outstretched there had been a magnificent American Eagle but a bomb splinter had neatly removed it. "Was this" they enquired "a bad omen?".

They told us how terrible life in Berlin was with the incessant air raids, of how, on occasion, when vast fires were raging, it was virtually impossible to breathe at ground level and, in particular, of the night of terror when we had, presumably in error, bombed the Berlin Zoo and released the lions, crazed with terror, and how the S.S., armed with machine guns, had had to be turned out to shoot them.

Then back we went by Underground to the station for our return journey. As we stood on the platform at which we expected to board the train, it came in at another and there followed a frantic rush to it to get seats. In the process I got separated from the two others and, without any identity papers, wondered what would happen to me if there was a check on those boarding the train. I managed to struggle aboard but we were well on our journey (it was a very long train) before I was able to discover the Obergefreiter and give myself into custody. At dawn the next morning, I became aware of the pulse of mighty pistons and, walking down the deserted corridor to the rear of the train, emerged on an observation platform. We were mounting a long incline and were being pushed by a very powerful engine, its pulse was so pronounced where I stood that it almost threw one off balance. There then appeared by my side a private soldier with a sense of fun for, pointing to a rifle standing against the guard-rail (which, to my shame, I had not noticed) he said, in German: "Your rifle?". Of course, I should have replied "Ja, Ja" and watched his reaction. Instead, missing the boat as usual, I said: "Nein". I then offered him a Red Cross cigarette and from his reiterated "Super", I gathered that we must be winning the war after all. After many, many hours (28 in all) we reached Salzburg, got a local train to Laufen station and arrived back in camp at about midnight. Berlin had been an abomination of desolation and never have I been more glad to reach a chosen destination than I was to be safely restored to my internment camp. It is ironic that this should be so but truth compels me to admit this strange fact.

10

DIARY KEPT IN ILAG VII LAUFEN 29/6/43 TO 3/6/45.

29/6/43   Elected British Camp Senior.

307 votes out of possible 456.

11 spoilt papers or no vote.

2.7.43.   Discharged from Revier & took over C.S.'s duties. Mr. Skingle returned unopposed as Deputy Camp Senior.

1.7.43.   Advisory Council formed. 5 Camp members whether Room Seniors or not. This approved by Camp. To be elected by Room Seniors.

Elected: Flint   President

Allin   Secretary

Wilcock

Boalch

Langlois

2.7.43.   Wynne Sayer and Flint resigned from Camp Tribunal (Wolfenden had resigned previously) to facilitate reconstruction. Camp procedure is that Room Seniors elect members of Tribunal, 3 in number. Accordingly, I have to-day requested Mr. Allin, President of Room Seniors, to convene meeting to nominate and elect members of Tribunal.

Made representations that Wireless and Loud Speaker sent from Feldkommandantur 515 (probably by Dr. Pelz) be fitted up.

3.7.43.   Boxing Tournament. Excellent show including Exhibition Fights between Raphaelito and Billy Bennett and Timms and Perriam.

During the week, as the result of great enthusiasm, organising ability and the great generosity on the part of Camp members, some RM.1000 have been collected for the Jersey and Guernsey Help the Children Funds. In addition, at the Boxing Tournament and afterwards, further sums have been promised for the same purposes.

5.7.43.   2 p.m.   Attended Advisory Committee Meeting which approved draft of letter to International Red Cross, Geneva, on subject of creation of reserve stock. Hitherto the Advisory Committee had formed part of Education Committee. It now recommends that Messrs. R. Wolfenden, Wynne Sayer and D.H. Savage be henceforth members of the Education Committee.

9.7.43.   Received visit from Mr. Berg, the Representative of the Y.M.C.A.

Mr. Berg has placed orders for

> Playing Cards
>
> Timber, Lathe and Tools
>
> 2000 Boxes of Matches
>
> Pipe cleaners
>
> 50 Tin Openers
>
> 100 Prs. Sun Spectacles

He was asked to procure Needles for use in Book binding, Exercise Books and manuscript paper, also some box files for Camp Senior's office. He also undertook to endeavour to obtain mat making materials (canvas etc.) and 100 prs of Ice Skates and Ice Hockey equipment including 30 sticks and a few Goalkeeper's Sticks and Pucks.

His next visit will be at the end of August. He will try to give ample notice of the date of his arrival and proposes to spend the day at the Camp watching Camp activities.

N.B.   Special preparations should be made to enable him to see as many Camp activities as possible.

He greatly praised the Report on Camp activities dated 21st June 1943 forwarded to the Y.M.C.A. by Mr. Stroobant and asked that similar reports should be prepared and forwarded half-yearly.

(N.B.   Next report to cover period up to 31/12/43.)

Mr. Berg has recently visited Oflag VIIB and had an opportunity of discussing the matter of the gift of RM.6000 to Laufen Camp and of RM.4000 to Tittmoning Camp. He made it clear that the RM.6000 sent to us was not intended only for the British Internees but for the benefit of all internees therein whether British or not. (Presumably, therefore, the 4000 RM for Tittmoning (where there are no British Internees) is for the benefit of Internees there without distinction or nationality).   The gift is to be used as may be decided in the Camp <u>but it is not intended for distribution among internees.</u>

It is possible to obtain books of all kinds through Y.M.C.A.   When writing Y.M.C.A. with list of books required, the censorship control in Camp Office will ensure that all books ordered will be acceptable to German Authorities and that none will be rejected on arrival.

7.7.43.	Meeting of Advisory Council.

Education Committee,   filling of Vacancies.   Deferred pending receipt of views of remaining members of Education Committee.

Red Cross Clothing Distribution.   Recommended: That all distribution of Clothing, Footwear etc. (except articles of special use) should be made in accordance with the needs of Internees.

(N.B. I concur AJS).

12.7.43.	Camp Senior appointed Major E.M. Langlois and Mr. H.F. Le Lievre as Black-out Inspectors and informed Room Seniors that he held the latter responsible for the efficient black-out of their rooms and for making such arrangements in that respect as are necessary. As regards Laundry Building, Mr. McQuade has undertaken responsibility for the Black-out. AJS
13.7.43.	Notices re. stealing of vegetables from Camp Garden and re. prohibition of use of Bathroom and Washroom between 10 p.m. and 5 a.m. posted.

13.7.43.   Despatched to Gy. and Jy. forms of authority re. Help the Children Funds Donations through Banks and P.O.

13.7.43.   Meeting of Advisory Council. Recommendations:-

(1)   That the Education Committee be composed henceforth as follows:-

(a)   One member of the Advisory Council to ensure liaison between that Committee and the Advisory Council.

(b)   Four persons (3 British and 1 American) specially interested in and qualified to further education in this Camp.

(c)   Three Teachers to be elected by the Staff of Teachers.

(d)   Mr. M. Cooper, the Education Officer, ex-officio.

(2)   That the Camp Senior forthwith appoints the Members referred to in (a) and (b) above and that Mr. Cooper be asked to arrange for the election of the Teacher Members.

(3)   That the Camp Senior express to Mr. Cooper the thanks of the Camp for his valuable and untiring work in regard to Education in this Camp.

15-16.7.43. Air Raid Alarm 2.15 a.m. Proceeded to Shelters on ground floor.

18.7.43.   Notified by Education Officer that the following 3 Teachers have been elected as Members of the Education Committee by the Teaching Staff:-

1343 M. Troman	12 votes
326 W.H. Kennett	11 votes
1344 M. Maclaren	10 votes

AJS

19.7.43.   Visit of M. Friedrich the representative of the International Red Cross Committee. See Report dated

	20.7.43. submitted to Advisory Council and Room Seniors' meeting and posted on Notice Board.

20.7.43.   Decided outside workers shall receive a food parcel per week.

AJS

22.7.43.   Lieut. Colonel F. Stevenson O.B.E. South African, Corps of Signals, taken at Tobruk, arrived in Camp awaiting escort to Italy.

30.7.43.   Advisory Council recommended gift of RM.80 to 598 USA Internee Jacob van Dougue on his release from interment on recommendation of American Camp Senior.

AJS

Do British Internee 1175 McCulloch H. RM.50 on loan.

AJS

31.7.43.   Borrowed 8 R.C. Terry Towels from Revier to issue to Btsh Niederstrass workers; towels borrowed to be replaced by Clothing Committee when access to Clothing Store can be obtained.

AJS

2.8.43.   Loaned RM. 50 to 1175 H. McCulloch to be repaid through States Supervisor Guernsey.

Repaid /12/43.

5.8.43.   Reveille for Departures 4.30 a.m. B'fast 5 a.m. Examination of hand luggage and return of issue articles 6 a.m. Left Camp 7 a.m. Departures for Biberach & (1) for Wurzach left Laufen Station at about 8.30 a.m. Camp Senior and Major E.M. Langlois, W. Arrowsmith and Mr. Wilcock saw them off. "40 hommes" to Freilassing, then passenger coach. Lt. Col. Stevenson also left for the Brenner Pass by train at 8.50 a.m. Said goodbye to him on platform.

5.8.43.   Rec' first next of kin parcel from Posy. Contents intact. A delightful surprise.

11.8.43.	One hour in basement last night. Party of 5 Br and Americans (including House) left for Vittel.
12.8.43.	Rec' 420 cigarettes from Lieut. P. Martel.
13.8.43.	Despatched Vitamins, Choc. and Cigarettes to Vaudin, Granville for May.
16.8.43.	1020 Lingshaw J.G. (of Jersey) saw me and explained very frankly the nature of the work he is undertaking in Berlin. He is to coach 15 girls in English. I ascertained that these girls are to be employed in some connection by the German Radio propaganda service. I explained to Mr. Lingshaw that, in my view, such work was incompatible with his duty as a British subject, that I should be compelled to regard him as a renegade Englishman and that he should consider the matter carefully. The interview was entirely without acrimony on either side. I also told him that I would on no account issue any Red Cross parcel to him or for forwarding to him after his departure. I further interviewed Sonderführer Gallhöfer and informed him, with Mr. Lingshaw's permission, of what I had said.
17.8.43.	I again saw Sonderführer Gallhöfer and repeated that I would on no account issue a Red Cross parcel henceforth to Mr. Lingshaw and he assured me he would never ask me to do so. Lingshaw left Camp to-day for Berlin.
17.8.43.	With approval of Advisory Council Mr. E. Vanderpool (Vice Mr. C.L. House) transferred to Vittel and Mr. H. Pierre appt. to Education Council, thus increasing American representation from 1 to 2 thereon.
21.8.43.	Doig, Lean and Skinner for Guernsey accompanied by Reid and Cranch, and Chapman, Morley & Proteau for Jersey accomp' by Brennan and Campbell left in charge of Oberjäger Knauer at 9.05 a.m. from Laufen Station en route to St. Malo via Ulm and Paris. Train (7.50 a.m.) running 75 minutes late. Wellborne, Ward, Boalch and I saw them off. Sfhr. Oswald in charge of embarkation.

| 22.8.43. | Local festival with armed bands passing down river and ferry, sham fights in neighbourhood and Band in scarlet. Schifferschutzen Tag 22.8.43. |

22.8.43.   Local festival with armed bands passing down river and ferry, sham fights in neighbourhood and Band in scarlet. Schifferschutzen Tag 22.8.43.

23.8.43.   Rec' 3000 food parcels as reserve to be utilised in accordance with instructions contained in letter dated the 16th Aug 1943.

27.8.43.   Visit of Messrs. RODOLPH BURCKHARDT and RUDOLF E. DENZLER, Attachés, representatives of the Protecting Power. Arrived 8.30 a.m. Met them at 9 a.m. Detailed visit of Camp. Conference $1^1/_2$ hrs between Mr. McQuade and myself and Representatives. Discussed position in C.I. Was promised representations to Swiss Minister in Berlin.

See my memo of 17.VIII.1943.

30.8.43.   Mr. Weissmann, A.J. No. 1121 died 4 a.m.

2.9.43   Funeral of Mr. Weissmann Laufen Cemetery 10 a.m. Both Camp Seniors - Father Cherie Zaberwoski officiating - 16 Internees attended. Two lovely wreaths 1 of which was from our Camp.

2.9.43.   Mr. Berg's visit (World's Alliance of Y.M.C.A.s) See detailed report in file.

6.9.43.   Report from Sports Council re. Le Breuilly, Houillebecq, Moss and Le Riche for insulting behaviour at Football Match on 2.8.43. Accused elected to take my award. Debarred them from Island until 1/10/43. Note Houillebecq acquitted.

8.9.43.   Dunkley went out to Niederstrass.

7.9.43.   Investigated assault by Guille on Wilkinson.

8.9.43.   Reviewed written evidence and recommended to Kommandant 48 hrs in close confinement.

9.9.43.   Sonderführer Gallhöfer photographed groups on Island.

11.9.43.   Interview with Kommandant. Camp Senior to have virtual freedom.

13.9.43.	873 Herrington P.F. taken seriously ill and transferred to Laufen Hospital.
7.9.43.	Camp Senior heard charge against 1085 E.J. Guille, Room 86 of assaulting 1156 Eric Wilkinson of the same room and sentenced Guille to 2 days close confinement and passed papers to German Kommandant. German Kommandant in due course gave effect to Camp Senior's decision.
21.9.43.	1026 Le Breuilly, S. 1027 Moss. S. - 1024 Marie. K were tried by Camp Senior with a jury of 7 persons drawn from a panel selected by the Advisory Council. Marie found not guilty of charges against him. Le Breuilly and Moss found guilty of certain of the offences charged against them and not guilty of others. Le Breuilly and Moss sentenced to loss of 2 Red Cross parcels and 2 weeks cigarettes each. Mr. D. Savage prosecuted and Mr. G. Frazer defended.
27.9.43.	Visited Castle Trierbach.
20.9.43.	Camp Senior and Deputy (Mr. Eveson) granted personal passes for certain districts 8 a.m. - 5 p.m. Must be in Camp on week-days other than Saturdays by 5.30 p.m. on Saturdays 5 p.m. and on Sundays by noon.
1.10.43.	Did the Grand Tour including Sillersdorf. About 23 miles.
12.10.43.	Instructed Mr. Ayres to give American C.S., 1 Btsh R.C. parcel and 50 cigarettes for Mr. Welch of Tittmoning in gratitude for his work on piano. Also to reimburse American C.S., 2 R.C. parcels in respect of American issue to Refail and Fraser on first arrival. N.B. They then received no cigarettes from American C.S.
24.10.43.	Party of 14 British subjects arrived in Camp from Italy, having travelled extensively in Germany.
28.10.43.	Hutchesson, Fisk, Dale and Russell left Camp 7 a.m. on transfer to Tost, Silesia (following upon their attempted escapes).

2.11.43.	Party of 11 (6 Guernsey & 5 Jersey) left on repatriation on medical grounds accompanied by Sanitäters P. Treanor, Bransbury (on 1 month's leave) and 6 porters.
5.11.43.	Party of 16 British Nationals from Albania arrived in Camp - were housed temporarily in 66 and 84.
6.11.43.	Party of 100 Italians arrived in Camp and were housed in 64 and 32 and 32A. They are headed by Gabrio Sigray di San Marzano, Italian Consul, Mattacotta, de Rege & Paulucci, adherents to the Badoglio Govt. 1132 Raisse arrived in Camp from Stuttgart and 1133 Lomax, L. from Prague.
10.11.43.	Visit of Representatives of Protecting Power, Messrs. Edmond A. Navelle, Attaché, and Rudolf E. Denzler, Attaché.
11.11.43.	Placed flowers on graves of 2 Officers and 1 L/Cpl. and Solomon and Weissmann in Laufen Cemetery. Padre Gerhold, L. Hewkin and I observed the 2 minutes silence by the graves.
9.11.43.	First film show (4 German culture films from Munich).
13.11.43.	Dr. Roscoe and Messrs. Honey, Burgess and French arrived from Wurzach.
15.11.43.	Snow.
22.11.43.	The 100 Italians left for Venice via Vienna. di San Marzano, Mattacotta, de Rege and Paulucci called on me 21.11.43. to say au revoir.
26.11.43.	Mr. Berg paid visit 9 a.m. - 4.30 p.m.
11.12.43.	Bentley transferred to Laufen Hospital.
14.12.43.	Bentley transferred to Salzberg Hospital.
20.12.43.	Tetley to Salzberg for observation (Diphtheric Throat).
26.12.43.	1319 H. Bentley died 6.30 a.m. at Salzberg Hospital.
29.12.43.	Funeral of 1319 H. Bentley at Salzberg Cemetery at 3 p.m. Party of 20 attended, including representative of American Camp Senior, Room Senior of 87 and Dr.

Roscoe and A.J.S. 2 beautiful wreaths taken, one from whole Camp and one from his friends.

9.2.44. Dr. Oliver arrived from Biberach.

27.2.44. Mr. H. McQuade and 30 other Americans left Laufen by 12.05 train on their departure for repatriation to the U.S.A.

2.3.44. Mr. Percey Herrington died 4.45 p.m. in Laufen Hospital.

6.3.44. Funeral of Mr. Herrington. 3 wreaths. Funeral party of 20. Padres Leedham and Gerhold officiated.

9.3.44. Sutton, Ommaney, Mackensie, Gale, Watson S.C., Dick, Ager and C.G. Smith accompanied by Cookson as Sanitäter and 6 porters left for Jersey and Church and Smith (of Rm. 66) left for Guernsey. Train left at 8.10 a.m. They are to pick up the Vienna-Paris Rapide at Freilassing.

17.3.44. Twelve British (C.I.) Internees arrived from St. Denis.

23.3.44. McLaren M.S., Kennett W.H., Duke, and Troman M. left for Vittel at 4.30 p.m. to take up teaching there.

25.3.44. New Internee H.J. Sockelt arrived from Neuhausen.

4.4.44. No. 2178 A. Dimery died in Revier 5.30 a.m.

6.4.44. Funeral of A. Dimery Laufen 3 p.m. Padres G & L took service. 2 wreaths, one from Camp and one from his comrades from St. Denis.

6.4.44. Visit of Protecting Power.

17.4.44. Internee No. 1316 Ernest Coniring arrived from Hamburg.

12.4.44. Pass to visit outside workers granted.

21.4.44 1167 F. Smith left for

RESERVE LAZARETT (Kgf)

ELSTERHORST

über HOVERSWERDA

(SACHSEN)

22.4.44.	V. Gontier (1137) and H. Gontier (1138) arrived from Saarbrucken.

22.4.44.   Visit of I.R.C.C. representatives.

24.4.44.   Interview with Dr. Schneider of German Foreign Office.

2.5.44. & 4.5.44.

Visits of Mons. Aubech de la Räe of Swiss Legation, Berlin.

6.5.44.   W. Evans No. 64260 arrived from Stalag XXA.

15.5.44.   The first Contingent of 105 Internees from Tittmoning arrived in this Camp this evening. I had to clear 86, 87, 622 and 662 for the purpose of accommodating American Internees and obtained 64 as a living room.   2$^{D.}$ Contingent arrived on 17.5.44. and 3$^{D.}$ on 19.5.44.

22.5.44.   Visited Salzberg and saw Everson, Topp, Stapleton and Ardley. Afterwards visited City and viewed Cathedral, Franciscan Ch. (beautiful architecture inside) and St. Peters.

24.5.44.   1127 H.J.D. Fraser left for Stalag 194/2, Giromagny, Frankreich.

28.5.44.   N. 1255 Dilwyn Davies died 7.30 p.m. 28/5/44 in Laufen Hospital. Tubercular Meningitis.

31.5.44.   461 Porter R., 617. Berry S.W., 83 Bryant J. and 401 Motto R. left by 9.30 p.m. train for Wurzach to rejoin parents.

1.6.44.   Funeral of Dilwyn Davies at 4 p.m.   Padre Flint officiated. Attended by Dr. Oliver, J. Aughton, S.C. Smith and Poole (the latter 3 personal friends) & 19 from Room 66 i.e. all in Camp except Chatburn and Withington who did not wish to attend. 4 wreaths, 1 from B & A Camp Seniors and all internees, 1 from his Room Mates and Mum, Dad and family, 1 from the Outside workers and 1 from W.J. Stewart and J. Lambon.

1.6.44.   Propaganda Circular inviting joining of British Free Corps to fight Bolshevism circulated at Camp by German Authorities. Apparently supply brought to Camp by

British non-German speaking Corporal in German uniform with 3 Lions on collar and Union Jack and inscription "British Free Corps" on right sleeve. Told to-day of his visit yesterday.

4.6.44.   988 S.F. Perkins informed me to-day that he wished not to be repatriated to England. I enquired why & was informed that he wishes to remain permanently in this country & not to return to England. I informed him that, in my view, it was wrong to issue him with any further Red Cross supplies of any kind. He agreed this to be logical. Accordingly I have passed instructions this day to all Red Cross Depts. in Camp to refrain from making any further issues to him.

N.B.   A.J. Sherwill cancelled this above entry and wrote in the margin against it: "Vide note 18.6.44".

5 - 6.6.44.   Channel Invasion started.

6.6.44.   Arranged to supply 11 Egyptian members of crew of Egyptian Ship Zam Zan (torpedoed) at Lazarett with R.C. food and cigarettes during their stay here.

6.6.44.   1139 Moses Jacobsohn and his two sons 1140, Etan Jacobsohn (15 yrs) and 1141, Ori Jacobsohn (19 yrs) came into Camp from Lazarett. They are natives of Palestine (though the two sons were born in Berlin of a Viennese mother).

7.6.44.   Rec' complaint from Room 80 (the sanitorium) concerning 1027 S.A. Moss. Convened Advisory Council. In view of complaint and of many past complaints concerning this internee, applied to-day to Kommandant for his removal to another Camp.

15.6.44.   18 new internees (including Brigadier Best S.A. and 8 Hindoo traders (formerly in Gibraltar) and others captured by The Admiral Scheer) arrived from Milag Nord (MARLAG & MILAG NORD (MILAG), POST BARMSTEDT, BEZ, BREMEN).

16.6.44.   Took over Room 83 from Edn. Cttee. and turned it over to Hindoos.

18.6.44.	Saw 988 S.F. Perkins and ascertained from him that, whilst I had correctly understood what he actually said, his real attitude is that he is very happy on farm where he is treated with great kindness and would wish to remain there and not return to England. He disregards "politics" entirely but is definitely not pro-German in regard to result of this war. In his view nothing can justify violence. He appears to be a follower of One who had similar views and to whom homage (at least lip homage) is still paid. Have decided to restore parcels and cigarettes and have given instructions accordingly.
6.44.	No. xxx Hasboun T.I. (Palestinian) arrived from Graz, Austria.
22.6.44.	87481 Mollison, E.H. arrived in Camp from Milag Nord.
27.6.44.	No. xxx T. Voyle arrived from Vienna. Taken into detention in Budapest in March 1944.
4.7.44.	American Independence Day.
	British Camp Senior took part in Ceremony "Salute to the King" at 8.30 a.m. Greatly admired the magnificent decorations prepared by our American friends.
	Issued Notice as follows:- "England Expects"
	Mr. Berg arrived for tea.
	Soccer England v America 4-0 England.
	Hockey England v America 3-1 England.
	Wonderful tea at 5 p.m. Wonderful gala concert with inspiring address by Father Sledz. Dinner with Mr. Gompertz. Art exhibition.
9.7.44.	Visited St. Pancras and Big Tree with Cusilo and Garnett. Picked wild strawberries and startled a young deer.
10.7.44.	Machon returned from [indecipherable].
17.7.44.	A.H. Price (1144) arrived in Camp.
18.7.44.	Kitschbühel. Wonderful trip in mountains. Mr. Berg gassed but recovered.

18.7.44.	1145 H. Brockes arrived in Camp from Italy.

24.7.44.   229 Leslie Green left a.m. for Sanatorium.   Reserve Lazarett (KGF) Elsterhost, über Hoverswerda, Sachsen.

29.7.44.   1558 Percival arrived from Kreuzberg.

2.8.44.   1146 Nader Bey Khalil-Nia, Iranian, arrived from Vienna.

4.8.44.   23 Internees arrived from Italy.   Passing through Laufen en route to Liebenau & Vittel 30 British women, 2 men and 1 small boy.   They stayed at Laufen Station for about 4 hrs.   Provided them with soup from kitchen, red cross supplies for journey and cigarettes also beer at Gasthof at Station.   They were also supplied with dry rations for journey by German Authorities.   Among ladies were Miss Maria Sebire of Brock Road, St. Sampsons, Guernsey, a teacher in Italy for many years, also Miss Grindley, a friend of Mrs. Whittaker and Blad family, and Mr. Skinner (Henry) and Miss Elisa Skinner.   Italian party in Camp visited station and greeted relatives and friends. Most cheerful show; we delighted to help our kinsfolk.

10.8.44.   1170 Barra R. arrived in Camp on first internment.

10.8.44.   Went by train with Dr. Heule & Mr. Gomez to Niederstrass via Freilassing.   Had excellent lunch & tea & saw some of peat diggings & learned general conditions under which Internees work.   Formed excellent impression.   Back in Camp by 8 p.m. after most enjoyable afternoon.

21.8.44.   Afternoon visit of Mr. Berg.   Recordings of Camp activities.   Gave Mr. Berg tea and we all supped with Mr. Gompertz.

26.8.44.   Visit of International Red Cross Delegates, Messrs. Biner and Mayer.

29.8.44.   1171 Prince Charles de Rohan and 1172 Prince Louis de Rohan arrived in this Camp.

31.8. & 1.9.44.

Mollison put on "Present Laughter" by Noel Coward. Played to packed houses. Enormous success.

8.9.44.   992 H. Mackenzie and 168584 Felix Palmer arrived. They had been at Kreuzburg and had gone to assembly camp Lamsdorf Stalag 344 for repatriation but were removed from the party to be repatriated.

12.9.44.   Dr. Oliver and 35 British Internees left this Camp on their transfer to Spittal.

14.9.44.   T.H. Bayes left to rejoin his wife at Wurzach.

11.10.44.   Mixed Medical Commission arrived and departed after passing 62 British Internees for repatriation.

Brigadier Clifton, N.Z. Forces, visited Camp to see M.M.C.

15.10.44.   Dr. Oliver returned from Spittal.

21.10.44.   Dr. Oliver left for Biberach.

19.10.44.   16 Internees left for Spittal, including Khider D. (Egyptian).

21.10.44.   Visit of Protecting Power Delegate (M. Denzler).

23.10.44.   Placed order for printing Xmas card.

24.10.44.   Appt' Brigadier A. Best S.A. as member of Education Committee in place of Mr. Wynne Sayer, no longer available.

24.11.44.   Augustus Dunkley died at 12.05 a.m. Funeral 28.11.44. Improvised Union Jack. 4 wreaths and other flowers.

30.11.44.   Visit from General in charge of POW and Internment Camps in District VII & by commission from Reichsicherheitshauptamt including 2 ex-detainees (I.O.M. & S. Africa respectively) to examine conditions in German Internment Camps in comparison with British Internment Camps.

7.12.44.   E. Billenge ? left for Salzburg for treatment (returned 18.1.45.).

--.1.45.   No...... Green (father of Leslie Green) arrived from Buchenwald.

15-18.1.45.   Journey to and from Berlin to interview Dr. Frei of Swiss Legation with regard to repatriation matters.

21.1.45.   American Repatriation.

21.1.45.   Arrival of party of 66 from Spittal.

20.2.45.   Party of 11 left for Spittal.

26.2.45.   Repatriation party left here 26.2.45. at 6.25 a.m. (Laufen Station). McCallum and Stoled returned from Spittal.

6.3.45.   28 arrivals (24 from Biberach and 4 from Liebenau) arrived in the Camp.

17.3.45.   Search by Cripo.

4.5.45.   Relieved by American Troops.

10.5.45.   N.H. Hey (268) died in Laufen Hospital at 3.30 a.m. from malignant tumour of pancreas.

14.5.45.   Funeral of Mr. N.H. Hey in Laufen Cemetery at 11 a.m. The Rev. S.W. Gerhold and the Rev. T. Leedham officiated.

1.6.45.   At 1.30 p.m. it was reported to me by Mr. Woodruff that at about noon that day Henry Le Goupillot had been accidentally shot while sitting in a lorry near the Lazarett Baracke by David T. Fisher and that Le Goupillot had been taken to Hospital where he died within about 20 minutes of the occurrence. I interviewed David Thomas Fisher, Eric Geary and D. Mc A. Campbell, internees, briefly and reported the matter to the British Consular Mission now in Camp. I requested the witnesses to prepare statements in writing and sent a message to other witnesses Arthur Winterflood, Victor Gontiel, J. Jenkins and D. Munro also to prepare written statements.

Briefly, the accident appears to have occurred as follows:-

A number of Internees under the control of Internee Woodruff and including the deceased Le Goupillot,

Fisher, Geary & ors. were engaged in guarding Lebanese Prison enclosure where there is a typhus hospital and where also there are a number of German women prisoners. The guards are under the nominal control of the American Military Authorities and sleep at the Lazarett Baracke. Just before 12 noon 1/6/45 Fisher going on guard duty borrowed a German Automatic Pistol from Eric Geary and one clip of ammunition. Geary and Fisher both believed the weapon to be unloaded. Le Goupillot & Fisher (+ ors.) got into the lorry sitting face to face. Fisher had the pistol on his knee and appears to have been playing with the trigger. The gun went off, the bullet striking Le Goupillot in the stomach. Le Goupillot was removed immediately to the nearby Hospital where an operation was commenced. He died, however, at about 12.10 p.m. 1.6.45. before the operation could be completed. The guards were not provided with arms by the Americans but their possession of arms does not appear to have been discouraged. Geary picked the automatic pistol and ammunition in question off a dump of German arms about 3 weeks ago and appears to have had it in his possession ever since.

3.6.45.   Funeral of H.J. Le Goupillot at 11 a.m. Service taken Mr. Flint & Mr. Best. Masses of beautiful flowers. Large attendance.

Details of graves of Channel Islanders in Laufen will be found in *Appendix L* and a Commentary on the Laufen Diary in *Appendix M.*

11

MATTERS TOO SHAMEFUL TO RELATE

It might be thought that the head of the house having long since been imprisoned and, later deported to the continent and interned, his wife and two small sons would have been encouraged to behave themselves in the presence of the enemy, especially as some eighty of the latter were by then in occupation of the house itself, my wife and children being relegated to a 'grace and favour' apartment in that portion of the basement not occupied by the detachment's field kitchen.

My wife, admittedly, was a hard case and very different from her amiable complaisant husband. Had she not, in the very early days of the German occupation, already blotted her copy-book? Accompanying me on Aug. 1st 1940 to German Military H.Q. (the Channel Islands Hotel) to hear me do a recording for transmission to the United Kingdom from the German Radio at Bremen *(A copy of this message is reproduced in Appendix D)*, (the recording which got me into grave disfavour with - to use the elegant expression much in use by Lord Haw-Haw at the time – 'Churchill and his gang'), she was told, when I had finished, that there was still room for a contribution by her if she so wished. Quite unprepared for such an offer, she sailed right in and recorded the following:-

"This is Mrs. Sherwill speaking for the mothers of Guernsey. We are all quite happy and contented with life over here if only we could have news of all our children to whom we send our very dearest love. They are always in our thoughts and prayers.

The Guernsey woman is always cheerful and philosophical under adversity - and the following story is typical of the spirit of the Island both before and since the occupation. A Guernsey fish-woman in the market said to me just before the arrival of the Germans: "Ah! but ain't some people awful, say! There's a woman, she ses to me, she ses: 'The Germans is to the back of the Island.' 'Ah well!' I ses to her 'Tell them to come round to the front.'"

At the time, I had no hope that this would be transmitted and, so far as I am aware, it never was. The paradise under German rule depicted in the first paragraph was, I fear, marred in German eyes by the insolence contained in the second. (In speaking of the insolence towards them of the Guernsey populace, the Germans usually qualified it as either 'dumb' or 'polite.)

Then, one Sunday evening in later October 1940, - her husband having been grilled for quite a time by a German Counter Intelligence agent, she being meanwhile relegated to the kitchen and subjected to the indignity of having to apply her ear to the keyhole of the intervening door in order to follow what was taking place - she had attacked the unfortunate agent - who, after all, as he explained to her, was only doing his duty - with such verbal vigour that he cringed away from her and actually came to me for protection.

I have even more shameful things to relate but can only do so at second hand in that I had been plucked from the bosom of my family long before they happened.

One culprit was my youngest son, then aged nine.

Our particular Germans paraded occasionally in fatigue dress and without headgear on the lawn in front of the house. One of them was bald. Going on to the balcony at first floor level overlooking them, my little horror found, by trial and error that, given ordinary luck and an absence of wind, a direct hit was obtainable on the bald pate below him. It was only a matter of how often and how strongly he could spit. From time to time, he scored a bull. Naturally, German discipline being what it is, immediate reaction by the 'victim' was not possible. The parade over, however, I regret to say that the soldier concerned was so unmindful of the decorum which should be preserved in the presence of youth that he uttered the most terrible imprecations and, to cap it, did so not in words which my sweet innocent could understand but in a hated foreign tongue. He even went so far as to shake his fist in a most menacing fashion in the poor boy's face.

I feel, too, that I should tell you about what happened in the tunnel. This particular tunnel, starting at the bend in our road and going slap through the high ground that hid Fort George from us, came out near the entrance to the latter. Its purpose was never discovered by us although it is reasonable to suppose that, to the German troops or, at the very least, to the German contractor who constructed it, it had one. I can, however, tell you how it began. One morning, I was standing in our rose garden when my reverie was broken by a large stone falling from the inside of my garden wall. Another fell and, through the resulting aperture, the end of a crowbar protruded. I investigated and found a German contractor and two Organisation Todt workers at the scene of the crime. I learned that my garden was to be used as a dump for the spoil from the tunnel about to be pierced. I protested, to no avail, to the contractor and, later, at the Feldkommandantur. I then made friends with the contractor and asked: would he first remove and heap all the topsoil before starting to dump the broken stone etc. and, when the dumping was finished, restore the topsoil and level it? He said that he, too, had a garden at his home in Germany and that he would comply with my request. When, soon afterwards, I was deported to Germany, the dumping operation was in full swing with a small diesel locomotive bringing in loads of stone throughout the twenty-four hours. When I returned in 1945, I found that he had been even better than his word. He had stopped short of a most productive fig-tree, had formed stone wells to protect the fruit trees growing against the walls and, although the final surface was some eight feet higher than nature intended, the drainage was vastly improved and the garden no less productive than before.

Now, in that tunnel when completed, the Germans had stored quantities of expensive light engineering tools, all beautifully cased. My two boys, virtually the only children living in the immediate neighbourhood, naturally took a keen interest in local happenings and had spotted the tools. The elder of them, then aged twelve and very mechanically minded - he doesn't inherit it from me - decided that the opportunity to improve on his output of gadgets was too good to miss so, with their small handcart, they removed one large case of expensive tools and hid them in our basement, not as yet in German use. The case was missed and the Germans suspected the obvious. One morning, as with Ikey, the garden boy she employed, my wife was leading our goats out of the front garden gate to pasture, she was accosted by a member of the Feldpolizei who asked if Ikey was her son. She indignantly repudiated any such responsibility for Ikey who, though a grand lad, was not very presentable in his working clothes and was asked if her real son was at home. He was, indeed, engaged in gloating over his 'find'.

Returning to the house after dealing with the goats, she found both boys being grilled in the kitchen though not, fortunately, over the actual fire. They repudiated with great indignation the enemy allegations of dishonesty. The German officer searched the kitchen and other likely places in the house. Now, in the kitchen and giving on to stairs leading down to the basement, was what looked like a cupboard door. Through that and down the stairs and the loot would have been found reposing at the bottom. The German officer certainly looked at the door but did not even attempt to open it. My wife has always ascribed this negligence on his part to the efficacy of prayer in which three of the four persons present were by now heavily engaged. My wife, understandably furious at the slur on her darlings' characters, intervened and was rudely thrust aside by the German, who grasped and slightly bruised her upper arms in the process. The German officer then informed her that he was taking the boys away for questioning and did so. She, having to go to town to get the weekly rations (no come when told to, then, possibly, no rations that week) could not allow the loss of her sons to stand in her way and left to do her shopping. On her return, she found every door locked and concluded that the Germans had closed the establishment. It was not so. Climbing in through a downstairs back window, she found that her darlings, back from questioning and quite unmoved (as they had left under escort, she had reminded them that they were British and must on no account cry), had barred entry to all intruders and were engaged in digging a huge hole in the garden and therein interring the sacred chest. Nothing more happened expect that the Feldpolizei told them subsequently that they knew that it was they who had stolen the tools but couldn't prove it. By the afternoon, the bruise on her arms having become visible to the naked eye, my wife donned her most glamorous raiment and made all speed for Feldpolizei H.Q., housed, appropriately enough, in the Vicarage a few doors up our road. The officer listened gravely to her complaint then called in his subordinate to give his version of the affray. He then told the latter: "You should understand that any mother will always stand up for her children." Honour being satisfied, she left for home.

This incident did not, I am glad to say, prevent the Polizei, when they had an excess of what was extremely nourishing soup, from distributing it among my wife and boys and other equally deserving folk in the neighbourhood. (I recollect how, on an earlier occasion before I was deported, as I was passing the Vicarage, a German came out with a huge metal container half-filled with soup and pressed it on me and how I H.M. Attorney General (demoted by German order) called with it at every house in our road until the contents had been disposed of, and then, after scrupulously cleansing the container with my own fair hands, returned it with many thanks. The populace was under the impression that the Vicarage was, in fact, Gestapo H.Q. but this was not so. I recall, too, another occasion showing to what depths we had fallen. Passing an enormous pit into which German troops quartered elsewhere threw their rubbish, I saw, for the first time for years, several lemons. I was down in the pit in a flash and retrieved some almost perfect ones. I beat it for home and, returning with a basket, retrieved a lot more, most of them bad in places. Sugar came out of our store cupboard and my wife made eight or nine pounds of delicious marmalade.)

But, as is customary with me, I have digressed and must return to the shameful behaviour of my family. There was the children's party held in our basement to celebrate a birthday. Badly brought up as they were because of the German occupation and oblivious of other people's feelings (I refer to the German soldiers in and about the house at the time), my two boys threw open a window and, displaying thereout a Union Jack which they had secreted about the premises, led their misguided little guests in a lusty rendering of 'God Save The King' in direct contravention of para (9) of the German Kommandant's Orders of July 2nd. 1940. (As regards their use of the Union Jack, I have only just discovered, as I write this, that we were never formally forbidden to fly it. Such a prohibition would have been permissible under International Law and I must have assumed that grave trouble would follow if we attempted to fly it for I remember asking Dr. Lanz whether we might not fly the Guernsey flag (the red and white Cross of St. George) on public buildings and received an emphatic 'Nein'.)

All wireless sets were finally called in by the Germans in June, 1942 and this was a very grave hardship to people under enemy occupation. My household complied but a good many, risking the heavy penalties (six weeks imprisonment and a fine of up to RM.30,000) did not. The older of my two boys, the unconvicted tool thief, really coming into his own at last and being highly ingenious, made numberless crystal sets for distribution among his friends, keeping one for his mother. On it, she had the unspeakable pleasure of hearing Churchill say that: "To-morrow, our dear Channel Islands will be free."

In that this is a sober account of what really happened, I have felt compelled to relate the criminal activities in which my wife and younger sons indulged at a time when our daughter and two elder sons, in the W.A.A.F., the Royal Navy and the Indian Army respectively, were fighting for King and Country. I would wish, however, to end this Chapter on a more pleasing note.

The younger boy spent many a happy hour helping the German cooks in our basement peel potatoes. He excused himself to his mother by producing from his pockets the potatoes he had secreted during the operation. However, Nemesis struck at last. Equipped by his foreign friends with an ultra sharp knife, he cut himself quite badly. The blood was staunched and his hand swathed in (German) Red Cross bandages and four German soldiers, one at each corner, tenderly carried him in and laid him on his little bed.

My wife tells me that the behaviour of the troops in our house was immaculate and that, at least once a month, an officer called on her to ascertain whether she had any complaints. She became quite attached to 'German John' (so called by her because of a slight resemblance to our eldest son) in command of 'our' troops and told me about him in her letters to me. I never met him until, some years later, we did a cruise in 'Andes' and called at Hamburg. Having his home address, she had dropped him a line to say we were coming and, as we went ashore, there, at the foot of the gangway, were 'German John' and his wife, complete with car, ready to take us wherever we wished to go.

And then there was her 'dear old Fritz' the head cook in our basement. Many's the time, she tells me, he smuggled food in for the boys during the terrible shortages of late 1944 and early 1945. When she had to go to hospital for a sudden quite serious operation (by then, the surgical needles were so blunt as to be almost unusable and there remained only enough surgical gut for a few more operations - my God! what a job our local doctors and surgeons did in spite of their half-starved condition), Fritz took over the feeding of the boys and, murders of people (including an old couple living little more than a stone's throw from our house) for their newly arrived Red Cross parcels being not uncommon (Georgian soldiers or prisoners of war were suspected) Fritz slept in the boys' bedroom to protect them. Poor old Fritz - I never met him - with his home in what is now East Germany: we often wonder what became of him.

Then, at long last, came the German surrender. The Island, 'conquered' in 1940 by a small detachment of Luftwaffe and having been made into one of the most impregnable fortresses in the world bristling with guns, including a battery of (formerly Russian) naval guns of a calibre in excess of 13 inches, garrisoned by many thousands of soldiers and with 16,000 tons of ammunition in reserve, was 're-conquered' by an even smaller detachment of one Officer and 25 Other Ranks of the British Army.

The Germans in our house - unpatriotic devils - were delighted. On the morrow at first light, they were to withdraw to the far side of a line roughly bisecting the island preparatory to being concentrated in a yet smaller space to facilitate their collection for (a) embarkation for the United Kingdom as P.O.W. or (b) marshalling for the massive clearing-up operations to be performed before they were allowed so to depart. So, on this their last night of liberty, they threw a party in the attics of our house with their remaining bottles of wine. Their principal guests were my wife and those two arch-saboteurs, my - I mean her - two sons. Drink was pressed on all three and two quite lovely pictures painted and framed by some of the hosts were presented to her and still adorn the walls of our flat in Alderney. Delighted by the events of the day and - to quote her - being by now very tiddly, she stumbled down the steep attic stairs on the way to her lowly basement. The boys - by now aged 13 and 10 - were made of sterner stuff. Having drunk far more than she had, they took the steep stairs - the road to the freedom of the morrow - in their stride.

12

À Propos Des Juifs

There arrived on my desk fairly early in the German occupation a "VOBIF"[10] concerning the Jews and a direction from the Germans that it was to be registered on the Island records as part of the laws applicable to Guernsey.

By centuries old custom, registration, having the effect of promulgating an enactment, has to be authorised by the Royal Court sitting as a Full Court i.e. composed of the Bailiff or a Lieutenant Bailiff and at least seven of the twelve Jurats. This venerable custom, no doubt, came into being so as to protect the islanders against any encroachment on their laws and customs without their knowledge by the Sovereign or that Sovereign's Government. Perhaps I should explain that the Royal Court, sitting as a Court of Chief Pleas, had from time immemorial possessed limited legislative powers (not extending, for example, to making an enactment in conflict with any Order of the Sovereign in Council whether made for the purpose of approving a Project de Loi (Bill) passed by the States or for some other purpose, or to the imposition of taxation or of other than a limited period of imprisonment as a penalty) and had a number of other important functions. One interesting survival to this very day is the obligation of the Lords of the Manors in the Island, holding in chief from the Crown, of personal attendance at each of the three Chief Pleas each year (after Christmas, after Easter and after Michaelmas) to perform suit of court. They are (by Royal Dispensation dating back to the time when travel between the island and the Sovereign's Court was difficult and often hazardous) not required to do homage to the Sovereign except when He or She actually visits the Island in person.

With the passing of the years and long before my time, it became customary for the Royal Court, at any of its weekly sessions during Court term time, or, indeed, in case of emergency, at any sitting whether specially convened for the purpose or not, to pass pieces of legislation styled "Provisional Ordinances", which, to remain in force,

---

[10] VOBIF was the abbreviation for Verordnungsblätt des Militärbefehlshabers in Frankreich, and it was the Official Gazette of the German Military Governor of the German Occupied Zone of France. It was published in German and French.

had to be renewed annually. These only became permanent after being submitted to and approved by the Island Legislature styled "Les États de Deliberation" ("the States"). Under the post-war constitution now in force, the legislative powers of the Royal court have been abolished and power to make Ordinances, permanent until repealed, has been vested in the States.

To those unaccustomed to such a set-up, it will appear surprising. Yet it worked admirably. Of course, in pre-war days, the Jurats, as such, were permanent members of the States and their prestige both in and outside the States was, and to this day remains, very high. I can even remember the case (the only one, I believe) where the States refused to make permanent a provisional Ordinance of which a majority of its Members disapproved. Yet, at the next Chief Pleas, the Royal Court renewed it as a provisional Ordinance and continued to do so for many years and only repealed it when the danger (to health) it sought to guard against disappeared.

I read the "VOBIF", which applied primarily to Occupied France, and noted its provisions, which included the required wearing by all Jews of the yellow Star of David. It disgusted me and I visualised Jews being jeered at - not in Guernsey - in the streets, pelted with filth and generally harassed but I had no premonition of the appalling atrocities which were to be perpetrated on them by the Nazi regime.

I made such enquiries as I could and learned, accurately, as it turned out, that the few Jews who had settled in Guernsey had all evacuated. (It had been a pre-war joke that so careful was the Guernseyman with his "doubles" that it had been beyond the wit of any Jew to establish himself in Guernsey and make a living there.)

I am virtually certain that I conveyed to the Bailiff and Jurats in private, as they assembled for the sitting, that the VOBIF, to the best of my belief, would harm no one in the Island. It is my recollection that I was anxious at that time to avoid a collision with the Germans but until recently any particular reason for this eluded me. Then quite by chance, when re-reading Mr. Durand's book, the penny dropped. The clue is the date, 23rd October, 1940, on which the VOBIF was registered. Only two days before, my manoeuvre designed to save two British Officers, Nicolle and Symes, from being shot as spies and to secure instead for them the status of prisoners of war, had culminated in their surrender and I was awaiting confirmation of its success. I think that, at that time, I had had as much as I could take for the moment. Had I been able to foresee what, in fact, happened in relation to them, my disquiet would have been very much greater.

In these circumstances, I felt that no purpose would be served in opposing the registration of the VOBIF or in advising the Court to refuse to register it. Had I done so, presumably the Germans would have been difficult. They might perhaps have directed the Greffier (Clerk to the Court) to register it without reference to the Court. I do not know what they would have done.

Nevertheless, I still feel ashamed that I did not do something by way of protest to the Germans; a vital principle was at stake even if no human being in Guernsey was actually affected. The honour of refusing to concur in its registration fell to Sir Abraham Lainé, K.C.I.E., who, when called on as a Jurat to vote on the matter, openly and categorically refused his assent and stated his grave objections to such a measure. He has now gone to his rest but this courageous act of his should never be forgotten. As I sat listening to him, I realised how right he was.

Across the passage from my cell in the Cherche Midi Prison in Paris was one occupied for most of the time I was there by a Belgian. He was eventually given a month's imprisonment and at once released for he had been there for about three months. How had he offended the Germans? I suppose I heard him say why he was there at least a dozen times for, as cells were vacated and re-occupied, the newcomers were always interested to know what had brought about the arrest of their fellow prisoners and, when the German guards were off duty, we were able (the penalty for doing so was three days without soup) by placing our stools on our tables and clambering up and pushing outwards the movable ventilation panel above our cell doors, to converse with each other. It was the only relief from misery that we had. His reply was always the same: "J'avais deux Juifs dans ma voiture". He explained that he ran a bus service between Paris and Brussels and that he was arrested and his bus impounded because, being stopped at a German road block, it was found that two Jews (husband and wife) were among his passengers. He insisted that their papers were entirely in order and that, in taking them, he had no idea that he was committing an offence. His pathetic face at the panel and his reiterated "J'avais deux Juifs dans ma voiture" have remained in my memory ever since.

In the next cell to mine was another Jew named Roditti and he was still there when I was released. I believe he was accused of illegal transactions in gold. He told me a remarkable story. I cannot vouch for its accuracy although I believe it to be true: it certainly seems worth relating.

At the time of the persecution of the Jews in Spain in the reign of Ferdinand and Isabella, his forbears had escaped to and settled in Turkey and, he told me that, although they had long since adopted Turkish nationality and spoke Turkish fluently, at home, in the family circle, they still conversed in the Spanish of that earlier period.

He told me, too, that at the time of the trial of Nurse Cavell in Brussels during the First World War, his father was Turkish Consul in Brussels. When Nurse Cavell was sentenced to death by a German Court Martial, representations had been made by the Turkish authorities through his father that mercy should be extended to her. He went on to say that these failed because Nurse Cavell had, at her trial and subsequently, shown such complete contempt for everything German that no German could be found to recommend the commutation of her death sentence.

Roditti was an unhappy person. Often during the bitter cold of that winter (1940-41), have I heard him say "Oh! que je gèle" (I'm freezing) and on a few occasions when a German guard entered his cell, I have heard him shout with pain as he was obviously being cuffed. This never happened to me and I wondered why. I gathered that he kept his cell filthy but it may be that his principal offence was that of being a Jew.

Of course, many Jews are very resilient, no doubt, in part, as a result of the treatment to which they have been subjected by Christians through the centuries. Two instances of such resilience came very prominently to my notice.

In June, 1944, I learned that there were three British protected Jews at the Lazarett (the outside receiving station where newcomers were, if necessary, de-loused and otherwise made fit to join the select society housed in our Ilag). They were reported to me as being in poor shape. I went up to see them and issued a Red Cross parcel to each. They were Moses Jacobsohn, a native of Bethlehem, and his two sons, Etan and Ori, born in Berlin. I learned that Moses had migrated to Austria and had married a Viennese girl and subsequently moved to Berlin where he had set up in business as a hatter and prospered. His wife and daughter - I know not when or how or by what means - had got away to Palestine. He and his sons had suffered dreadful indignities but, as he spoke only German and Yiddish, I never discovered precise details. After some days, Sonderführer Henle sent for me and introduced the three Jacobsohns and told me that, although British protected persons, they spoke only German. This was a new element in camp life and it gave me a chance to pull his leg. I said: "In that case, I can't accept them." Henle was obviously perplexed and I went on to say: "I'll accept them on one condition and that is if they will give me a solemn undertaking that they will not indulge in German propaganda in my camp." Henle, knowing at least as much as I did about the German treatment already meted out to them, said "You seriously ask me to get such an undertaking from them?" Without moving a facial muscle I said I was only too serious. He then asked them in German if they would give a solemn undertaking not to indulge in German propaganda. As one man, they shouted "Ja, ja." I said that, in that case, I would accept them and, as Henle turned to leave, gave him a broad grin. The Jacobsohns were put in a room with a rather rough, though good natured, crowd as there was just nowhere else to put them. They settled down very quickly, however, and there was never a spot of bother concerning them.

Two days after we had been freed by the Americans (4th May 1945) I was amused to see Ori Jacobsohn (or was it Etan) in possession of a motor-bike. He must have been a fast worker.

And there was a sequel. Some years after the war, my wife and I did a car trip through France, Germany, Austria and Luxemburg. In the course of our journey we called on Colonel Bandelow, Sonderführer Gallhöfer, Unteroffizier Krafft and Baron von und zu Aufsess and decided to stay at Laufen for a day or so, if facilities for doing so existed. When we reached Laufen, we found that my former Camp Kommandant, Oberst Kochenberger, was still living in the village. He told us that accommodation in the local inn was very primitive and offered us the loan, for the duration of our stay, of a little house owned by him and normally occupied by Dr. Leidle, an extremely intelligent German girl who had worked in the Camp Office and was well known to me, and her husband, formerly one of my British internees, who were away on holiday. We gladly accepted it.

He took me to visit the Burgomeister and explained who I was and the Burgomeister insisted on giving me a book of photographs and asked me to sign the Golden Book of the municipality. Having done this, I asked the Burgomeister to clear up something which was puzzling me. "I was here before for quite a time. May I know why it was that I was not then presented with photographs and invited to sign the Gold Book?" My misguided sense of humour seemed to appeal to them for they laughed heartily.

Chatting with us afterwards the Colonel asked if there was anyone in the village I particularly wished to see and I could only say that I hadn't a notion whether anyone remained there whom I had known personally. The Colonel then mentioned Moses Jacobsohn and I said I'd be delighted to meet him again and along we went to his house.

It was certainly more opulently furnished than the Colonel's own, the womenfolk had been restored and an air of modest affluence was apparent. I gathered that Moses had set up several small shops in what had been our exercise ground (nicknamed by us "The Birdcage") and, I was told, though not by Moses and it may not even be true that, after his liberation, he had 'acquired' the very voluminous green velvet curtains which hung in the hall which we had used for Camp services for all the denominations and that, there not being a lady's hat or suitable material for making one on sale in that part of Germany at the cessation of hostilities, he had taken advantage of this unprecedented opportunity to pander to feminine desires and that the curtains had gone up, not in smoke, but in hats and in price.

As my wife and I were about to take our leave Moses said to me: "You were very kind to me and I have not forgotten it; is there anything I can do for you?" I replied: "As a matter of fact, it may be that you can." My immediate financial position was worrying me. Under the currency control regulations then in force, some of the banker's cheques I had bespoken for the journey were encashable only in Germany, the others in France and/or Austria. I had found prices in France sky-high and those in Germany much more moderate than I had expected. In consequence, I had masses of German marks which I would not be able to use and, per contra, the means of procuring food and shelter in Austria - and in France as we returned - so limited as to cause me deep apprehension, I explained my dilemma. Moses said "What about 10,000 Austrian schillings?" I said: "Good heavens, no; but could you perhaps exchange 400 schillings against their equivalent in German marks which I can hand you now?" He said: "Nonsense, there are wonderful things for sale in Salzburg and Madame (pointing to my wife) will certainly want to buy a souvenir." I said: "Want must be her master. Not a penny more than 400 schillings." He got pen and paper and gave me a note bearing an address just across the River Salzach in neighbouring Austria. In due course, after getting through rather tedious German and then Austrian Customs formalities on the bridge near our Camp which I knew so well and had, while a prisoner, crossed without let or hindrance on so many occasions, I found the address and handed the note to the woman who answered the door. She returned within seconds and handed me 400 schillings in notes; not one word was exchanged between us. Both of us were breaking Austria's laws and I, at least, was breaking those much nearer home.

I said to Moses Jacobsohn as we parted: "Had I accepted your 10,000 schillings, how on earth, having regard to currency regulations, could I ever have repaid you?" He said: "Simple, you could have sent British pound notes for the correct money to my cousin in London." I give Moses Jacobsohn full marks for being, despite all he had undergone, in full possession of his faculties.

My fears of temporary starvation were, despite Moses' intervention, justified by experience. We arrived back in Dinard one morning to catch the afternoon boat for the Channel Islands. We had almost no ready money left and, at lunch time, searched Dinard for a small eating-house where we could have the cheapest déjeuner advertised on its show card. There was not one within our means and we made do with a loaf and a small pat of butter and two bananas which had to suffice till we could get aboard the steamer and purchase a high tea with the £ notes we still had but were too proud to flog illegally.

And then there was Khider. He was an Egyptian Jew, a carpet merchant who, for some reason, was treated by the Germans as British and was in my part of the camp. He was in good shape and was apparently totally unconcerned about being interned. What troubled him, to the point of an obsession, was the fate of the stock of carpets he had had to leave behind when he was picked up by the Germans. He must have seen me dozens of times on the subject, urging me to make representations on the matter to the proper quarter. I had no expectation that he and his carpets would ever be reunited but, in any case, I pointed out that I hadn't the faintest idea to whom I could make representations, but a jolly good idea of the fate of any representations

I might make. Finally, completely fed up with him and his carpets, I told him I could do nothing and not to come near me about it again. To my surprise, he merely said: "Well, never mind, within a year of getting my freedom, I shall make another fortune."

Now, in the village of Obendorf (of "Silent Night, Holy Night" fame) just across the bridge from us was a cinema (to which we internees were, sometimes, allowed to go under escort) owned by a man reputed to be the most ardent Nazi in the district. At or just after our liberation by the Americans he died a mysterious death; it was rumoured that he had been killed by one of his own people whom he had terrorised. Within weeks, Khider had installed himself in the home of the Nazi's widow and, to all appearances, as they took their walks abroad, he was seeking her hand in marriage. I left soon after and never learned whether he had acquired the cinema as the first step towards that financial rehabilitation which he had predicted so confidently at the time of my last interview with him.

It would be very wrong of me to finish, on such a note, a chapter headed: "A propos des Juifs."

On the American side of Ilag VII, for which I had no responsibility, were many Polish Jews equipped with Central American Republic "passeports de protection" secured Heaven knows how, but certainly for large sums of money. Sonderführer Gallhöfer said to me one day: "Have you any influence with the Poles?" I replied: "None whatever". He went on: "We have their passports from Guatemala, Honduras, Costa Rica, Panama, Nicaragua, etc. in this office. They're always bringing grievances to me; do tell them to shut up. They're safe here but what do you think would happen to them if Himmler got to hear of them? I don't believe their passports would even serve to allow them entry into the countries concerned; do tell them to shut up." I did what I could but that didn't amount to much. They all survived but I do not know what happened to them after liberation. If memory serves me faithfully when an American Consul General arrived and screened those classed by the Germans as "Americans", out of a camp population of approximately 500, he found only seventeen having in his view the status of "United States citizen."

Among the Polish Jews were a considerable number of young men, some well-educated and all personable and in fair condition.

Now, in the very last days before the German surrender, there arrived in our village under guard a number of the wretched ex-inmates of Regensburg concentration camp. They still wore their striped pyjama type clothing, were in wretched condition and had been herded in our direction to avoid their being liberated by the advancing American Army. It was said that even more had fallen out unable to continue the march than had arrived and that these had been shot by the wayside by their guards but this may or may not be true. I gathered that these poor people were all, or mostly, German nationals. The condition of the majority was such that a large ward in the village hospital, hitherto unused, was cleared so that they could be accommodated on mattresses on the floor. There was, I remember, a grave deficiency of blankets. I went there to see if there were any British among them but there were none. So crowded were they that it was difficult to move between the mattresses. They were virtually naked and I was horrified at their state of emaciation. I would not have believed that life could continue in such skeletons.

The matron of the hospital was a rather forbidding character, who did her duty, but no more, to those of our camp who entered the hospital as patients. She was, by repute, a virulent Nazi. Earlier, I tried out an unusual tactic on her. On the discharge from the hospital of one of our own people, cured, I procured in the village a very nice bunch of chrysanthemums and went to the hospital to present it to her with the thanks of the British (who knew nothing about it) in our Camp. To my grave embarrassment, her eyes filled with tears and, excusing myself, I beat a hasty retreat.

Confronted with the emergency of the concentration camp survivors, she turned to with a vengeance and worked extremely hard to succour them.

Then a terrible thing happened. Typhus broke out among them and all of us in Camp and the villagers were inoculated.

An emergency typhus hospital was set up a few miles away in part of a Women's Prison, the patients were transferred there and a call went out in our camp to young and fit British and "Americans" alike to volunteer for the various transport and other jobs which became necessary. I particularly remember how a number of young Polish Jews volunteered as nursing orderlies, putting themselves in the most dangerous posts of all for attracting infection and how valiantly they worked at this for weeks on end.

I remember, too, old Dr. Schickehofer, our German camp doctor (who was not a Jew), the nicest of men who said to me: "Mr. Sherwill, I go to take charge of the typhus hospital, it will be a good end." I rejoice to say that for him it was not the end and that, when I last heard of him, he a lifelong bachelor, had married happily.

I had a curious encounter with him at the village hospital the night after we were liberated. I had called to visit a British internee, N.H. Hey, who was lying desperately ill there. (He died on May 10th). Beds had been set up in the corridor to cope with the rush of patients and in one, was a man, half-naked and of magnificent physique, unconscious and obviously in high delirium, tearing at his bandaged side and revealing an appalling gunshot wound, probably sustained as the Americans were nearing our village. As I passed, he murmured something which sounded to me to be in English. I bent over him to check from any further utterances whether he was English. And then Dr. Schickehofer came along and saw me and said: "Mr. Sherwill, do not distress yourself, it is only a German". It sounds irrational (of course I was) but I could have hit him. I didn't but visited my own dying internee.

There was Dr. Oshek, a Jew of Polish origin but a bona fide nationalised American citizen. He was a highly skilled physician and worked in the Camp Dispensary and in our Revier (Sick Bay) with great devotion. He was under the general supervision of our dear old German Doctor Schickehofer. The latter thought highly of him. This is not surprising for Dr. Schickehofer once said to me: "I am a Christian. I treat Jews and Gentiles alike."

I was able, early in 1944, when a party of British and American internees were transferred from our Camp to one at Vittel to strengthen the educational staff there working among many young internees, to persuade our Camp Office to allow Dr. Oshek, in recognition of the value of his medical services, a week's leave so that he might travel with them and pay a visit to his mother, interned in St. Denis. He returned much heartened at having met her again and told me what a joy it had been to her. It was one of her last joys on earth for, although we only learned of it after liberation, not long after his visit she, as a Jewess, was removed from St. Denis and met her end in the gas chambers. Dr. Oshek himself was transferred to another Camp to carry out medical duties there and I have no reason to think that any harm befell him. I am virtually certain in fact that he is still practising medicine in the United States.

I intervened effectively in the case of another Jew, Mr. A.J. Weissmann, a Roman Catholic, a brilliant musician, old and feeble and, for most of the time, a patient in our Camp Sick Bay, where he received devoted care from internee Cookson. Orders arrived early in August, 1943, that he was to be transferred to a destination not disclosed to me. I was becoming wise about what was happening to Jews though I did not know the full extent of the appalling treatment meted out to them. I refused to obey the order and insisted that he be left where he was while I reported his case to the International Red Cross in Geneva and received a reply from them. The German Camp Office agreed to this. What would have happened eventually I do not know. The pressure from above on our Camp Office would presumably have submerged any pressure I could apply from below. Mr. Weissmann solved the matter for us by dying peacefully in his sleep on the 30th August. We buried him in Laufen Cemetery on Sept. 2nd. Two R.C. Priests, Fathers Czerne and Zaberwoski officiated. Both the American and the British Camp Seniors and 16 internees attended and we sent two lovely wreaths, of which one purported to come from his widow.

One afternoon, I went down to the German Camp Office on some business or other and, in the outer office was an elderly Jew, a man of striking appearance, with a short jet-black beard. He was from the American part of the Camp. I had never spoken to him and did not even know his name. Standing by him and leaning against the wall were two German civilians whom I decided were members of the Gestapo or the Secret Feldpolizei. They were obviously about to conduct him somewhere. And then there emerged from the inner office, the Jew's Camp Senior. The latter was a United States citizen but, to the best of my belief, a German born Jew who had been naturalised. He passed through the outer office without a glance in the elderly Jew's direction. For some reason, this incensed me although I had no status of any kind entitling me either to feel or to act. Then I was told that the German officer I sought was free to see me. On an impulse, I strode across and shook the elderly Jew warmly by the hand and wished him all the best luck possible. My approach to him galvanised the two lounging Germans into activity. God knows what they thought I was going to do to him. Attack him? Rubbish. Secretly hand him a pill by which he would escape their clutches? I do not know. They did not physically intervene but they were ready to do so. All I could do was go about my business. When I emerged after my interview, the Jew and his attendants had left, to what destination, I never discovered but I can guess.

13

FINIS

Does this book contain any message worth recording? Even if it does will it be read by more than a handful of people? In other words was it worth the task of writing it?

It has at least enabled me to dig into my innermost self and to resurrect memories which some may think might be better left buried.

I am not financially dependent on it being a best, or even a good, seller. I should like it to be for the sake of my vanity. The filthy lucre would also be acceptable. My publisher's anxious doubts and touching faith are also worthy of reward.

As the German occupation became imminent I counselled those close to me that to expect to find pro-British Germans was to doom ourselves to severe disappointment. We should be abundantly satisfied when we came across good Germans. I proposed to myself that, with great moderation and discretion I would, being utterly powerless to employ other means, exploit any such good Germans in the interests of my own people. To the best of my ability, I consistently carried out this policy, in Guernsey, to an extremely limited extent when questioned by the Secret Military Police in Guernsey and in Paris and, later, to a much greater extent, as British Camp Senior at Ilag VII, Laufen, in Bavaria.

Let me admit quite frankly that despite my earlier counselling of others, the coming to Guernsey of men like Major Lanz, Dr. Maass, Dr. Brosch and Unteroffizier Krafft disarmed me. They were better Germans than I had expected. So was Rittmeister Prince von Oettingen who might well have been a typical English aristocrat of the old school. I never met Count Graf von Schmettow, the Commander in Chief of the Channel Islands, to whom my fellow prisoners and I undoubtedly owed our liberation from prison and some of us, including probably myself, our lives. Within the last twelve months he spent a holiday in Guernsey and telephoned[11] to me in Alderney. It was the first occasion on which I could thank him personally.

---

[11] The date of this call would have been in the nineteen sixties

I quickly realised the sterling honesty of the average German.

I recall certain acts of mine which might be termed gratuitously honest, flamboyant or actuated by sentimental mawkishness.

When a German officer broke into our airport terminal building on June 30th, 1940, and hurriedly withdrew and jumped into his plane at the approach of British aircraft, he left his loaded revolver behind. It was brought to me and, at my first meeting with the Germans at the Royal Hotel that night, I handed it over still loaded to the senior officer explaining in what circumstances it had come into my possession. That same night, on his question as to whether we possessed any military weapons, the reply "None" came from one of my companions who was uninformed on the matter. I intervened and said "We have twelve service rifles without ammunition" and these were handed in the next day.

At the preliminary court of enquiry by the Germans into a particularly nauseating case of rape of an elderly lady by a German soldier (admittedly far gone under the influence of drink), when the Germans behaved to the lady with far greater delicacy and tact than would have been possible under the rules of procedure of our own Royal Court, it was confidently predicted to me by the German officer who conducted it that the soldier would undoubtedly be shot, as he was. I at once said that as the Guernsey Public Prosecutor I sought no greater penalty for him than would have been inflicted by our own Court. This was waived aside as irrelevant. I insisted on my submission being inserted in the German record of the proceedings. After considerable argument it was.

Why take such a line in these cases? Was it honesty in the first two and compassion in the third? Perhaps, to some slight extent; I regret - or rather do not regret - to say that my purpose in the former was to impress on the Germans that I was scrupulously honest and, in the last, that I was consistent. I anticipated having, in the future, to intercede quite often on behalf of my fellow islanders who, wittingly or unwittingly, committed offences against German enactments. I was not going to risk a sneer that "you didn't make any such plea when a German soldier was concerned".

In Ilag VII, soon after I was elected British Camp Senior, one of our internees working on a farm, out of the kindness of his heart, brought me in an egg. This was forbidden but tolerated and honoured more in the breach than its observance.

I took the egg with me on my next visit to the German office and placed in on Sonderführer Gallhöfer's desk. I told him of the gift but not the name of the donor and said: "This is for your little daughter". At the time, I had never set eyes on the brat; I have since met her and her very charming mother and I think I can say that we are fast friends. Such an act was bound to excite comment in the German office (I can imagine the ribald comment it would have provoked among my own people in the Ilag had they known of it). I cannot say whether it had any practical effect but I do know that the German Kommandant gave orders to the guards that I was never to be searched when I returned to camp after my visits to the internees working outside.

I said earlier in this book that at the time of the occupation I had little or no knowledge of the German character. Since writing that I have remembered something. My paternal grandfather migrated to Guernsey from Devonshire in the 1850s and so there was a break in tradition and an absence of memories about our forbears who lived at Widecombe-in-the-Moor and had farmed land beside the River Dart, probably for centuries. My mother[12], dead these sixty years and more, to whom my mind goes back with deep and abiding affection, also came from Devonshire and I have only just remembered her telling me, when a small child, that, according to a story current in the family, one of her distant forbears was a very musical German who played the fiddle in Exeter Cathedral before the installation of the organ. If this be true, I certainly inherited no musical sense of any kind from him; did I inherit something which appealed to the Germans and conditioned my reactions to them? I shall never know.

---

[12] Elizabeth Annie Sherwill, née Roberts, died on 6th December 1907.

Appendices

APPENDIX A

German Orders

German Orders of Sunday, 30th June, 1940, but bearing date July 1, 1940, the date of publication.

ORDERS OF THE COMMANDANT OF THE GERMAN FORCES IN OCCUPATION OF THE ISLAND OF GUERNSEY

(1)   All inhabitants must be indoors by 11 p.m. and must not leave their homes before 6 a.m.

(2)   We will respect the population in Guernsey, but, SHOULD ANYONE ATTEMPT TO CAUSE THE LEAST TROUBLE SERIOUS MEASURES WILL BE TAKEN AND THE TOWN WILL BE BOMBED!

(3)   All orders given by the military authority are to be strictly obeyed.

(4)   All spirits must be locked up immediately, and no spirits may be supplied, obtained or consumed henceforth.   This prohibition does not apply to stocks in private houses.

(5)   No person shall enter the aerodrome at La Villiaze.

(6)   All rifles, airguns, pistols, revolvers, daggers, sporting guns and all other weapons whatsoever, except souvenirs, must, together with all ammunition, be delivered at the Royal Hotel by 12 noon to-day, July 1.

(7)   All British sailors, airmen and soldiers on leave in this island must report at the police station at 9 a.m., to-day and must then report at the Royal Hotel.

(8)   No boat or vessel of any description, including any fishing boat, shall leave the harbours or any other place where the same is moored, without an order from the military authority, to be obtained at the Royal Hotel. All boats arriving from Jersey, from Sark or from Herm, or elsewhere, must remain in harbour until

251

permitted by the military authority to leave. The crews will remain on board. The master will report to the harbourmaster, St. Peter Port, and will obey his instructions.

(9)   The sale of motor spirit is prohibited, except for use on essential services, such as doctors' vehicles, the delivery of foodstuffs, and sanitary services where such vehicles are in possession of a permit from the military authority to obtain supplies. These vehicles must be brought to the Royal Hotel by 12 noon to-day to receive the necessary permission.

The use of cars for private purposes is forbidden.

(10)   The black-out regulations already in force must be observed as before.

(11)   Banks and shops will be open as usual.

(Signed)

....

[13]THE GERMAN COMMANDANT OF THE ISLAND OF GUERNSEY

July 1, 1940

---

[13] The German Commandant who signed the first set of German Orders was Hessel

German Orders of Tuesday, 2nd July,1940, published in the Press on that day and in the Star on Wednesday, 3rd July, 1940.

ORDERS OF THE COMMANDANT OF THE GERMAN FORCES IN OCCUPATION OF THE BAILIWICK OF GUERNSEY DATED THE 2nd DAY OF JULY, 1940

(1)   The German Commandant has taken over the military powers of the islands of Guernsey and Jersey.   The population is hereby required to retain calmness, order and discipline.   If this is assured, the life and property of the population will be respected and guaranteed.   The German Commandant is in close touch with the Civil Authorities and acknowledges their loyal co-operation.   The German Commandant expects that every effort will be made to adjust the economic life of the island to the changed circumstances arising out of the evacuation and occupation and to preserve its economic structure and life.

(2)   The Civil Government and Courts of the Island will continue to function as heretofore, save that all Laws, Ordinances, Regulations and Orders will be submitted to the German Commandant before being enacted.

(3)   Such legislation as, in the past, required the sanction of His Britannic Majesty in Council for its validity shall henceforth be valid on being approved by the German Commandant and thereafter sanctioned by the British Civil Lieutenant-Governor of the Island of Guernsey.

(4)   The orders of the German Commandant will automatically have effect in the Island of Sark on promulgation by the German Military Authorities.

(5)   The orders of the German Commandant heretofore, now and hereafter issued shall in due course be registered on the Records of the Island of Guernsey in order that no person may plead ignorance thereof.   Offences against the same, saving those punishable under German Military Law, shall be punishable by the Civil Courts and the Royal Court shall, with the approval of the

German Commandant, enact suitable penalties in respect of such offences.

(6)   All clocks and watches are to be advanced one hour as from midnight of the 2nd/3rd July, 1940, to accord with German time.

(7)   Assemblies in Churches and Chapels for the purpose of Divine Worship are permitted. Prayers for the British Royal Family and for the welfare of the British Empire may be said. Such assemblies shall not be made the vehicle for any propaganda or utterances against the honour or interests of or offensive to the German Government or Forces.

(8)   Cinemas,   concerts   and   other entertainments are permitted subject to the conditions set out in Order No. 7 above.

(9)   The British National Anthem shall not be played or sung without the written permission of the German Commandant. This does not apply in private houses in respect of a British Broadcasting programme received therein.

(10)   The use of wireless RECEIVING SETS is permitted.

(11)   No increase in the price of any commodity shall be made without the previous assent of the German Commandant. On any contravention of this order taking place, then without prejudice to any civil penalties thereby incurred, the business premises concerned will be closed by the Military Authorities.

(12)   For the purpose of removing doubts, it is hereby declared that the prohibition of the supply and consumption of spirits applies to all Clubs.

(13)   The sale and consumption of wines, beer and cider is permitted in such premises as are licensed in that behalf by the civil authorities.

(14)   Holders of licences for the sale of intoxicating liquors shall take the most rigid precautions for the prevention of drunkenness.

If drunkenness takes place on licensed premises then, without prejudice to any other civil penalty, the island police shall, and are hereby empowered to, close the premises.

(15)   All traffic between Jersey and Guernsey, whether direct or indirect, is prohibited.

(16)   The rate of exchange between the Reichsmark and the Guernsey Pound has been provisionally fixed at 5 marks to the £.   A definite rate will shortly be fixed.

(17)   The continuance of the privileges granted to the civilian population is dependent on their good behaviour. Military necessity may from time to time require the orders now in force to be made more stringent.

    (Signed)   THE GERMAN COMMANDANT,

....

Dr. Lanz

Dated this second day of July, 1940

APPENDIX B

A Reassurance To The People Of Guernsey

A Written Statement by A.J. Sherwill published in the Star Newspaper of Monday, 8th July 1940.

On the evening of Sunday last, the 30th June, this Island was occupied by German Forces.

As the troop-carrying planes came in I telephoned to the Home Office and to the Bailiff of Jersey to acquaint them of the position and to say au-revoir.

The moment of greatest tension - that of making the first contact with the occupying Forces - had arrived. Arrangement had been made which were designed to avoid untoward incidents and these worked admirably.

Soon a car driven by a Police Sergeant brought a German Officer to my house. The Officer was the embodiment of courtesy and consideration.

I went with him to the Lieutenant Governor's house and the Lieutenant Governor, the Officer and I drove to the German Headquarters where we were received by the Commandant and his Staff. Again every courtesy and consideration were shown to us. Mr. Isler acted very ably as interpreter.

Questions were asked of us and were replied to with the utmost frankness. Directions were given and these were embodied in the first Orders in English issued by the German Commandant.

Then, on Monday, the German Commandant informed me that he was leaving, thanked me for the way the people of Guernsey had behaved in relation to himself and those under his command and introduced me to Dr. Lanz, the new Commandant of Guernsey and Jersey.

Courtesy visits were exchanged between the new German Commandant and the Lieutentant Governor.

I was then requested to attend on the German Commandant to give him such information as he might require and to receive such instructions as he might wish to give.

I was received by the Commandant and his Staff with every courtesy.

I felt it my duty at the outset to make the position clear, namely, that, as loyal subjects of His Britannic Majesty, we deeply regretted the German occupation but that, in the circumstances imposed upon us, the Commandant could rest assured that the attitude of the Civil Authorities and of the population towards himself and the Officers and Soldiers under his command would be correct in every respect. I also undertook personally to co-operate in every way towards that end and to behave with the utmost frankness in my relations with the Commandant and his Staff. It is my firm intention so to continue during the occupation.

The German Commandant gave me personal assurances as to the safety of the lives and property of the people of this Island which he subsequently embodied in his Orders.

I made a number of requests to him on behalf of the people of this Island, all of which were granted.

I am certain that everyone can rest assured that, going quietly about his or her business and refraining from any hostile act or speech directed against the German Government and Forces, no apprehension of any kind need be felt of any repressive measures being taken against the civilian population.

At the same time, the standard of discipline expected of each one of us is more rigid than we have been accustomed to. That standard must be observed and, if it is not, the consequences to the offender may well be serious.

The situation arising out of the cessation of our exports and imports and the severance of our communications with the United Kingdom is receiving the very earnest and continued attention of the various Departments of the Control Committee of the States of Guernsey and plans are being worked out to meet it. We ask for the sympathy, patience and co-operation of all in bringing those plans to fruition.

The German Commandant has repeatedly stressed the point that it is the policy of the German Government that the economic life of every community within its power and under its protection should be preserved to the greatest extent that circumstances permit and has expressed his intention of doing everything in his power towards that end.

It will be our endeavour to provide work for all capable of undertaking it and sufficient food for all.

May I express my deep gratitude to those who are collaborating with me in this task.

We have fallen temporarily on very hard times and those who are used to a high standard of living will have to accustom themselves to a very much lower one. It is in times of adversity rather than in those of prosperity that the best human qualities emerge and I am confident that these will see us through.

A.J. SHERWILL

July 6th, 1940

APPENDIX C

Letter From A. J. Sherwill To Home Office

Being a letter dated 18th July, 1940, from A.J. Sherwill addressed to C.G. Markbreiter. There is no evidence that it was ever delivered.

18th July, 1940.

C.G. Markbreiter Esq., C.B.E.,

Home Office,

Whitehall,

London, S.W.1.

My dear Markbreiter,

On the night of the 14th-15th July, an armed British force landed in Guernsey. They assaulted an old man living in the vicinity of the landing place, cut some private telephone wires, erected a barricade across a road and left behind a quantity of arms, ammunition, clothing and accoutrements. Certain of their number became detached from the force and have been taken prisoner. There were no casualties.

I do not know what the object of the landing was but to us it seems senseless.

Until it was definitely established that an armed force had landed, the German Military Authorities quite naturally suspected a locally staged incident and, although the truth soon became apparent, certain restrictions have been imposed as a result of the landing.

The object of this letter is to ask that you will make the strongest representations in the proper quarter to the effect that, it having been decided by the British Government, in the interests of the people of the Channel Islands, to demilitarise them, military activities of the kind referred to above are most unwelcome to us and are likely to result in loss of life among the civilian population and generally to make our position much more unpleasant than it is. Please urge this very forcibly. The Bailiff was amazed when he learned of the landing and in writing you thus I know I am expressing his views and that of many prominent people here.

The local officials have been and are being treated with the greatest courtesy and consideration by the German Military Authorities and the general behaviour of the German Troops is excellent.

The severance of communications with the United Kingdom has given rise to many problems with which we are grappling to the very best of our ability.

The German Authorities have undertaken to provide us with essential supplies and we anticipate that, shortly, seaborne trade with France will begin.

We very much hope that great discrimination will be exercised in regard to offensive action against any ship plying between the Channel Islands and the French coast and between Jersey and Guernsey. Such a ship may well be carrying essential supplies to us or taking our tomatoes in exchange for such supplies.

It would be most helpful if some arrangement could be made between the British and the German Admiralties for the return to us, for trading between Guernsey and Jersey and France, of the steamer "New Fawn" (Capt. F. Noyon) whose port of registry is Guernsey. She is presumably lying somewhere on the South Coast.

If she could be despatched with a mixed cargo of

(a)   flour,

(b)   salt,

(c)   margarine and cooking fats,

(d)   tea, and

(e)   sugar

we should be most grateful and payment could be obtained out of the funds belonging to Guernsey in London.

The German Commandant trusts the Island Officials and conversely the Island Officials trust the German Commandant who has proved just and humane and I am satisfied that stores sent here in this way would not be interfered with but would be available for consumption and use by the civilian population.

The Civil Lieutenant Governor and Bailiff is well and carrying out his duties.

My kindest personal regards to Sir Alexander Maxwell, yourself and Martin-Jones.

Could you as a personal favour drop a line to my boy of 15, Richard F. Sherwill, Elizabeth College, C/O Education Office, Oldham, Lancs. and say that his Mother and I and Joly and Rollo are quite well and send their love and ask him to so inform his elder sister Mary Rose and his brother John.

Very sincerely yours,

....

APPENDIX D

Message From A. J. Sherwill Transmitted By Bremen Radio

A message from A.J. Sherwill, recorded in Guernsey on 1st August, 1940, and transmitted soon after by Bremen Radio.

This is His Britannic Majesty's Procureur in Guernsey, Channel Islands speaking to the people of the United Kingdom, and in particular to those who left Guernsey and Alderney during the evacuation which preceded the German occupation.

I imagine that many of you must be greatly worried as to how we are getting on.

Well, let me tell you. Some will fear, I imagine, that I am making this record with a revolver pointed at my head and speaking from a transcript thrust into my hand by a German Officer.

The actual case is very different.

The Lieutenant-Governor and Bailiff, Mr. Victor Carey, and every other Island official has been and is being treated with every consideration and with the greatest courtesy by the German Military Authorities.

The Island Government is functioning. Churches and Chapels are open for public worship. Banks, shops and places of entertainment are open as usual.

Naturally, the sudden and entire severance of communications with the United Kingdom created innumerable problems with which we have wrestled and are still wrestling.

Perhaps the best indication of the measure of our success will be shown by the latest figures of unemployment, which are as follows: Males unemployed (of whom hardly any are fit for manual labour) 186; females unemployed, 191. Relief by way of public assistance is not above the normal figure.

The States have set up a Controlling Committee to speed up public business. My friends, Sir Abraham Lainé, A.M. Drake, R.O. Falla, R.H. Johns, John Leale, Stamford Raffles, and Dr. A.N. Symons are collaborating with me on this Committee and are working like trojans.

The conduct of the German troops is exemplary.

We have been in German occupation for $4^{1}/_{2}$ weeks and I am proud of the way my fellow-Islanders have behaved, and grateful for the correct and kindly attitude towards them of the German soldiers.

We have always been and we remain intensely loyal subjects of His Majesty, and this has been made clear to and is respected by the German Commandant and his staff.

On that staff is an officer speaking perfect English – a man of wide experience, with whom I am in daily contact. To him I express my grateful thanks for his courtesy and patience.

And now let me end on a more personal note.

To Elizabeth College, the Guernsey Ladies' College, the Guernsey Intermediate Schools, the Guernsey Primary and Voluntary Schools, to both Teachers and Scholars, all our love and good wishes.

To all men of military age who left here to join His Majesty's Forces, God speed. To all wives and mothers and sweethearts, God bless you. To all Guernsey children in England, God keep you safe.

God bless you all till we meet again.

And to Mary Rose, to John and Dick, Mummy and I send our fondest love and best wishes.

Tell Diana Raffles that her parents are well and send their love.

Will the B.B.C. please re-transmit this message and will the daily papers please publish it.

The following comments were made in a Leading Article in the Guernsey Evening Press of 2nd August, 1940, regarding A.J. Sherwill's message.

TELLING BRITAIN

We feel sure that everyone in Guernsey will feel a thrill of joy that a message from Mr. A.J. Sherwill, President of the States Controlling Committee, was recorded by him yesterday, and is to be broadcast in the near future from the Bremen Station in Germany, and that the B.B.C. are being asked to re-transmit the message and the daily papers to publish it.

The message has been made possible by the kind permission of the German Commandant, and it was made on a gramophone record, which has been sent to Bremen for transmission.

The possibility of some such transmission of good news was made to our Information Officer some days ago, by a representative of this paper and we are glad that a means has been found for putting it into effect.

The actual time of transmission by wireless from Germany is not yet known: it may be expected in the near future, and if Mr. Sherwill's request is carried out, it is safe to assume that every Sarnian now on the mainland will hear it and, still better, read it at leisure.

Mr. Sherwill's message, in well chosen words, is one that is at once homely, loyal and true to the history of the Island since the evacuation of part of the population and of our life, under changed, but not unhappy, conditions since the German occupation. It is a message such as any Guernseyman, anxious to reassure his loved ones beyond the reach of correspondence, would have himself wished to send, and it is therefore one voice speaking for all and with the heart of each with it.

APPENDIX D   MESSAGE FROM A. J. SHERWILL TRANSMITTED BY BREMEN
RADIO

The thanks of Guernsey will be given to the German Commandant for this happy and considerate gesture, one which all islanders will deeply appreciate.

APPENDIX E

Report Delivered To States Of Guernsey By A. J. Sherwill On 7th August 1940

Being a copy of the Report delivered to the meeting of the States of Guernsey held on 7th August, 1940, by A. J. Sherwill, President of the Controlling Committee.

On the 21st June last, after the partial evacuation of the Island following its demilitarisation, the States met informally, that is to say, they were convened at shorter notice than is provided by law, and appointed a Committee styled "The Controlling Committee of the States of Guernsey" with the extraordinary powers set out in the Resolution.

After some discussion, I was appointed President of the Controlling Committee and was empowered to nominate the other members of the Committee.

I proceeded immediately to form the Committee and invited Mr. Drake to become responsible for Horticulture, Mr. R.O. Falla for Agriculture, Mr. R.H. Johns for Unemployment, Re-employment and Public Assistance, Sir Abraham Lainé, K.C.I.E., for Essential Commodities, Mr. John Leale for Economics, Mr. Stamford Raffles for Information and Dr. Symons for Public Health Services.

All these gentlemen accepted the invitation and have laboured unceasingly ever since.

When the export of tomatoes to the United Kingdom ceased on the 28th June, it was felt that it was unnecessary to retain a department for Horticulture, and accordingly Mr. Falla became responsible for the utilisation of our soil, whether bare land or land covered by glass, and Mr. Drake was asked to become President of the Glasshouse Utilisation Board under Mr. Falla while remaining as a very valued member of the Controlling Committee.

Sir Abraham Lainé's Department was extended so as to include Essential Services while Mr. Raffles was asked to undertake the difficult and responsible task of dealing with the large number of people normally in receipt of income from outside the Island who as a result of the severance of communications with the United Kingdom were or would shortly be without means of subsistence.

May I take this opportunity of expressing my deepest gratitude to these gentlemen for all they have done and are doing. And working with and under them there has been a whole army of willing helpers, in the vast majority of cases receiving no salary of any kind, and all working long hours and tackling difficult problems with courage, determination and quiet confidence.

And I should be lacking in gratitude if I did not mention specifically H.M. Comptroller, the States' Supervisor and the States' Civil Service, the Inspector of Police and the Police Force, the various States' Departments, Boards and Committees who have co-operated so loyally, the Voluntary Organisations, and particularly the A.R.P. personnel and the St. John's Ambulance Brigade, who have done such yeoman service and the men and women unattached to any particular organisation who with patience and dignity have followed their callings and have accepted sacrifices and borne discomforts with cheerfulness and unselfishness.

You will remember that, except for a few persons, Alderney was completely evacuated. Those remaining were fetched in the lifeboat. The cattle and most of the horses and pigs were brought away and dogs and cats were destroyed.

This dangerous and unpleasant task was performed by a band of volunteers who knew the risks they might encounter but did not flinch from them. These were indeed men of whom Guernsey may be proud. The harvesting of the crops and the removal to Guernsey of stores and crops is still proceeding.

Then came the Air Raid of the 28th June. The *Courier* narrowly escaped disaster. Disaster came that evening in this Island and with it heroism and magnificent service by the A.R.P. personnel, the St. John's Ambulance Brigade, the Police and the medical profession. Death and bereavement, injury and suffering. Our hearts go out to the bereaved and to those still in hospital recovering from their wounds.

Next, the occupation of this Island by the German Forces on Sunday the 30th June, which took place without incident.

The cost of that occupation falls on the States of Guernsey, the rationing of the troops, the provision of premises, the wages of the civilian personnel such as interpreters, cooks and various helpers and the expense of transport, all these have been directed to be borne out of States' funds.

Arrangements had been made before the occupation for the functioning of the Banks under States' instructions, and these arrangements appear to have worked well.

Unemployment has been tackled vigorously and for some types of work it has been difficult to find the necessary labour.

We were instructed to keep half the tomato crop going in order that it might be exported to France against payment. This continues, but only a small proportion of the fruit available has been exported. As regards the other half, this was taken out and the soil prepared for beans and such like crops and these were planted and are doing well.

The Committee offered to take over the use and occupation of glasshouses and the employment of staffs, and their offer was accepted by the majority of growers. Only in this way could a vast amount of unemployment and distress be

avoided.   The   men   concerned   form   a   pool   from
which   we   can   gradually   draw   for   essential
services.

There should be a considerable quantity of fresh
vegetables and dried beans this winter, and the
latter will provide proteins to supplement the
somewhat slender supplies of meat which will be
available.

The meat in cold storage will not last for many
more weeks, and when that is exhausted we shall
have to depend upon the beef and pork which we
can produce locally together with the stocks of
preserved meats which exist.

We hope to be able to ensure a sufficient, if
somewhat meagre, butter ration throughout the
winter, but, although we anticipate that there
will be an abundance of skimmed milk, we cannot
promise whole cream milk except to children,
expectant and nursing mothers and invalids.

Now this Island has specialised for many years in
growing tomatoes, flowers and other crops of
lesser importance for export and with the
proceeds has purchased goods of the most varied
descriptions which it imported, some of which can
be produced here, but many of which cannot in any
circumstances.

We shall have to do without those things which we
cannot produce or import, and this means a very
great drop in the standard of living.   It is no
use blaming the Controlling Committee for this,
for it is beyond their power to remedy.

Already, in the interests of the whole community
drastic cuts have been made in the use of what we
have regarded as essential commodities.   Other
cuts will undoubtedly follow.   These cuts are
designed to make commodities last as long as
possible.

We have been assured repeatedly that the German
Government feels responsibility for ensuring that
we have the means of subsistence and that
essentials such as flour and coal will be sent

in, but the Controlling Committee feels the very gravest responsibility for conserving and providing such stocks as exist or can be produced locally and every effort is being and will be made in that direction.

Without any supplementation from without our stocks of flour should last for a further four to four and a half months. There should be no shortage of potatoes.

We are proposing so far as possible to collect the Income Tax for 1940. We cannot estimate its yield, but it is clear that in existing circumstances it will be very much less than the figure which we estimated originally.

At the present reduced rate of use, petrol will last for some months yet and it is hoped to keep the water and electricity undertakings going through the winter. Every effort will be made, too, to ensure a supply of gas.

Paraffin available for household consumption is very limited, and it is not possible for us to promise more than a very small quantity weekly, barely sufficient for lighting purposes. We deplore this but we cannot help it.

We have tried to the utmost of our ability to make such arrangements as will secure equality of sacrifice between users of gas, electricity and paraffin. But we cannot work miracles.

The Civil Service has received a drastic cut in the remuneration of its members. The salaried staff has been cut to the extent of one half of the difference between £100 and the salary previously paid. This meant that the more highly paid the official, the more drastic the cut.

The partial evacuation, and then the severance of communications with the United Kingdom have dealt a terrific blow to Island economics, and we have had to deal with innumerable and pressing problems, many almost and some quite insoluble, without time to sit back and think, without precedent to guide us. We have had to take charge of abandoned businesses, of abandoned dwelling houses, to destroy abandoned pets, to collect abandoned crops and abandoned stores.

We may have disappointed you sadly, no doubt there is much that you would have done otherwise. But at all events we have worked as a team, and in only one instance have I had to exercise my right to a casting vote on the Controlling Committee.

I was never under any illusions as to the difficulty of the task which you entrusted to me. If I have succeeded, or not wholly failed, it is because I was able to call upon men of tried capacity, and there is but one thing on which I pride myself and it is this : I believe firmly that I chose the right men, men who would draw to themselves and retain the support of a whole host of others.

Too much has happened during the past five weeks for me to do more than give a general account of it. If I started on details I should be merely wearisome and probably misleading.

I would mention, however, that the Country Hospital is now the general hospital for the whole Island, and that we hope to give special attention to the improvement of conditions there in the very near future.

Our tree-felling campaign is well on its way and, without in any way spoiling the Island, we hope to provide a reasonable amount of fuel for everybody this winter.

A considerable part of my time has been spent in acting as liaison officer between the German Commandant's staff and the Control Committee. My relations with the Commandant and his Staff are of the best, and throughout I have been treated with the greatest courtesy.

It would be idle to pretend that it is a bed of roses, but by frankness in my relations with the German Commandant I hope that I may have been of some slight service to the people of this Island.

We are, let us remember, in enemy occupation and are treated with consideration. So long as we continue to comport ourselves as we have during the past five weeks, refraining from provocative behaviour and going quietly about our daily tasks, there is no reason to fear harm to anyone. May this occupation be a model to the world, on the one hand tolerance on the part of the military authority and courtesy and correctness on the part of the occupying forces, and on the other dignity and courtesy and exemplary behaviour on the part of the civilian population. Perfect obedience to law and order, conformity, the strictest conformity, with black-out regulations and with orders and regulations issued by the German Commandant and the Civil Authorities. I do not know how long the occupation will last, but it will not last for ever. When it is over, I hope that occupying force and occupied population may each be able to say : Of different nations, having differing outlooks, we lived together with tolerance and mutual respect. The German Forces, fighting troops flushed with success on the continent, came to Guernsey and found the civilian population calm, dignified and well-behaved. Having us in their power, they behaved as good soldiers, *sans peur et sans reproche*. And we the civilian population were sober, law-abiding, giving no cause for offence, courteous and polite. We did our utmost, without exception, to avoid incidents and to assist in the maintenance of perfect order. This was the only contribution we could make in the circumstances in which we were placed and we made it. We were civilians and we behaved as such in the strictest sense in accordance with the usages of war. We did not shed and were not asked to shed our loyalty to our King and Country. In one of the greatest tests which could befall us we tried to justify the words of Victor Hugo when he called us "Ce noble petit peuple de la mer".

You have placed before you by the President of this House a proposition to the effect that the resolution of the 21st June last be confirmed. You should know before you vote that it is unquestionable that a large debt will be piled up to be dealt with after the war. I do not see how this or any other administration can avoid it in the circumstances in which we are placed. At the moment, the over-riding consideration is that the stocks of essential commodities that we possess and may produce shall be as fairly distributed as possible among our population and that the means of subsistence should be available to all.

You will remember that I associated myself with the view taken in this House by a number of members that Jurat Leale and not I should be the President of the Controlling Committee. I have frequently during the past six weeks been perplexed and baffled by the problems which have arisen. But for Mr. Leale's penetration and unremitting activities, I think the picture I have tried to sketch, grim as it may be, would be grimmer yet. Many a time since the 21st June have I wished that I might have been doing the type of work to which I was accustomed and where I more or less knew my way about. As the result of being a dictator for six weeks I think I'm a much humbler person than I ever was before. I certainly never realised before how little I knew about anything. But that's probably because I'm not made of the stuff of which dictators are ; which leads me to my final remark : When the time comes to discard me, as come it will, whether to-day or later, you can be sure that such service as I can give will be given gladly to whoever may be appointed in my place and, if that successor should be Jurat Leale, no one would be happier than myself.

APPENDIX F

Milk Orders

Containing the following:-

(i)   The Milk Order, 1940, together with that Order's two Appendices.

(ii)   The Milk Consumers Registration Order, 1940.

(iii)   The Milk Rationing Order, 1940.

(iv)   Order Relating to all Retailers of Milk.

(v)   The Milk and Butter Prices Order, 1940.

The Milk Order, 1940

Evening Press - Saturday, September 28, 1940.

"LA GAZETTE OFFICIELLE"

The Controlling Committee of the States of Guernsey

THE MILK ORDER, 1940

The Controlling Committee of the States of Guernsey, in virtue of the powers conferred upon it under Ordinance of the Royal Court No. LXVIII of 1940, hereby makes the following Order :-

PARAGRAPH 1.

1. -   All owners of cattle shall deliver the cow's milk produced on their premises to the Milk Depôts (see Paragraph 2) established by the States Dairy Committee.

2. -   The duty of delivering milk to the Milk Depôts applies with regard to all milk produced in so far as no exceptions are made under this Order or, in any individual case, by written authority of the States Dairy Committee.

3. -   Cow's milk (whether whole milk or separated milk) shall be supplied to retailers only by the Milk Depôts and to consumers only by the Milk Depôts or Retailers licensed by the States Committee for the Control of Essential Commodities and every such supply shall be made in accordance with the provisions of this Order and every other Order for the time being in force governing such supply (including any order for the time being in force governing the rationing of whole milk and separated milk) and in accordance with the directions given from time to time by the President of the States Committee for the Control of Essential Commodities. The supply of whole milk or separated milk, whether by way of sale, gift or otherwise, directly to a retailer or consumer by an owner of cattle, not otherwise authorised under this Order to effect such supply, and the separation of milk elsewhere than at the separating depôts established by the

States Dairy Committee, are prohibited. The States Dairy Committee is hereby authorised to take all necessary steps to render milk separators inoperative.

PARAGRAPH 2.

1. - Milk Depôts are (a) the States Dairy and (b) the Milk Depôts (that is to say the Separating Depôts and the Road Depôts) established by the States Dairy Committee.

2. - In the Appendix particulars are given as to the Milk Depôts established by the States Dairy Committee. Individual owners of cattle are required to deliver their milk to the Milk Depôt nearest to their farm premises or, if so required by the President of the States Dairy Committee, to such other Milk Depôt as is indicated to them by or under the authority of such President.

3. - The delivery of milk to the Milk Depôts is the obligation of the owners of cattle.

4. - The price payable in respect of the purchase of whole milk delivered at the Milk Depôts and the price payable in respect of the purchase of whole milk and separated milk from Milk Depôts and retailers will be fixed and made public by the Controlling Committee of the States of Guernsey.

PARAGRAPH 3.

1. - The States Dairy Committee will appoint a person in charge of each Milk Depôt and each such person so appointed is hereinafter referred to as "the Milk Depôt Manager."

2. - That Committee will be responsible that milk to be delivered under this Order to each Milk Depôt is so delivered by owners of cattle.

3. - The Milk Depôt Manager will be responsible that the milk delivered at the Depôt of which he has charge is handled properly, especially in regard to the prevention of waste and contamination, and that it is disposed of in accordance with the provisions of this Order and

with the directions given by the States Dairy Committee under Section 2 of Paragraph 9 of this Order.

4. - The States Dairy Committee and any member or representative thereof thereunto appointed by that Committee shall be entitled to inspect all premises in which milk or any milk product is produced, kept, processed or sold and may demand information of the occupier in regard to any matter relating to the production, keeping, processing, sale or delivery thereof. If any information demanded under this Section is refused or if incorrect or incomplete information is given, the person demanding such information may by order in writing addressed to any owner of cattle, or his representative, direct the delivery of a specified quantity of milk to the appropriate Milk Depôt, such quantity being fixed upon the basis of an examination of the relevant circumstances. Failure to obey any such order so given shall constitute a contravention of this Order and shall be reported to the States Dairy Committee by the Milk Depôt Manager.

PARAGRAPH 4.

The States Dairy Committee shall keep exact daily records of :-

(a) all milk delivered at each Milk Depôt ; and

(b) all milk and milk products disposed of at that Depôt.

PARAGRAPH 5.

Each Milk Depôt Manager shall supply milk only to persons who establish their right so to be supplied and to the extent only of the right so established. Every such person shall establish his right to be supplied :-

(a) if he is a retailer, by presenting a permit issued under the authority of the States Committee for the Control of Essential Commodities upon that Milk Depôt setting forth the quantity of milk and the period for which the permit is valid.

(b) if he is a consumer, by registering in the milk supply list "A" or "B" of that Milk Depôt.

In the milk supply list "A" those consumers are to be registered who   establish their right to be supplied with whole milk and in the milk supply list"B" those entitled to be supplied with separated milk.   Registration shall be effected in the manner prescribed and published in "La Gazette Officielle" by   the States Committee for the Control of Essential Commodities.

(c) if he is an owner of calves, pigs or poultry, by presenting a permit for separated milk for animal feeding issued upon that Milk Depôt by the States Dairy Committee and setting forth the quantity of separated milk and the period for which the permit is valid.

PARAGRAPH 6.

1. The supply of milk by retailers to consumers shall be governed by the principles set forth in Paragraph 5 (b).

2. Milk (whether whole milk or separated milk) may be supplied by a retailer only to consumers who are registered under the provisions of this Order in the list of customers of that retailer.

PARAGRAPH 7.

Hotels,   boarding   houses,   restaurants, institutions and other establishments with a changing number of consumers require, in order to obtain a supply of milk, a special permit issued upon a definite supplier (Milk Depôt or Retailer) by the States Committee for the Control of Essential Commodities. This special permit shall include the requirements of milk of the resident owner or manager, his family and the resident staff. Such persons may not also register in a milk supply list under Paragraph 5 (b) or Paragraph 6.

PARAGRAPH 8.

Owners of milch cattle are entitled to retain for their own use and the use of members of their family and of their staff residing with them from the milk to be delivered by them to the Milk Depôt such quantity of whole milk as is prescribed under the Milk Rationing Order, 1940, as the ration to which those persons are entitled.

PARAGRAPH 9.

1. This Order shall be carried into execution by the States Committee for the Control of Essential Commodities and by the States Dairy Committee, each in so far as those Committees are concerned therewith respectively.

2. The States Dairy Committee, taking into account the actual quantity of milk produced from time to time and the probable requirements of consumers, shall instruct each Milk Depôt Manager as to:-

(a) the quantity of milk to be distributed as whole milk or to be delivered to the States Dairy;

(b) the quantity of cream to be separated and delivered to the States Dairy;

(c) the quantity of separated milk to be distributed and what is to be done with the surplus;

(d) the quantity of milk products to be manufactured by the States Dairy and what portion thereof is to be distributed immediately and what portion is to be conserved for future distribution.

3. In planning the disposal, distribution and conservation of milk and milk products, account shall be taken of all Orders for the time being operative in relation to the rationing of milk and milk products.

4. Permits and special permits issued by the States Committee for the Control of Essential Commodities and permits for milk for animal feeding issued by the States Dairy Committee shall be in the Forms 1, 2 and 3 respectively set out in Appendix 2.

PARAGRAPH 10.

This Order is without prejudice to the continued operation of the provisions of Part IV of the Public Health Ordinance, 1936, which relate to the inspection of farms, dairies and other places wherein milk, butter or other dairy produce is kept, treated, prepared, blended, sold or offered for sale and to the taking of all such steps in relation thereto as are necessary to safeguard health.

PARAGRAPH 11.

Every retailer of milk trading as such before the date of the coming into force of this Order shall thereafter continue to trade as such in accordance with the provisions of this Order until permitted by the States Dairy Committee, after consultation with the States Committee for the Control of Essential Commodities, to relinquish his milk retail business.

PARAGRAPH 12.

The provisions of the Defence Regulations (Guernsey), 1939, apply in relation to the enforcement of this Order and to the punishment of contraventions thereof.

PARAGRAPH 13.

Such of the provisions of this Order as relate to the fixation of the purchase price of whole milk and separated milk, the appointment of Milk Depôt Managers, the issue of permits and special permits for the supply of whole milk and separated milk, the registration of consumers, and otherwise to the taking of such preliminary steps as are deemed necessary for the purpose of bringing this Order into operation, shall have effect as from the date of this Order, and the remaining provisions of this Order shall come into operation on the 13th day of October, 1940, to the intent that this Order shall be fully operative as from the commencement of the date last mentioned.

....

A. J. SHERWILL,

For and on behalf of the Controlling Committee of
the States of Guernsey,

Dated this 27th day of September, 1940.

Genehmigt   (Approved),

Feldkommandantur, 515,

Nebenstelle,

GUERNSEY.

....

DR. REFFLER.

Kriegsverwaltungsrat.

Den 27. 9. 40.

APPENDIX 1.

MILK DEPOTS

SEPARATING DEPOTS

1. Cliffdale, Torteval.
2. La Houguette, St. Peter's.
3. Myrtle Place, King's Mills, Castel.
4. The Old Testing Station, Lilyvale, Castel.
5. La Ramée, St. Sampson's.
6. The Rectory, Vale.
7. The States Dairy, St. Martin's.

ROAD DEPOTS

1. Luff's Corner, St. Martin's.
2. Chêne Hill, Forest.
3. Forest Schools.
4. La Villiaze, Forest.
5. La Croix, St. Peter's.
6. Sion Chapel, St. Peter's.
7. Sous L'Église, St. Saviour's.
8. Les Buttes, St. Saviour's.
9. Les Picques, St. Saviour's.
10. Le Gron, St. Saviour's.
11. Candie, Castel.
12. La Chaumière, Castel.
13. Les Galliennes, St. Andrew's.
14. Bailiff's Cross, St. Andrew's.

APPENDIX 2.

FORM No. 1.

PERMIT for the supply of Milk to a Retailer.

To the States Milk Depôt,

....

....

This permit authorises the supply to ....

of .... daily for the purposes of his
retail business of the following quantities of
Milk :-

.... Pots of Whole Milk.

.... Pots of Separated Milk.

This permit is valid for the period ending on the

…......... , 19 ....

....

President,

States Committee for the Control of Essential
Commodities.

.... , 19 ....

FORM No. 2.

SPECIAL PERMIT for the supply of Milk under Paragraph 7.

To ....

....

....

This permit authorises the supply by you to ....

of .... daily for the purposes of his retail business of the following quantities of Milk :-

.... Pints of Whole Milk.

.... Pots of Separated Milk.

This permit is valid for the period ending on the .... , 19 ....

....

President,

States Committee for the Control of Essential Commodities.

.... , 19 ....

FORM No. 3.

PERMIT for the supply of Separated Milk for Animal Feeding.

To the States Milk Depôt,

....

....

This permit authorises the supply to

....

of .... daily , for the purposes of feeding the same to

Calves*

Pigs*

Poultry*

of .... Pots of Separated Milk.

This permit is valid for the period ending on the

.... , 19 ....

....

President,

States Dairy Committee.

...., 19 ....

* Delete inapplicable words.

The Milk Consumers Registration Order, 1940

Evening Press - Saturday, September 28, 1940.

"LA GAZETTE OFFICIELLE"

States Committee for the Control of Essential Commodities.

THE MILK CONSUMERS REGISTRATION ORDER, 1940

WHEREAS on and after the 13th October, 1940, no person will be permitted to purchase milk without having previously registered with a licensed retailer in that commodity, and then only from the licensed retailer with whom he or she has registered.

AND WHEREAS a licensed retailer is a retailer who has obtained from the States' Committee for the Control of Essential Commodities, Ladies College, a licence to trade as such.

NOW THEREFORE the States' Committee for the Control of Essential Commodities, in exercise of the powers thereunto enabling it, hereby makes the following Order :-

1. - The registration of milk consumers shall be effected as follows :-

A milk registration card will be delivered to every house through the post in the same way as was done in the case of census cards. If no card has been so delivered by the 3rd October, 1940, to any house, or to any family requiring one, the head of such house, or family, must apply to any Post Office for a card. Cards must be obtained for every family, that is to say, every milk customer, and completed in accordance with the instructions given thereon. Separate cards may be handed in for individuals whose anticipated domestic arrangements in the near future may be thought to warrant such action ; e.g. young people about to marry and change residence on doing so, and so on.

Registration cards must be completed and posted in a letter box on or before the 4th

October, 1940. They must not be stamped, folded or enclosed in an envelope.

Hotels, boarding houses, restaurants, institutions and other establishments with a changing number of consumers must apply for a special permit issued upon a definite retailer by the States Committee for the Control of Essential Commodities. The application for such permit must contain the same information in respect of consumers as would have been furnished had a registration card been used, and, in those cases where whole milk is claimed on medical certificate, the relative certificate must be attached to the application. Should a certificate not be forthcoming when the application is made, it should be sent as soon as received to the Committee for the Control of Essential Commodities, Ladies College, accompanied by a reference to the original application.

2. - Consumers will not be permitted to change their retailer except with the consent of the Committee, which will be granted only in the event of removal necessitating a change of retailer, or other special circumstances.

3. - It is emphasised that registration must be completed by the 4th October, 1940, so as to enable the Committee to arrange with the States Dairy Committee for the necessary supplies to be made available at the depôts to registered retailers.

This Order shall come into operation forthwith.

....

A.   J.   LAINÉ,
President,

States' Committee for the Control of Essential Commodities.

Dated the 27th day of September, 1940.

Genehmigt (Approved).

Feldkommandantur, 515.

    Nebenstelle,

        GUERNSEY.

....

        I. V. DR. BROSCH.

        Kriegsverwaltungsrat.

Den. 27. 9. 40

The Milk Rationing Order, 1940

Evening Press - Saturday, September 28, 1940.

"LA GAZETTE OFFICIELLE"

The Controlling Committee of the States of Guernsey

THE MILK RATIONING ORDER, 1940

It is hereby ordered as follows :-

1. Whole cow's milk and separated milk shall henceforth be rationed foods.

2. The amount of the ration shall be as follows :-

(a) Whole Milk

(i) For a child over two years of age and under fourteen years of age	1 pint per day.
(ii) For a child up to two years of age, for an expectant mother during the last three months of pregnancy, for a nursing mother for a period not exceeding nine months following the birth of the child, and for an invalid	Such quantity per day as shall be prescribed from time to time in a written certificate of a medical practitioner authorised to practise in this Island and deposited with the Committee for the Control of Essential Commodities. In no case, save in the most exceptional circumstances, shall the daily quantity so prescribed exceed 2 pints.

(iii) For an owner of milch cattle, each member of his family residing with him and each member of his staff residing on his farm premises, such owner, member of his family or staff not being a person entitled to a ration under clause (i) or (ii) of this sub-paragraph	One half pint per day.

(b) Separated Milk

For every person not being a person entitled to a ration of whole milk	One half pint per day.

3. For the purposes of this Order, "invalid" means   a   person   suffering   from   some   illness, weakness   or   disability   which   necessitates   a ration of whole milk or whose health would be seriously impaired were he or she to be deprived of a ration of whole milk and who is certified as such   by   a   medical   practitioner   authorised   to practise in this Island.

4. Not more than one sixth of a pint of separated milk   shall   form   part   of   any   meal   or   of   any beverage   consumed   at   any   one   time   as   is   or   are partaken   of   in   an   hotel,   restaurant,   or   other place by a person not residing therein.

5. This   Order   shall   come   into   operation   on   the 13th day of October, 1940.

....

A. J. SHERWILL,

For and on behalf of the Controlling Committee of the States of Guernsey.

Dated the 27th day of September, 1940.

Order Relating to All Retailers of Milk

Evening Press - Saturday, September 28, 1940.

"LA GAZETTE OFFICIELLE"

The Controlling Committee of the States of Guernsey

ORDER RELATING TO ALL RETAILERS OF MILK

The Controlling Committee of the States of Guernsey, in exercising powers conferred thereon by Ordinance of the Royal Court, hereby makes the following Order :-

Every retailer of milk in this Island must, on or before Tuesday, October 1st, 1940, furnish the President of the States' Committee for the Control of Essential Commodities, Ladies' College, with the following information :-

(a)   Full name, address and telephone No.

(b)   Number of regular customers who themselves fetch their milk from the retailer's premises.

(c)   Number of regular customers to whom milk is delivered by the retailer.

(d)   Total quantity in pots of milk supplied weekly by retail.

....

A. J. SHERWILL,

For and on behalf of the Controlling Committee of the States of Guernsey.

Elizabeth College,

Guernsey.

Genehmigt   (Approved).

 Feldkommandantur 515

 Nebenstelle, Guernsey.

....

     DR.REFFLER,

     Kriegsverwaltungsrat.

 Den. 27. 9. 1940.

The Milk and Butter Prices Order, 1940.

Evening Press - Wednesday, October 2, 1940.

"LA GAZETTE OFFICIELLE"

The Controlling Committee of the States of Guernsey.

THE MILK AND BUTTER PRICES ORDER, 1940.

It is hereby ordered as follows :-

MILK

1.- The price payable by the States Dairy Committee in respect of whole milk delivered by the producer to the States Dairy and the Milk Depôts established by the States Dairy Committee shall be at the rate of 11d. per pot.

2.- The price payable by a retailer to the States Dairy Committee in respect of milk supplied to the retailer at the States Dairy or at any milk depôt established by the States Dairy Committee shall be as follows :-

As regards whole milk, at the rate of 1/- per pot.

As regards separated milk, at the rate of 6d. per pot.

For the purpose of this paragraph the expression "supplied to the retailer" shall include :-

(a) the supply for the purposes of his trade or business to any person engaged in the trade or business of supplying milk or things prepared wholly or partially from milk or to which milk is usually added before delivery thereof, but only as regards any calendar week during which the amount of each such supply is not less than one pot.

Provided that the expression "trade or business" shall not include the provision by any person of board or board and lodging for any relative or member of the household of that person.

(b) the supply to a States Council, Board, Committee or Institution.

3.- The price payable by consumers to retailers shall be as follows :-

(a) As regards whole milk fetched by the consumer, at the rate of $3^1/_2$d. per pint.

(b) As regards whole milk delivered at the residence of the consumer, at the rate of 4d. per pint.

(c) As regards separated milk fetched by the consumer, at the rate of 2d. per pint.

(d) As regards separated milk delivered to the residence of the consumer, at the rate of $2^1/_2$d. per pint.

BUTTER

4.- The price payable to the States Dairy Committee in respect of Guernsey butter purchased from that Committee for the purpose of resale shall be 1s. 8d. per lb.

5.- The price payable to retailers by purchasers of butter from such retailers shall be at the rate of 1s. 10d. per lb.

GENERAL

6.- The provisions of the Defence Regulations (Guernsey), 1939, apply as regards the enforcement of this Order.

7.- This Order shall come into operation on the 13th day of October, 1940.

....

                                    A. J. SHERWILL

For and on behalf of the Controlling Committee of the States of Guernsey

          Dated the 27th day of September, 1940.

                    Genehmigt   (Approved)

                    Feldkommandantur 515,

                    Nebenstelle, Guernsey.

          K.V.R.   DR. REFFLER

....

          Den 1 Okt. 40.

APPENDIX G

The Mulholland And Martel Affair

The paper which Sherwill wrote regarding this occurrence has unfortunately been lost but not before it had been used by Alan and Mary Wood as the basis for the account, concerning these two young officers, in their book *"Islands in Danger"*. The following details have been obtained, in the main, from that source.

At a little before midnight of the 9th July, 1940, H.M. Submarine H 43 (Lieutenant G.R. Colvin) surfaced off the south coast of Guernsey. Two Guernseymen, Second Lieutenant Desmond Mulholland, of the Duke of Cornwall's Light Infantry, and Second Lieutenant Philip Martel, of the Hampshire Regiment, together with Sub-Lieutenant J.L.E. Leith, the submarine's navigation officer, transferred to a Berthon dinghy and paddled ashore to Le Jaonnet Beach, landing through the breakers with considerable difficulty. Here, awaiting them in accordance with plan, was Second Lieutenant H.F. Nicolle, ready to return to England, having successfully completed his first reconnaissance visit. All three of the Army officers were dressed in civilian clothes. Nicolle quickly briefed Mulholland and Martel about the situation on the island but Leith was having difficulty preventing damage to the dinghy in the rough seas and was anxious to get away, with Nicolle, from the beach. The Berthon set off but was quickly swamped. The four of them managed to drag the boat out of the water, bail out and successfully re-launch her. Leith and Nicolle were lucky to get back aboard the submarine by 02.18 hrs.

This landing, and the earlier one by Nicolle, were intended to prepare the way for a full-scale Commando Raid on Guernsey, planned for the night of July 12-13th. Their orders were to reconnoitre routes for the raid and then to act as guides to the landing parties, with Mulholland to meet a party at Moye Point and Martel performing a similar function at Petit Bôt.

In the event, the Commando Raid was postponed for 48 hours and, when it did take place, the two young officers were unable to make contact with the raiding parties. They were left stranded and on the run.

After failing to get away in a boat which they stole at Perelle, on the west coast of Guernsey, they crossed over to Sark, mingling with German officers on the small inter-island vessel, but found escape from that island to be impossible. Unwilling to further compromise friends and relations, they decided to contact Sherwill with the intention of seeking his aid in surrendering to the Germans.

Early one morning later in July, Sherwill had gone down to the basement at the back of his home, Havelet House, to stoke the boiler, only to find the two officers at the back door. He knew Desmond Mulholland well and was introduced to Martel. They rapidly told their story and of their determination to give themselves up. Sherwill immediately realized that, having landed in civilian clothes, they were liable to be shot as spies and that the only way of saving their lives was to obtain uniforms for them. First of all he consulted his wife, warning her of the grim penalties for helping spies, but she brushed aside his warnings and immediately set about preparing breakfast which the two young men ate ravenously. They were then hidden in an attic bedroom to rest and to sleep.

Sherwill believed that military uniforms might be found in the unoccupied houses of Guernsey Militia officers who had evacuated to England. He felt that his friend, Don Bisset, a builder and licensee of La Fontaine inn, who had a distinguished record in the Royal Guernsey Light Infantry in the First World War, would make an ideal accomplice. "Don," he said, "put all your keys in your pocket – we're going burgling." Bisset, a captain in the Militia, pointed out that there was still a stock of uniforms at the Town Arsenal and to the Arsenal they went, driving past a German soldier who took no notice of them. Here they selected two sets of uniform. Medal ribbons had to be removed and Militia buttons replaced. Mrs. Dawes, wife of the Arsenal caretaker, did a heroic high-speed job of sewing on British Army buttons. Sherwill loaded the uniforms into the little Baby Fiat car he was using, dropped off Bisset and returned safely to Havelet House. He woke up Mulholland and Martel who, after a meal, dressed themselves in the uniforms.

He then rang German Headquarters and spoke to Dr. Maass, saying:

"Two British officers have surrendered to me."

"Two officers?"

"Yes."

"When?"

"I won't lie," said Sherwill. "It was two or three hours ago. They were in a pretty bad way, so I gave them a chance of some food and a rest before telephoning you."

"Are they in uniform?" asked Maass.

"Yes."

"At your house?"

"Yes."

"You mean they were able to walk through the streets to you in British uniform without being seen?"

"Of course not," he said quickly. "Do you think they are mad? They landed in uniform, but they had some civilian clothes to come here. I've kept the clothes to show you.

They then set off for the German headquarters and on the way Sherwill impressed on the two young men that they must reveal nothing but their Name, Rank and Number. "Otherwise you'll be shot, and I'll be shot too."

On arrival at the Channel Islands Hotel, the then German headquarters, the sentries outside reacted in panic at the sight of the two British officers but Sherwill waved them aside and asked for Dr. Maass.

Maass shook hands with all three of them, was most charming and, with the air of merely making conversation, asked Martel and Mulholland when they had arrived. To Sherwill's horror, one of them told him and he felt that it could only be a matter of time before the whole story came out. After the two young offices had been led away he determined to make a last attempt to put them on their guard.

"Do you mind?" he asked Maass. "I meant to give them cigarettes, but forgot". He went to the guardroom, handed around some cigarettes with a cheery smile and a whispered mutter of:-

"You bloody fools, nothing but Name, Rank and Number!"

Some days later, when he could stand the suspense no longer, Sherwill asked Maass as casually as he could manage:- "By the way, have you heard anything about how those two young officers are getting on?" To which Maass replied:- "They'll be all right if their story holds."

They were eventually treated as Prisoners of War.

APPENDIX H

Draft Letters Between A. J. Sherwill And Major Bandelow

The following two letters were based on drafts submitted by A.J. Sherwill to Major Bandelow and they were published in the Guernsey Evening Press on Saturday, 12th October 1940.

Draft Letter from Bandelow to Sherwill:

Guernsey

11th October 1940

The President,

Controlling Committee of the States of Guernsey,

Elizabeth College,

Guernsey.

Dear Mr. President,

Will you please inform the population of Guernsey that Colonel Count von Schmettow has been appointed German Commandant of the British Channel Islands with Headquarters in Jersey and has confirmed my appointment as Commandant of the Island of Guernsey.

After having had the opportunity of becoming acquainted with conditions on the Island, I wish to express to you, Mr. President, my pleasure in finding that the Island Authorities and Civic Population show towards the German Forces an attitude which enables me to continue the pleasant relations which have existed hitherto between the Occupying Forces and the population.

As I have already expressed to you orally, you will understand however that, in the fulfilment of my duty, I cannot tolerate conduct which might militate against the interests of the German Reich.

After it had been found that, contrary to regulations, eight Islanders had departed for England in a boat, strict watch over all available boats has been found necessary as it is by no means unlikely that information of military importance may reach England in such manner.

Furthermore, there exists the possibility of British soldiers still being on the Island in hiding with the assistance of the inhabitants. These may be soldiers who either stayed behind at the time of the evacuation or who have since entered the Island.

I draw your attention and that of the inhabitants to the fact that the civilian population of an occupied area are only entitled to immunity from military action for so long as they abstain from any military activity and that the affording of assistance to or the concealment of any member of the armed forces of a Power at war with the German Reich, participation in espionage, or any act of sabotage, would be severely punished by military tribunal in accordance with the relevant enactments. In war, harsher measures are necessary than in time of peace.

I intend to arrange with you a certain date by which all members of the British Armed Forces still in hiding here will have to report. Those reporting up to that date will be treated as prisoners of war, also no measures will be taken against their relatives who had assisted in hiding them.

Those members of the British Forces who may be found after this time limit must expect to be treated as agents of an enemy power. At the same time, all those who have been aiding them will have to take the consequence.

I hope that after the carrying out of these measures all difficulties still existing between the Army of Occupation and the Island population will then be removed and I would like to ask you always to approach me with full confidence in case you should require my help in the carrying out of your official duties.

With the expression of my deep respect.

....

BANDELOW

Draft Letter from Sherwill to Bandelow:

The Controlling Committee of the States of Guernsey,

Elizabeth College,

Guernsey.

11th October 1940

The German Commandant

Insel Kommandantur,

Guernsey.

Dear Herr Commandant,

I have the honour to acknowledge the receipt of your letter of to-day's date.

In the first place, I welcome your kind message to the effect that having acquainted yourself with conditions on the Island, you can assure me of the continuance of the pleasant relations which have hitherto existed between the Army of Occupation and the population.

I will gladly avail myself of your kind suggestion that I should approach you in all confidence for your help in relation to the carrying out of my official duties. You have already in a number of matters on which I have approached you, given tangible proof of your goodwill towards the Island Administration and population.

I fully appreciate the responsibility which rests upon you in the execution of the duty entrusted to you and consistently throughout the command of your predecessor, Dr. Lanz, every effort was made by the Island Administration to ensure that no incident should arise which might imperil the correct and courteous relations which existed between the German Military Authorities and the Island Administration. You may rest assured that those efforts on our part will continue during your command and you may rely with confidence upon my own personal energies being continually directed to that end.

You refer in your letter to the departure of a boatload of persons from the Island and the consequences which have followed. The Island Authorities deplore the incident which they would have prevented had they been aware of it. I would draw your attention to the Notice which I caused to be published in the local newspapers on the 28th September 1940. I also instituted police watching the bays and harbours but at our recent interview you kindly relieved me and the police of all further responsibility as regards this.

I accept unreservedly your statement that no civilian may participate in any military activity without incurring the gravest penalties.

As from the military evacuation of this Bailiwick by the British Government it became imperative, as was and is recognised by the Island Authorities, that military activity, direct or indirect, of any nature by the Island Administration and the civilian population must be abjured.

The Island Administration has problems of grave complexity to grapple with, problems of finance, supply, etc, and nothing would embarrass it more in the execution of its formidable task than that the Island should be the scene of activities forbidden by the law and usages of war and of the consequences which might ensue.

I have noted that you intend to arrange with me a time limit within which any personnel of the British Armed Forces in hiding in this Island (if such there be) must surrender and that, if this direction is complied with, such personnel will be treated as prisoners of war and no measures will be taken against any of their relatives who may have given them assistance.

This, Herr Commandant, is a generous gesture on your part, I appreciate that, thereafter, you will be unable to afford such immunity.

Whilst these considerations are clear to you and to the Island Administration I think a useful purpose would be served if you would allow your letter to me and this my reply to be published in order that no one, however un-tutored in the laws and usages of war he or she may be, may henceforth be ignorant of the consequence of illegal action of the nature referred to.

Such publication will also acquaint Islanders of the appointment of Colonel Count von Schmettow as German Commandant of the British Channel Islands and your own nomination as German Commandant of this Island.

It gives me grounds for confidence that, at a period when nations to which we respectively belong are locked in a combat the consequences of which will be momentous to Europe and the whole World, it is possible – though only in the Channel Islands – for a German Officer and a British Official to enter into friendly correspondence, to engage in full and frank discussions and to exchange courtesies. This I hope and anticipate with every confidence will always be possible throughout the German occupation of this Bailiwick;

I beg that you will acquaint me of any happenings to which you may take exception and I ask that, with that humanity of which you have consistently shown yourself to be possessed, you will permit me to intercede on behalf of anyone who, unwittingly or without appreciation of the consequences, may offend against the German Military Code.

I convey to you, Herr Commandant, the expression of my deep respect and my sincere appreciation of the many courtesies accorded to me by yourself and your Adjutant Oberleutnant Schnadt.

....

A.J. Sherwill

The following Notice was subsequently published:-

Members of the British Armed Forces in hiding in Guernsey and persons who are assisting them in any way must report at the Island Police Station, St. Peter Port at the latest by

6 P.M. ON MONDAY, 21st. OCTOBER 1940

Members of the British Armed Forces obeying this order will be treated as prisoners of war and no measures will be taken against persons who have assisted them.

Any Member of the British Armed Forces who may be found after this time limit must expect to be treated as an agent of an enemy power. Also all those who have assisted in hiding such persons or in any other way will have to take the full consequences of such actions.

Feldkommandantur 515

Nebenstelle Guernsey

....

i.V. Signed DR. BROSCH

Guernsey, 18th October, 1940.

APPENDIX I

The Cherche Midi Diary

7.11.40.   Left Aerodrome about 3.30 p.m.   Beautiful take-off. Given fire bucket in case I'm sick. As we banked to head for France, Island appeared to stand up on its side. Went out over Moulin Huet. Cliffs and sea lovely. As we left the cliffs we dropped sickeningly in air pocket. Sark and Jersey very visible. Journey good.   Saw St. Malo and landed Dinard for few minutes.   Then on to Paris. Bumpy at times. Landed Villacoublay Aerodrome 5.50 p.m. Had tea, bread, sardines and biscuits in Aerodrome Canteen. Then on by car to Paris to the Kommandantur and then to the Hotel des Ambassadeurs, Boulevard Haussmann.

Treated like a prince, bedroom with private bathroom and lavatory.

Dinner and then bed.

8.11.40.   Breakfast 9 a.m. Dr. Mette, an interpreter, is deputed to accompany me everywhere, it being explained to me that I am only Englishman under 65 at large in France and that I might be picked up by German Police.

Go for ¾ hr. walk. Paris much as usual except much less traffic.

Provided with newspapers. Excellent lunch and nap and then a long walk. Difficult to judge but Paris does not appear too unhappy under the occupation. The Germans appear to be behaving very well and Parisians appear unconcerned. Major Schoenmeyer who accompanied me to Paris a very charming and cultured man. He returned to hotel today for few minutes. I had mentioned that I should like to call on M. Regnault and his colleague who were so charming to us at the Semaine de Droit Normand in 1938. I am asked not to do so and to give my word of honour that I will not. I do so.

I think I detect a slight change in Major Schoenmeyer. Why, I wonder.

Then dinner. No coffee is served and with morning coffee no milk is obtainable. By the way, I must be a Jonah. Paris had its first air raid alarm since the 7th June on the night of my arrival.

Hotel a mass of uniforms. I certainly am in the centre of things. One elderly colonel has a mass of medal ribbons and appears to be very popular.

I was not sick in the plane nor did I feel any after effects till tonight but have now started a headache and upset tummy. Then at about 10 p.m. just as I am deciding to go to bed, an officer comes in and speaks to my interpreter companion. We are to go elsewhere. I have a sense of foreboding. Away we go in a car and I am told I am under arrest and that we are heading for Versailles. At Versailles I am taken to the prison with two others, one apparently an Englishman and one a Frenchman.

I am put into Cell No. 54 on the top tier of the prison. Cell 13 ft. long by 6'6" wide. One straw mattress on floor. No blankets. A hot water pipe, a primitive washbasin with running water, a table and form, and in one corner a filthy lavatory and a metal jug which leaks. Window apparently unopenable.

Am appalled at the sudden change in my circumstances but curl up in my fur coat, (thank God May made me bring it) and go to sleep.

Called at about 8.30 a.m. Cell more appalling than ever in daylight.

Coffee (?) without milk or sugar and black bread very stale. Not very successful breakfast.

My braces and nail scissors were taken away so that I can neither hang myself nor cut my throat.

I have no towel but have some sort of a wash and dry with a handkerchief. Determine not to let it get me down and feel better.

German warders not unkind but know no English. I feel so desperately alone and my moods move from utter depression to elation and back again. If only I could talk to someone. I had never realised before what solitary confinement means particularly when one doesn't know how long it will last, what one is charged with or one's ultimate fate.

Dinner: potatoes and fat meat and gravy. Can eat only a little. Then am dished out with about 1 ½ oz. butter and some sausage which I eat with bread and with unsweetened black coffee for supper.

No one comes near me and I have not left my cell.

The prisoners tap morse messages to each other which for some reason annoys me.

I shave as best I can without a mirror and go to bed. I am at least holding my own.

10.11.40.   Sunday. Try my electric razor on electric light and it works. Enjoy shave. Wash and dry as before. Read book on Verdun. The trials of those heroic defenders cheer me up when I compare their lot with mine. Yesterday I was allowed to send out for apples and biscuits.

Dinner: good boiled meat and potatoes and gravy. Eat it all. For supper bread, butter and cheese and an apple and sweetened black coffee.

Clean my W.C. and scrape and scrub seat. It is now spotless and the brightest thing in my cell. Can do nothing with washbasin. Clear up generally and with my nail brush scrub off the walls the more obscene drawings. All this does me good. I am conquering depression and adapting myself. My cigarettes are nearly gone but I have bought some cigarillos.

Bed at 8 p.m. I have got a blanket now and the pipe is warm at night. I have found out how to open my window and do some physical jerks and inhaling exercises.

Say my prayers very earnestly asking that God will bless and preserve all my dear ones and will help me to bear whatever is coming to me with dignity and resolution. I am definitely feeling better. The food is sufficient and nourishing and the rest is doing me good. Air raid warning 10 p.m. Heard many planes passing over.

11.11.40.   Sweetened coffee and stale bread and good butter for breakfast. I estimate my fat allowance at about 10 oz. per week.

Still great difficulty in making myself understood but guards kinder. Borrowed towel (very dirty) and mirror. My electric razor causes much interest.

Feeling calmer and better. Allowed to walk along corridor for few minutes. Like heaven to get out of my cell.

At noon – 11 a.m. British Time – kept 2 minutes silence.

There was a short Air Raid Warning at 7 a.m.

Then good nourishing meat soup for dinner. I eat and drink everything out of a metal bowl which I clean as best I can. I am not allowed a knife.

For supper, bread, lard and boiled beef.

3 p.m. Have been outside in a triangular yard 37' x 17' for exercise for 20 minutes but quite alone.

Apparently I am to be kept in solitary confinement. That is the worst to bear but, fortunately, I have plenty inner reserves to draw upon.

Very rough night, strong gale.

Another Air Raid Alarm this morning. Am I a Jonah? Have burnished my water tap till it is a joy to behold and have, with a razor blade, scraped clean part of one wall of my cell. In time I shall get the place clean. Have got hold of a second blanket at last. Am buying a dictionary so as to make myself understood. The German warders speak no English at all.

Good dinner of boiled beef, potatoes and broth. Supper to be bread and butter and sausage.

Had ½ hour's exercise in yard by myself. This reminds me of the Lycée de Cherbourg, only more so.

Tried to get permission to write to May but no luck yet.

Feeling much rested and more balanced today.

13.11.40. Weather wet. Get sugar in my "café succédané" now. English speaking German warder on duty. Very kind. Warders change every day so one never really gets to know them. The cook is constant. Very friendly and kind. Gets me apples, cigarettes etc. in the town.

At last I have a towel or rather a length of towelling the only material procurable. There's a French girl in Cell 56. I wonder what she's guilty of. There's a nice Frenchman in here too but I don't see much of him and am not allowed to talk to him.

During my "break" I amassed 3 sycamore leaves blown into the yard by the gale, 1 multi-coloured as an ornament and the other two as plates to hold my bread and butter.

I take my meals out of an iron bowl which I clean with cold water and paper. Have started scraping my table to the bare wood. With my limited appliances I have weeks of work cleaning. If I am to stay here, I will buy distemper and brushes and decorate my cell.

Good dinner of boiled beef and potatoes and gravy. Supper, bread, butter and meat loaf. Am well fed. Health good, morale fine. Since I have to be out of the world temporarily, I will be so happily. I am quite adjusted and since I am helpless to change my circumstances I will make the best of them. Got some chocolate today. Wrote long letter to May enclosing 5 £1 Notes towards Joly's bike and my last month's salary cheque which I forgot to cash in Guernsey.

With my new French-German dictionary I can make myself understood if that is not putting it too high.

Get a great kick and about 2 hours interest reading "Le Matin".

Very clever but very anti-English.

The news of the Russo-German rapprochement and of sinkings of our merchant tonnage look to me grave. Unless I am mistaken the menace in the near East will become increasingly grave. I think when I am really settled in, I will try to write a book on the German Occupation of the Bailiwick of Guernsey. Not a thriller but a fair and honest book. It ought to sell well. Perhaps I may thus restore the shattered family fortunes.

8 p.m. Must soon turn in. Last night I left it too late and the light went out while I was undressing. Goodnight to all my darlings and God bless and protect you.

14.11.40.   Mornings drawing in. Towel a great success. Went on with scraping my table with razor blade. Wood coming up nicely. If I'm to stay here will buy some distemper, paint and brushes and colour walls primrose, wash-basin green, lavatory base and dado red with green line against primrose and window green. Will keep table scrubbed. How much sweeter cell is than when I came. It amazes me that I am so peaceful and contented. How adaptable one is and what a blessing that one is. I can understand the old lag being unwilling to leave gaol. A few days ago this was incomprehensible to me.

Prepared request through Red Cross to Montague for news of children, Mrs. Sutcliffe etc.

Friday 15.11.40.   Told I am going to Paris at 3 p.m. False alarm, it's tomorrow. I wonder why. At 6 p.m. cell door opened and told to pack and come to Paris. Drive there in open car with French girl prisoner. Nice to see country and Place de la Concorde again.

Driven to Cherche Midi Prison in centre of Paris. Discipline very, very strict, no smoking, no luxuries. All except toilet things taken from me. No money, no anything.

Cell much smaller and no sun penetrates. Difficult keep warm without exercise. Have spent most of day restoring my morale. My letter to May and communication to Red Cross returned to me and then sealed up with my other goods. Disappointment upon disappointment. I must indeed keep calm and of good courage. May will soon be beginning to worry.

X Wrote to May.

Saturday 16.11.40.　No change. Good soup lunch. Bread, butter, cheese and apple for supper. Cell very cold and dull. No sun ever enters. Lack of exercise and solitude tend to get one down but one must not let that happen. Spotted Emile Nicole among the poor devils I met on the stairs this morning. There must be a great deal of human misery per cubic foot of Cherche Midi but there is also much kindness and gentleness and goodness. I pin my faith to these to save the world. Have written to May today. It did me good to do so but I fear she will be very worried, poor darling.

Sunday 17.11.40.　Wet day. Have been allowed electric light in my cell so can read. Otherwise cell very dull and depressing. Only possible read and write by natural light in middle of day. Met. E.W.N. on stairs yesterday and today. Poor devil, caught in grip of same circumstances as myself.

This is the prison where Dreyfus was incarcerated. Old, grim and cold and situate in heart of Paris.

It's the little things that get one down i.e. lack of light, a chilly atmosphere etc., rather than big things. Surprising how my e.l. bulb has cheered me up.

But why must man heap such indignity upon his fellow man and deprive him (as we are) of human companionship and all the minor conveniences so that we live almost like animals and yet, pathetically, we all try to preserve our dignity, courtesy and humour. Never had I been in touch with so much misery at the same time. Sunday does not differ from any other day here.

Monday 18.11.40.   Nothing happened except that W. Allen arrived tonight and I believe other Guernsey people are in here. Issue of sugar today.

Nothing happened.

Wednesday 20.11.40. Quite uneventful.

Thursday 21.11.40.   Nothing happened. I thought this place without exercise or sun would get me down but I am beating it. Very depressed sometimes but generally speaking morale good.

Friday 22.11.40.   Had my hair cut. How terrible and demoralising it is to have absolutely nothing to do or to see. Difficult to sleep at night.

Saturday 23.11.40.   Nothing happened. Of good courage.

Sunday 24.11.40.   Nothing happened. Cell very cold.

Monday 25.11.40.   Nothing happened except that stoves were lighted today. The chill has been most depressing.

Tuesday 26.11.40.   Life much more comfortable now that stoves are lighted. Nothing happened. I pass part of my time casting my bucket down into the well of the past. Occasionally, nay often, I bring up precious memories. Visited by American Quaker who is going to arrange to have my washing done and give me a clean towel. Thank God for a spot of human kindness.

Wednesday 27.11.40. Nothing happened.

Thursday 28.11.40.   Away from home 3 weeks today. Nothing happened.

Friday 29.11.40.   Nothing happened. I wonder if it is possible that Providence or chance has decided that, in our family, I and not any of the others, shall be selected for the suffering which this war is spreading abroad. If this is indeed the case, how proud I should be and how patient I ought to be. Never have my thoughts been with Mary Rose, John and Dick as they have been since my arrest. I doubt if the food is sufficient in quality or quantity to support health for very long.

Substitute Coffee

11 a.m. Soup ($^3/4 - 1$ pt.)

2 p.m. Substitute Coffee

3 p.m. Bread (something under 1 lb.) a small pat of butter or margarine or lard and a piece of sausage or some potted meat or a little jam.

Saturday 30.11.40.   Nothing happened.

Sunday Dec. 1st, 1940.   Nothing happened.

Monday Dec. 2nd, 1940.   Nothing happened except that we got out in the yard for ten minutes to refill our mattresses with straw. It was like heaven after the cell.

Tuesday Dec. 3rd, 1940.   Nothing happened except that I have been given a travel book to read supplied by the Americans. This will help to relieve the monotony.

Wednesday Dec. 4th, 1940.   Visited today. Am to be questioned tomorrow or Friday.

Thursday Dec. 5th, 1940.   Nothing happened. I left Guernsey a month ago.

Friday Dec 6th, 1940. Interrogated today at length by very sympathetic Sous-Officer, who took long typewritten statement. Smoked innumerable French cigarettes during interrogation.

X Saturday Dec. 7th   Nothing happened. Wrote to May

Sunday Dec. 8th.   Nothing happened.

Monday Dec. 9th.   Visited by Inspector who is hopeful there may be no trial and that all except officers, may be released and returned to Guernsey. Inspector charming, friendly and sympathetic. Last Friday I put in a statement and pleading running to nine sheets of foolscap and he told me he translated it into German on Sunday afternoon and had placed it in the dossier. He thought it set out the case from my point of view very thoroughly.

Tuesday Dec. 10th   Nothing happened.

Wednesday Dec. 11th Only a fortnight to Christmas. Nothing happened except that Jack Doyle and a lot of other British soldiers left for a P. of W. Camp today.

Thursday Dec. 12th Nothing happened. Have been in this prison 28 days and 6 at Versailles.

Friday Dec. 13th Nothing happened.

Saturday Dec. 14th Nothing happened except that No. 36 left for an unknown destination. (He was a 2ième Bureau man & I fear he was executed).

Sunday Dec. 15th. Nothing happened.

Monday Dec. 16th Nothing happened except that there being no sausage or other delicacy to serve with our "casse-croûte", we were given a second bowl of soup this afternoon. Today, for the first time this month, I have had enough to eat.

Tuesday Dec. 17th Nothing happened except that there is a change of regime. Till today we went down to the yard to empty out slop-pails and draw water and fetched our food from the end of the corridor. Now we do not leave our cells.

Wednesday Dec. 18th Nothing happened.

Thursday Dec. 19th Nothing happened.

Friday Dec. 20th Nothing happened.

Saturday Dec. 21st Nothing happened.

Sunday Dec. 22nd Nothing happened.

Monday Dec. 23rd Nothing happened. xxx L.M. Symes found dead.

Tuesday Dec. 24th Nothing happened except that we had an extra ration of bread, lard, sausage and a supplementary ration of butter and honey and some raisins. Our sugar ration was also issued today. So even in Cherche Midi Prison the spirit of Christmas is not absent; thank God for it, may it soon return in full abundance and redeem Europe and bestow peace in our time and restore goodwill among men. My dear family, so scattered this Christmas, may God's richest blessing fall on you all and may we be soon re-united. Figs and dates and an apple and an orange have just been given us.

Wednesday, Christmas Day.

The first Christmas that the family has not spent together. May God bless each of my darlings and protect them from harm and may I soon have definite news concerning myself. I pray that all is well with dear little Guernsey. Nothing happened. I started the day with a bad bilious attack but it cleared during the day.

Thursday Dec. 26th   Nothing happened.

Friday Dec. 27th   Nothing happened.

Saturday Dec. 28th   Nothing happened.

Sunday Dec. 29th   Up early and ready in case anything happens. Rumour Guernsey women left for unknown destination reached me last night. Something is afoot for girls have been visited and asked for particulars of Guernsey party and told they are going to camp or home and boys to be prisoners of war. 9 a.m. Bell rings and we are unlocked. I am ready to leave at a moment's notice. It is a presentiment. Sgt. Fach comes to my cell and says "English partir tout de suite" and calls me to roust out Bill Allen which I do. I walk along corridor giving away my bread and cheering up and thanking prisoners for their kindness and bidding them au revoir. Down to the salle where we all assemble.

Rumour women to go to Guernsey, men internment cap. Marquand very downhearted. I am fairly bright. Would have preferred prison sentence and then home.

Definitely told women going home. No news men but no hope Guernsey held out. Kiss women. Give Mrs. Nicolle affectionate messages for May and financial advice and for Bird and Allen.

Get our belongings. Then told whole party to Guernsey. Don't believe it. Then told officially. Given hot "sweetened coffee" and bread. Everybody kind and helpful and friendly. The terror of our corridor shakes hands and bids me a friendly farewell.

Bus waiting. Feld Gendarmerie in attendance as escort to Guernsey. We are under surveillance till Guernsey then free on condition reside there till end of war.

Leave for Granville. Stop at Dreux for coffee, patisseries and eau de vie. Bread, butter and pork en route. Arrive Granville 7 p.m. Got only supply of Coramine (for Col. de Putron) and chemist's shop at Dreux opened specially for me.

Put up at Hotel Pellerin. Leaving morrow for Jersey.

Monday Dec. 30th. Driven to Port. There told too rough, storm expected. Ship very small. Wait for "Holland" morrow.

Shop. Call on Guernsey-Jersey Office Les Hirondelles, Rue de Falaise, Granville. Tea M. et Mme. Mauduit, Rue Couraye. Met Captain Sowden. At Mme. Mauduit met his son. Invite to Guernsey? Saw "Normand" flying Jersey flag on staff.

APPENDIX J

A Case of Telepathy?

Two days before my fellow prisoners and I were returned to Guernsey after release from the Cherche Midi Prison in Paris, my wife went out leaving our youngest boy, aged 6, alone at home. On her return, he told her that two German soldiers had called and told him to tell her that her husband would be home on the morrow.

Nothing had been heard in Guernsey concerning our whereabouts or fate and, in a great state of excitement, my wife telephoned the Controlling Committee for further details. They knew nothing about it but immediately despatched someone to the Feldkommandantur to find out.

Now it seems certain that the Germans in Guernsey were aware of what was afoot for soon afterwards they published a notice announcing that we were being freed. They protested, however, that they knew nothing about the matter and my wife and the small boy had to attend at the Feldkommandantur and a number of soldiers were paraded for the boy to inspect so that the two soldiers who had delivered the message might be identified. He failed to identify them. My party returned to Guernsey on December 31st 1940 and the mystery was never solved. The Germans were virtually certain that they had two "traitors" among them and those of us who had heard the story were convinced that two German soldiers at the Feldkommandantur had, out of the kindness of their hearts, sought to alleviate a wife's natural anxiety as to her husband's safety.

Years afterwards, the boy told us that no German soldiers ever called or delivered such a message. It had suddenly come into his head to tell his mother what he did. He was terrified when she telephoned for more information and from then on felt that all he could do, to avoid dreadful things being done to him by the Germans, was to stick to his story and bluff the matter out. This he successfully did. Yet what he said was going to happen - and there was no possibility of him having any knowledge of it - did actually occur.

318

APPENDIX K

Letters Exchanged Between A German Ex-Soldier And Sherwill In 1950

RUMMELSTR 12,

(22b) WEILERBACH/PRALZ,

GERMANY.

22nd September, 1950

Dear Mr. Mayor,

At Christmas it will be 10 years since I, as a German soldier, received the order to drive to Paris in order to take English civilians from a Prison there to Granville on the Channel coast.

I was then Lance Corporal and Motor Driver to the Staff of a General-Commando, and it was my first encounter with English people. I should like, therefore, to set down my impressions on paper and perhaps, dear Mr. Mayor, would you be so kind as to put me into touch, by correspondence, with those people. Unfortunately the list of the people concerned is no longer in my possession, as the War has also made itself felt in my Fatherland, and I am now living, the victim of heavy damage, in a small village of South Germany.

I will now try to report on those events. On December 30th, 1940, I received from my superiors instructions to drive my bus to Paris. I was accompanied by 3 soldiers of the Feldgendarmerie. At the beginning, the exact mission was unknown to me, but I heard from my comrades that we were going to Paris to fetch English families imprisoned there under suspicion of espionage. At about 10 a.m. we reached Paris, on a Sunday, I think. After a little waiting, the prison gates were opened and the distressed persons got into the bus. Unfortunately none of us could speak English, but in spite of this we tried to make ourselves understood. I can say that during the 2 days we spent together we were like a big family. Unfortunately I have forgotten the names, except that a young girl was named Mary, and a gentleman had the same Christian name as myself i.e. Albert. I was thinking at the time how can it be that we are at war with a people that is so closely related to us?

On the way we made a small stop and went to a restaurant to eat something. I should like to express renewed thanks for the friendly way in which we were treated, as, strange as it may seem, we felt as if we were the guests of persons belonging to a Nation with which we were then at war. Although they had been imprisoned by the occupation troops, we felt no trace of hate for us, and I am still sorry I could not speak English then.

When we reached Granville in the afternoon, the people could not be put on board for crossing to their country. The harbour Commandant had received a gale warning so that the small patrol boat could not sail. So the crossing was postponed until the next day. My mission was really fulfilled and I had to return to my headquarters. However, I asked the Officer in charge of the English people for permission to accompany them to their Island. We spent the evening very pleasantly with the English party. On the next day, New Year's Eve, we went on board at noon. The crossing was quiet and we reached Jersey.

Unfortunately we had to part, as from there the Island Kommandantur took over the escorting to Guernsey. The leave taking was very cordial and we regretted not to be able to accept the invitation for New Year's night. On the 1st January, we returned to headquarters.

I should very much like to get in touch with those people and sincerely hope that all of them have stood the trials and tribulations of war without damage. Although I am a simple man, I have preserved humane feelings all through the time of war and never felt any hate for people who did their duty in a war imposed upon them.

Let me know how you are and please write in English because I can read them better than write or can speak. I learned it during the time as driver by the British Occupation Armee. My best regards to all the English people who remember that days. I don't hope I make you trouble with my writing because of little time to hand them to the interested persons. I will be very glad to hear from you.

Affectionately,

ALBERT ZIEHLKE.

7th October, 1950

Herr Albert Zichlke,(sic)

Rummelstr. 12,

(22b) Weilerbach/Pralz,

Germany.

Dear Mr. Zichlke,(sic)

A copy of your letter of the 22nd September has been sent to me by the States Supervisor of Guernsey, to whom it was delivered. I understand that he is sending a copy to all the other members of the party which you drove from Paris to Granville on Sunday, December 30th, 1940.

I well remember the occasion in question. You may perhaps remember me when I say that I am tall, fair and that I was wearing a fur coat.

We were all very happy at getting back to Guernsey after our stay in the Cherche Midi Prison in Paris and I remember we stopped at Dreux and got some refreshments at a restaurant and then bought cakes at a confectioner's and, after driving all day, reached Granville after dark and were billeted that night (and the next night because of the gale which delayed our departure) at the Hotel Pellerin.

I remember, too, that, in charge of the whole party, was a very tall Oberfeldwebel who was terribly sick on the passage from Granville to Jersey and that you were all very disappointed not to be able to come on from Jersey to Guernsey.

So far as I know, all the members of the party driven by you are alive and well though not all are living in this Island. I see some of them frequently.

The Mary you speak of was Mary Bird who has since married and Albert would, I think, be Mr. Marriette.

I was interned at Laufen in Upper Bavaria from February 1943 until May 1945.

May I congratulate you on your very excellent English. It is really amazingly good.

Like you, I have no feelings of hatred for those who were on the opposite side in the last war and, as for you and your comrades of the 30th December, 1940, no one could have been kinder or more courteous.

Let us hope that your country and mine may never again in the future find themselves opposed to each other in war but that all our efforts may be put to co-operating for the preservation of a lasting peace.

My wife and I spent a fortnight in Germany last year and renewed many acquaintances and received much friendship and kindness.

With all good wishes for a happy future,

Yours very sincerely,

....

(Sir Ambrose Sherwill)

APPENDIX L

Details Of Graves Of Channel Islanders In Laufen[14,15]

IN

AFFECTIONATE REMEMBRANCE

OF

PERCY FRANK HERRINGTON

BORN AT HALLING, ENGLAND ON 12.12.1891
DIED AT LAUFEN ON 2.3.1944.

Erected as a token of esteem and regret by his fellow British
Internees at Ilag VII, Laufen

****

---

[14] Hermon Bentley of Jersey, an internee at Laufen, has not been included in the List.
He died in Salzberg Hospital on 26.12.43. and he was buried in the Salzberg
Cemetery.

[15] Augustus Dunkley of Guernsey, a retired Royal Navy Chief Petty Officer, died at
Laufen on 24.11.44. and he was buried in the Laufen Cemetery. His name has, for
some reason, been omitted from this List.

IN

AFFECTIONATE REMEMBRANCE

OF

ARTHUR DIMERY

BORN AT CHELTENHAM, ENGLAND ON 7.11.1892
DIED AT ILAG VII, LAUFEN ON 4.4.1944.

Erected as a token of esteem and regret by his fellow British
Internees at Ilag VII, Laufen

****

IN

AFFECTIONATE REMEMBRANCE

OF

DILWYN DAVIES

BORN AT THORNE, DONCASTER, YORKS, ENGLAND ON
6.7.1919.
DIED AT LAUFEN ON 28.5.1944.

Erected as a token of esteem and regret by his fellow British
Internees at Ilag VII, Laufen

****

IN

AFFECTIONATE MEMORY

OF

<u>NORMAN HEATHER HEY</u>

BORN STRETFORD, ENGLAND 22.9.1883.
DIED AT LAUFEN 10.5.1945.

Erected by his fellow British Internees at Ilag VII, Laufen

****

IN

AFFECTIONATE MEMORY

OF

<u>HENRY JAMES LE GOUPILLOT</u>

BORN AT MIDDLESBOROUGH, YORKS 25.10.1923.
DIED AT LAUFEN 1.6.1945.

Erected by his sorrowing friends at Laufen Internment Camp.

APPENDIX M

A Commentary On The Diary Kept By A.J. Sherwill In Ilag VII, Laufen, Bavaria

In the autumn of 1941 Britain interned a number of Germans living in Iran. Hitler was outraged and ordered punitive reprisals to be made by the deportation of Englishmen from the Channel Islands. The Feldkommandantur was ordered to prepare to deport 5,000 British civilians from the Islands.

By September, 1942, because of logistical and political problems, no deportations had in fact taken place. In discussions at that time between the German and the Swiss Governments regarding the exchange of seriously-wounded prisoners of war it was suggested by the Swiss that some Channel Island residents might be included in the exchange. Hitler immediately guessed that his earlier deportation order had never been obeyed and the Führer's order was issued again. As a result, the first party of deportees from Guernsey, made up in the main from people not born in the islands, finally sailed on 26th September, 1942. Most of the unattached men were sent to ILAG VII, Laufen, in Germany.

Laufen is a little Bavarian town on the River Salzach, on the Austrian border. ILAG VII, for single unattached male internees, was established here in the centuries-old Schloss Laufen which was formerly the country summer residence of the Archbishops of Salzburg. (Prior to 1816 Laufen had been part of Austria).

The first group to arrive from the Islands was a Jersey contingent with Roy Charles Skingle as its leader and he became British Camp Senior. On the arrival in October, 1942, of a larger Guernsey contingent Skingle stepped down to become Deputy to Frank Stroobant of Guernsey.

Another party, from Guernsey and Sark, apparently made up of potential trouble makers and officers of the First World War, and including Ambrose J. Sherwill, sailed from St. Peter Port for St. Malo on 12th February, 1943. On reaching St. Malo they had to wait in a train for almost a day for a Jersey party delayed by the engine failure of their ship. A.J.S. had been given the responsibility of looking after the Guernsey and Sark contingent by the German Feldkommandantur and the Germans left it to him to break the awful news, once their journey was underway, that the families would be split up; the women, children and men over 63 were to stay in a camp at Compiègne, near Paris, while the younger men were to go on to Laufen. In his book *"Islanders Deported"* Roger E. Harris wrote:-

"The separation of families on the 1943 deportations was probably the most callous act committed by the Germans during the whole of the deportation saga, the more so because they had given many of the men the option of taking their families with them, only to separate them once they reached French soil. To be fair to the Germans this separation was probably not planned and was not part of the "punishment" of the Channel Islanders, but was indicative of the crowded state of the internment camps organised by the Oberkommando der Wehrmacht in 1943 and especially the lack of facilities for women and children."

In a letter written in Laufen on 21st February, 1943, to his wife in Guernsey, A.J.S. wrote:-

Arrived here Tuesday (Feb. 16). First three hours sea journey beastly, then good. Travelled comfortably. Ample food. Left women, children and most elderly men in France, probably temporarily

Express to Bailiff and Controlling Committee and helpers, heart-felt gratitude of all Guernsey and Sark evacuees for great kindness on departure.

Those left behind at Compiègne were eventually reunited with their families many months later at Biberach.

On arrival at Laufen A.J.S. was content to settle in as an ordinary internee. However, in May, 1943, Stroobant joined a party of Allied Prisoners of War sent to the Forest of Katyn, in Russia, to witness the exhumation by the Germans of the graves of some 5,000 Polish Army Officers who had been murdered by the Russians. On his return to Laufen some of his fellow internees regarded his action in going on this trip with suspicion. Furthermore his prudent proposals to husband Red-Cross food parcels against a time when supplies might dry up was most unpopular. Fed up with the continual fault finding, Stroobant resigned as British Camp Senior and on 29th June, 1943, despite making it plain that he fully supported Stroobant, A.J.S. found himself elected in his place. On his discharge from the Revier, the Camp sick-bay, A.J.S. took over the Camp Senior's duties on 2nd July, 1943.

(This German word "Revier" is also used in the entries dated 31.7.43. and 4.3.44.)

There were internees other than Channel Islanders at Laufen. For example there were other British citizens and a large group of Americans, the majority of whom claimed American citizenship through their fathers who had emigrated to America and had since returned to Europe; some could speak very little English.

The entry dated 9.7.43. refers to a Mr. Berg of the Y.M.C.A. Mr. Erik Berg was the Swedish representative in Germany of the World's Alliance of the Y.M.C.A. and he was very popular with all the internees. Frequent references to his visits will be found throughout the diary.

Many of the diary entries are records of the transfer of internees to and from Laufen by railway. In the entry dated 5.8.43. A.J.S. describes how a party on transfer to Biberach and Wurzach were to travel by box-car type freight wagon (Dix Chevaux ou Quarante Hommes) from Laufen as far as Freilassing and then onwards by passenger coach.

In the second entry dated 5.8.43. "Posy" is Mary Rose, A.J.S.'s daughter who was serving with the W.A.A.F. in England.

Lieutenant P. Martel, named in the entry of 12.8.43. was Philip Martel, a Guernseyman of the Hampshire Regiment who was taken prisoner in Guernsey together with Desmond Mulholland. Appendix "G" describes how A.J.S. became involved in equipping these two officers with British Uniforms and helping in their surrender to the Germans in Guernsey in 1940.

In the entry dated 13.8.43. A.J.S. records the despatch to his wife, May, in Guernsey of a parcel via Mr. G.M. Vaudin who was a member of the States of Guernsey Purchasing Commission based in Granville.

There are references to a renegade Englishman, J.G. Lingshaw, in the entries of 16.8.43. and 17.8.43. Stroobant, in his book "One Man's War" also mentions this incident but without naming the man, and adds: "He received his just reward in Prison when the War ended".

An account of the repatriation detailed in the entry dated 21.8.43. is given in the book "Islanders Deported". There it is stated: "In August

1943, Messrs. A. Doig, Danny Skinner and D. Lean were repatriated to Guernsey, on medical grounds, in the company of W.P. Reid, a hospital orderly and Donald Cranch, a deputy of the Red Cross Department. Unfortunately, the escorts had to return to Laufen within a few days, but before going they were able to reassure many Islanders that their relatives were reasonably well cared for in the camps".

The entry dated 22.8.43. refers to a local festival "Schifferschutzen Tag 22/8/1943." An internee at Laufen, Gerald Webb who also kept a diary, wrote that this event was held annually and was to celebrate the Trade Agreement between Laufen and Austria, which brought to an end a turbulent time of violent cross-frontier smuggling and which introduced a new period of prosperity to the town. He described the Band in old Bavarian uniforms of about the year 1800, with scarlet tunics, white drain-pipe trousers, black hats decorated with feathers, white belts and equipment.

A.J.S., in the entry dated 6.9.43. gives details of disciplinary action taken against four Jersey internees as a result of which they were "debarred from Island until 1/10/43". There is a small island in the River Salzach which was linked at that time to the Laufen camp by a wooden footbridge. This island had a football-pitch, one-third normal size, and it was also used as a walking ground for the older men. It was the internees' main recreational area and to be "debarred from the Island" would have been a considerable penalty. There is a further reference to this island in the entry dated 9.9.43.

On 2.11.43. A.J.S. gives an account of another repatriation on medical grounds and in which mention is made of "Sanitäters" accompanying the party. These were fellow internees, acting as medical orderlies. The use of the German word "Sanitäters" occurs also in the entry dated 9.3.44.

The entry dated 13.11.43. records the transfer of four internees to Laufen from Ilag VC Wurzach. This transfer is fully detailed in the book "Islanders Deported". Wurzach was a family camp but with antiquated accommodation, unsuitable for the purpose, and with poor sanitary facilities. The rooms were over-crowded and smelly. These factors, coupled with the weak leadership of the Camp Senior, the purported presence of ghosts and the existence of a Hitler Youth Training Camp immediately adjacent, all contributed to this being a very unhappy camp with continual conflict between the internees, culminating in the transfer of these four men who were thought to be the main trouble makers.

In the entry dated 21.4.44. A.J.S. mentions the Reserve Lazarett. The German word "Lazarett", which is also used in the entries dated 6.6.44, 24.7.44 and 1.6.45, refers to the German Military Hospital, or Medical Facility, which served as a receiving and quarantine station for Ilag VII.

A.J.S. refers to "The Admiral Scheer" in his entry dated 15.6.44. This was a German Naval pocket-battleship which had a successful career in the early years of the War attacking British merchant ships in the Indian Ocean and South Atlantic.

In the entry dated 4.7.44. the name "Mr. Gompertz" appears. At this time Mr. Herbert Gompertz was American Camp Senior.

On 18.7.44. A.J.S. recounts a recreational visit to Kitschbühel in the mountains with Mr. Berg of the Y.M.C.A. From Gerald Webb's diary it is known that the senior Sonderführer accompanied them. It is believed that, in fact, they visited Kitzbühel in the Kitzbüheler Alpen, now a noted winter sports centre in Austria, to the south of Laufen. It is recalled from many years ago that A.J.S. told of how Mr. Berg had been overcome by fumes from a faulty charcoal gas generator which supplied power for the engine of their car.

In his entry dated 24.11.44. A.J.S. records the death and funeral of Augustus Dunkley, who was a retired Royal Naval Chief Petty Officer, and mentions an "improvised" Union Jack. It is recorded that this flag was made out of a white linen sheet by Padre Gerhold, using water colours. A.J.S. wrote about Padre Gerhold's flag in the foreword to Stroobant's book "One Man's War" as follows:

"Until needed, it was kept in the Sondeführer's cupboard. When American tanks rumbled into our village in the early afternoon of May 4th, 1945, it was displayed at our most prominent window. The effect was dramatic: the column halted and an American officer came to investigate. We were free. That flag flew proudly over our Schloss for many days until, alas, the rains came and gradually obliterated its colours. Before that happened, it had attracted to us many escaping British prisoners-of-war, one party of whom, I remember, arrived in a German staff car fitted with inch-thick bullet-proof glass".

The entry dated -.1.45. records the arrival at Laufen of Stanley Green from Buchenwald Concentration Camp but makes no mention as to how Green was moved from Buchenwald to Laufen.

It happened as follows:-

Stanley George Green was arrested in Jersey, suspected by the Geheime Feldpolizei of having wireless equipment. After imprisonment in France he was moved to the notorious Concentration Camp at Buchenwald. In the book "Islands in Danger" by Alan and Mary Wood it is recorded:- "Green owed the recovery of his liberty, and probably his life, to Major Sherwill. By now his elder son, Leslie Green, had been deported to Laufen, where Sherwill was the British Camp Senior. Green managed to smuggle out of Buchenwald a letter to Leslie telling him of his whereabouts, and Leslie took it to Sherwill. Thereupon Sherwill went to his German Camp Commandant, secured his help, and in less than a week Green had been transferred to Laufen."

The entry dated 15.1.45.-18.1.45. mentions a journey to Berlin. A.J.S. gave a full and exciting account of this visit to Berlin, at the height of the R.A.F.'s assault on that city, in the Chapter "MY WINTER VACATION".

On 17.3.45. A.J.S. wrote:- "Search by Cripo". The story of this search of the camp by the Bavarian Criminal Police, the part A.J.S. played in saving the internees' hidden wireless set from discovery and the German Camp staff from probable transfer to the Russian Front, is given in the Chapter "A GUEST OF HITLER'S REICH".

A.J.S. twice refers to the "Lazarett Baracke" in the entry dated 1.6.45. which tells of the tragic accidental shooting of an internee. As previously stated, "Lazarett" is the German for Military Hospital, while "Baracke" is the German spelling of Barracks.